Charaiveti

Praise for *Charaiveti*

'Pranab Bardhan is one of the pioneers of modern development economics. He has also had a ringside view of sixty tumultuous years and more, both for India and the economics field. This is the story of those years, told in a voice gentle and yet incisive—like the author, always amusing and yet deeply humane.'
—Abhijit V. Banerjee, Professor of economics, Massachusetts Institute of Technology

'Pranab Bardhan is a man of exceptionally wide scholarship, of a fiercely independent turn of mind and one who has always been deeply immersed in literature and cinema. His observations of his times, in different parts of the world, and of the many people whom he has known, are always entertaining, his insights often profound. This memoir is a joy to read.'
—John Harriss, Professor Emeritus, International Studies, Simon Fraser University

'Economist Pranab Bardhan recounts, in engaging prose, his remarkable journey from childhood in a rough Kolkata neighbourhood to the high tables of the intellectual world in the West. The persistence of inequality in the world has remained for him an abiding concern.'
—Indira Rajaraman, Indira Gandhi Institute of Development Research

'*Charaiveti* is written with Pranab Bardhan's customary charm and wit. In documenting his personal journey, he weaves together reflections on the world with recognizable themes from his

academic writings and offers us insights into why he has been such an important figure in humanizing and broadening the discipline of economics.'
—Tim Besley, Professor of economics and political science, London School of Economics

'Pranab Bardhan proves that he is not only an exceptional scholar but also an expert raconteur. He has written a fascinating memoir that is highly entertaining and full of insights about academia, economics, India—and indeed, the world at large.'
—Dani Rodrik, Ford Foundation Professor of International Political Economy, Harvard University

'In his "travels"—for that is how he describes his memoir—through fast-changing times, continents, cultures, economies and the portals of academe, or in his interactions with almost all the major economists of the time, Pranab Bardhan remains passionately engaged with the political–economic problems of India and other such "extremely unequal" developing countries: relentlessly seeking ways of redressal, and lovingly reliving and objectively unfolding his Kolkata of the 1950s.'
—Samik Bandyopadhyay, editor, translator and film, theatre and art critic

Charaiveti

An Academic's Global Journey

Pranab Bardhan

HarperCollins *Publishers* India

First published in India by HarperCollins *Publishers* 2023
4th Floor, Tower A, Building No. 10, DLF Cyber City,
DLF Phase II, Gurugram, Haryana – 122002
www.harpercollins.co.in

2 4 6 8 10 9 7 5 3 1

Copyright © Pranab Bardhan 2023

P-ISBN: 978-93-5699-574-1
E-ISBN: 978-93-5699-575-8

The views and opinions expressed in this book are the author's own and the facts are as reported by him, and the publishers are not in any way liable for the same.

Pranab Bardhan asserts the moral right
to be identified as the author of this work.

All rights reserved. No part of this publication may be reproduced, stored in a retrieval system, or transmitted, in any form or by any means, electronic, mechanical, photocopying, recording or otherwise, without the prior permission of the publishers.

Typeset in 11.5/15.2 Adobe Caslon Pro at
Manipal Technologies Limited, Manipal

Printed and bound at
Thomson Press (India) Ltd

This book is produced from independently certified FSC® paper
to ensure responsible forest management.

Contents

Preface ix

1. A Child in Kolkata and Santiniketan 1
2. Life in Kolkata's By-lanes and College Street 19
3. A Foreign Student in Cambridge, UK 44
4. A Young Faculty in Cambridge, Massachusetts 64
5. Grappling with Life in Delhi and with Data 89
6. The Social and Intellectual Milieu in Delhi and Kolkata 112
7. Exploring Kerala and Surviving Delhi under Emergency 131
8. A Newcomer to Berkeley 152
9. Exploring China 179
10. Reflecting on Comparative Systems and Marx 201
11. Wearing Multiple Hats 223
12. Life in English Academia 245
13. Policy Economics and the Indian Elite 265
14. Academic Life in Berkeley 293
15. An International Research Network and Travels 308
16. At Journey's End 340

Index 345

Preface

In this preface, let me mainly say what the book is not about. This is not an autobiography; it is more an academic's quasi-memoir. The former is usually about a whole life filled with personal details, relations and inner struggles. This book is instead more about an academic's interactions with others and observations on the society both in India and abroad. There is the occasional personal detail, but it is mainly to provide some background—the emphasis is on academic or social interactions and various related anecdotes. While my life course provides some chronology for the narrative, and I have not been exactly self-effacing in it, my attempt has been to keep the interaction with others and the social commentary in the foreground.

While the book is about an academic's journey, I have taken some care in keeping the interest of non-academic readers alive in much of the writing, particularly through general political and social observations, and a profusion of stories and anecdotes. In fact, a few of my economist colleagues have complained that there is not enough about some of the economic debates on policies and methods that have been important in the profession. I have tried to avoid technical issues and, even when I talk economics, it is more about political-economy and institutional-systemic issues which can be of general interest for the non-economists. Even when I write about economists, there is usually as much on human-interest stories about them as on their economic views.

The book also deliberately avoids some unpleasant or embarrassing events (both about others and myself) that I have encountered in my journey. Herman Melville once wrote (in his short story, 'Billy Budd, Sailor'): 'A truth uncompromisingly told must have its ragged edges.' I think, in this book, I am not that uncompromising, and I may have rounded and smoothened some of the edges. I have seen some people writing memoirs partly to settle scores or to air grievances about injustices done to them, or to answer unfair accusations. While I cannot say that some of these unseemly things have been entirely absent in my academic life, I think I am against taking these too seriously—particularly when I am telling stories to readers who may not have much patience with them. Of course, this creates the opposite danger of presenting an overly smooth narrative, of a journey that looks much too orderly and coherent, glazing over much of the churn and trials and tribulations that usually afflict all lives, and reeking of what my leftist friends call 'bourgeois complacency'. I have not been entirely unmindful of this danger in my writing, and I have not avoided some impersonal or social unpleasant issues.

Also, I have generally felt that a memoir like this is not the right place or device to capture some of the complexities and nuances of human character or the generally crooked timber of humanity or what the writer Iris Murdoch called 'the opacity of persons'. I have often felt that fiction is a better way of handling those complexities, opacities and nuances in some people I have met in my life. Of course, in literature there is now a whole genre of what is called 'autofiction', a blending of autobiography and fiction. But this is not a work of autofiction—at least, not consciously.

I have never kept a diary in my life. So my narrative plucked from a porous memory may not have done full justice to things as they happened, some of them in the distant misty past. In any case an act of narration is not an act of relentless truth depiction. As Lila, a main character in Elena Ferrante's novel, *My Brilliant Friend*, says: 'Each of us narrates our life as it suits us.' The book is full of meandering memories and anecdotal detours, with stories leading to other stories, and plenty of flashbacks and flash-forwards. I hope my readers will look at these with an indulgent eye and may even be amused by some of the digressions from time to time. While off and on I have discussed some serious issues, I have taken some care to not let their solemnity overwhelm the narrative, with what may seem like professorial gravity. Some readers will note that levity lurks in many corners of the book (just as a friend of Samuel Johnson once told him that he had tried to be a philosopher, but cheerfulness kept breaking in). This is also a way of suggesting that my whole enterprise here is not to be taken too seriously. But the reader will also note that for all the levity the book ends on a note of some despair.

1
A Child in Kolkata and Santiniketan

I do not sleep well on long plane journeys. But some years ago, in one such journey, I was tired and fell fast asleep. When I woke up, I saw a little note on my lap. It was from the captain in charge of the plane. It said, 'I did not want to disturb you, but from our computer log I could see that your total travel so far with our airlines group just crossed 3 million miles. So congratulations! It seems you travel almost as much as I do.' I made a quick calculation: Three million miles is like six return trips from the earth to the moon. With a deep sigh, I chanted to myself, as our plane was hurtling through the night sky, a word from an ancient Sanskrit hymn: *charaiveti* (keep moving)!

There was a time when, for me as a young boy, a rare trip from one part of my city to another was a breathless adventure. I grew up in the mean streets of Kolkata (then known as Calcutta). I spent much of my boyhood and youth in a cramped rented house on a narrow by-lane of north Kolkata, with no running water or flush toilet, and all the rooms packed with refugee relatives from East Bengal, recently displaced by the violent Partition of India. My father, an educator, was not very poor by Indian standards, but, for a time, he had to support most of those relatives. He had no savings as whatever was left of his paltry income he spent on good food and books. Very early in my childhood, he instilled in me an appetite for both, and also the habit of rational, irreverent thinking and a deep sense of irony.

He had plenty of opportunity to do so as he had decided to home-school me. As a result, my early education was heavy in areas of his interest and expertise (mathematics, literature, history, politics, economics, and discourses in his pugnaciously atheist and sardonic attitude to life), and less in some branches of science or art practice. I was very weak, for example, in chemistry, or even in simple hand drawing—underneath most things I drew, I took care to describe in words what it was, as otherwise there was a good chance of people being misled. Since we did not have TV or internet those days, books and magazines were our main sources of learning (even the radio came to our house rather late—I remember the first few days after it arrived, I listened to all the programmes non-stop). The other great source of learning was observing the social interactions of the people swarming around me, and not all the lessons there were edifying.

My father was also a good raconteur; he relished telling stories of even everyday happenings spiced with ironic wit and great style, which made him popular with many of our acquaintances. My mother used to complain that even when a mishap struck our family, he spent less time in handling the situation than in polishing the narrative for when people would come and ask him about what happened. As a child, I dreaded his occasional temper tantrums and resented his domineering ways of controlling his family, but I also closely and admiringly observed how meticulously he collected his materials from the teeming life around him, in the streets or marketplaces (going out to the bazaars in search of food items that he considered best both in quality and bargain was his daily preoccupation), and how he turned them into masala ingredients for his colourful stories. It was not until much later that I realized how much of his wit and humour actually served as a shield against the frustrations in his life and against an unfair society that simmered inside.

Since my home-schooling hours were quite flexible and depended on when he was free, I spent much of the day playing with the street kids who came from much poorer families in the neighbourhood (including some whose mothers were sex workers in the brothels nearby). Since the narrow by-lane of not more than 10-feet width in front of our house was the playing field, you may imagine how the rules of football or cricket were mangled and adapted to our limiting circumstances—for example, in our cricket, usually played with tennis balls, if you catch the ball off the bat after it hit one wall, then the batsman was out, but if it had bounced off both walls on the two sides of the narrow street, the batsman was safe.

In periods when our house was particularly overcrowded with relatives, my father often sent me, my sister and mother off to our maternal uncle's home in Santiniketan, a small town about a hundred miles north of Kolkata. This town was famous in India for having the residential educational institution established by Rabindranath Tagore. Santiniketan's wide open fields and ravines gave me a great deal of freedom to wander about, exploring nature, playing, plucking fruits and catching fish with children from extremely poor families from the neighbouring village (most of their parents worked as rickshaw-pullers and maids), who also did not go to school. My father would occasionally visit for a short time and give me homework for the next few weeks, which I frantically finished in less than a week, so that I had all the time to play with those friends.

My uncle's home had several ducks, and we the children were put in charge of them. There were three ducks under my watch. In the morning, I'd let them off into the nearby interconnected ponds, and they would go very far through across those ponds. My task in the evening was to bring them back to the house. Standing on the embankment near a pond, I'd make a special sound calling them; they'd recognize my call and respond to it, and soon would come to me. One evening, I was a bit late after my football game and when I made my special call, two of the ducks came but not the third. I ran along the banks of the ponds for quite some distance, but did not find it. As dusk was falling, I became frantic and would not come home. I remember it was quite dark when people dragged me back, telling me that maybe a fox had pounced on the duck. That night, I felt feverish.

In Santiniketan, those days, there was only one doctor who served the relatively small population. This doctor was very popular even though he did not have any advanced medical degrees. He knew every family and would make house calls riding on his bicycle with a palm-leaf hat on. He was brimming with empathy and while visiting a household, he would not merely check the patient; he'd also spend a few minutes asking after the general well-being of the whole family. He knew which family member had a history of which ailment, and, in cases where he thought the ailment was more psychological than physical, he'd sit down and talk tenderly with the patient like a concerned uncle. I still remember his affectionate eyes and reassuring voice.

Even though I was not a student at Santiniketan, I used to accompany my friends in the neighbourhood who studied there to attend the numerous cultural events that took place in the campus every week. Every Wednesday morning, there used to be a solemn gathering where the master of ceremony was Kshitimohan Sen (Amartya Sen's grandfather), a professor of Sanskrit, who used to recite verses from ancient texts and interpret them, which were almost completely unintelligible to us children; we all used to wait for the beautiful Tagore songs that the sermons were frequently interspersed with. Amartya-da's (I have always addressed Amartya in that typical Bengali younger-brotherly way) mother told me that when he was a small child, she once took him to that Wednesday gathering where Tagore himself was the master of ceremony. The child was obviously bored by Tagore's sermons and the hushed silence around him, so he started blabbering away, and his mother shushed him. At this, the child pointed his finger at Tagore, and loudly said, 'Why is that fellow talking then?' Clearly a pointed argument from an 'argumentative Indian'!

My young days in Santiniketan were immersed in Tagore's music, poetry and drama. In our neighbourhood, I once acted as the sick and dying, but dreamy child, Amal, in his famous play 'The Post Office'. (Much later, I came to know that this play was staged in the orphanage run by Janusz Korczak in the Warsaw ghetto, just before he and the children were taken by the Nazis to the Treblinka concentration camp. The French translation of this play by André Gide was read on the radio the night before Paris fell to the Nazis.) In the house next to ours in Santiniketan lived Nilima Sen, and a few houses away lived Kanika Bandyopadhyay, two of the best singers of Tagore songs; to this day, their voices and the melody from a distant past ring in my ears. Nilima Sen was a friend of my mother's and, as a child, I often spent some time at her home; in the warm evenings, she'd sit on the floor of the portico of her house and sing in a lusty heart-rending way into the gathering darkness. My cousin Sudhir Chanda, who lived with us and learned Tagore songs in Santiniketan, later started a well-known Tagore music school in Delhi.

Santiniketan used to attract a lot of foreign scholars, artists and students, which was a boon to a young stamp collector like me. Every day, the sorting at the small post office was completed by mid-morning, and many of the residents used to come and collect their mail themselves. I, along with a couple of other children, used to wait there for the foreigners to collect their mail. As soon as one was spotted, we used to scream 'Stamp! Stamp!'; they obliged us by tearing off the stamps on their envelopes. Soon, I had a thick album of foreign stamps. I used to linger wistfully over every stamp and imagined things about those distant foreign lands. (I remember Swiss stamps said only 'Helvetia' on them, which I could never find in the only world map I had at home.)

The other times I used to go to the post office was to mail my grandmother's frequent letters, which she had dictated to me the previous day. She was a marvellous cook, spent long hours in the kitchen despite her osteoarthritic stoop, and then, after everybody, had been fed, she'd sit down in the kitchen with her own food and call me to take the dictation of her letters. She was not illiterate, but she liked my way of phrasing in an organized way the outpouring of her emotions and frustrations in those letters to her near ones. My skill at concisely expressing intense personal feelings, honed in my grandmother's kitchen, was later tested in a crowded Kolkata post office. There, an illiterate migrant worker from a Bihar village approached me for help filling the money-order form that he required for remitting a meagre amount of money to his family back in the village. When it came to filling the measly little space at the end of the form, where you were allowed to send a brief message along with the money, this worn-out man sat on the floor, on his haunches, and told me what to write there in sporadic bursts of raw emotion (an incoherent mixture of his affection, anxiousness and longing) for his daughter and wife in the village whom he had not seen for many months. My skill was sorely tested, and I think I failed, particularly because the language had to be Hindi, in which I was deficient.

I was my grandmother's favourite, who got to have the first taste whenever she cooked something special. She tried to inspire me to follow in the hallowed footsteps of one of her uncles, Dr P.K. Roy, who in 1902 became the first Indian to be the principal of Kolkata's premier Presidency College. She also told me that this uncle, despite being revered, was ostracized by her Hindu orthodox family as he had converted to the Brahmo religious faith, a reformist sect that arose in nineteenth-century Bengal (its principles were first codified by Tagore's father). Roy's wife, Sarala, was a famous pioneer in women's education in Bengal. My grandmother's elder brother remained in Dhaka, even though most of his family moved to West Bengal before and after Partition. He was a stubborn, opinionated patriarch who dismissed his sons' repeated requests to him to join them in India. He was furious about the Partition, and used to blame Jawaharlal Nehru for it, and told his sons that if he were to go to India and chanced upon Nehru, he'd 'cut him up with an axe'. Maybe in consideration of Nehru's safety, his sons gave up.

I, as a child, did chance upon Nehru once during a convocation ceremony in Santiniketan. All the children in our neighbourhood were seated on the ground of a famous mango grove where the ceremony used to take place. We expected Nehru as the chancellor of the university to be on the dais, but shortly before the ceremony started, he was still loitering around. Suddenly, we found him standing in the area where we were seated. We were awestruck by his presence in our midst. I remember one of the children softly touching him and pointing my attention to his pink Kashmiri skin colour. Those were days when the Prime Minister of India could move around masses of people without much security or protection. This is unthinkable today in most countries, though I understand that the Prime Minister of the Netherlands still bikes regularly to his office.

Every night, sitting by a dim hurricane lamp (those days in Santiniketan the rationed electricity went off at 8 p.m.) and with jackals howling in bushes nearby, it was my grandmother's unfailing duty to tell me bedtime stories, which included stories about her family, but more often magical fairy tales of a distant time—tales that she herself learned from her mother while growing up in a village near Dhaka. I always talked to her (as to my parents) in the Dhaka dialect of Bengali, even though, as I was born in Kolkata, I was more familiar with the Kolkata dialect. As with the French, language is an essential, even sacred, part of the Bengali identity (linguistic nationalism was later at the root of the birth of Bangladesh); and just as in France until late in the nineteenth century where the majority of people spoke not the standardized Parisian version of French, but a diverse array of patois, in riverine Bengal, the different districts speak quite different dialects. My father was adept at mimicking the dialects of at least ten different districts of (undivided) Bengal.

I frequently write (and give lectures) in Bengali, and it is a motto with me to try to avoid using English words even when the subject is complex and technical. This grew out of a habit acquired during my college days—whenever I wrote letters to my friends it was a clear understanding among us that we'd meticulously avoid English words. This is not always easy (and nowadays almost an obsolete practice even among many Bengalis), and I have to often coin new words for which English words are more common. In this task, I have been immensely helped by my early love of Sanskrit, which I studied both in high school and college, and which provides a rich repository of ingredients to draw upon. (Once, in the pre-email days, Amartya-da complained that in being compelled to reply to my letters in Bengali, he had to keep track of his rusty Bengali spellings.)

All through my youth, until I went abroad, I was not fluent in common conversational English, though I had read many English books and, starting from high school, recited poems and participated in debates in English (not to speak of the pathetic attempts to mimic radio commentaries of cricket games, from the top of a guava tree by the Santiniketan playing field, when my side was batting). Even after going abroad, in conversations initially, my English was halting and kind of 'bookish' (this reminds me of a story a Bengali friend told me, that when he first had an affair with a woman in the US, at an intimate moment she said, 'Why are you talking to me in seminar-speak?'). I was also conscious that in my English conversation I was regularly translating from Bengali thoughts; over time, I just became a faster and more efficient translator. Even today while talking, some of my occasional slips are tell-tale signs of the translation effort (for example, in Bengali, the pronoun is gender-neutral, so in my translated conversation the occasional his–her confusion turns up—the recent currency of the gender-neutral 'their' is a help).

Finally, rather late in the day, I succeeded in persuading my father to send me to a nearby school, which happened to be one of the best schools of Kolkata, public-funded and with a long history (in 2017, the school celebrated its 200th anniversary). The day I went for the entrance examination for the school, one of the street kids I used to play with decided to take the same exam. His father took leave from his day job and accompanied us. Just before the exam started he instructed his son to sit close to me and copy every line that I wrote; as an explanation, he told him something that to this day haunts me, 'Don't try to write anything on your own; you know your head is full of cow dung.' Throughout history, this is how working-class parents have often psychologically disabled their children. Needless to say, the boy did not pass, either because of inefficient copying or inner resentment.

By the time I started regular school, my father's home-schooling had prepared me enough to sail through the various half-yearly and annual examinations relatively easily. Indian exams, certainly then and to a large extent even now, do not test your talent or learning ability—they are mainly a test of your memorizing capacity and dexterity in writing coherent answers in a frantic race against time. I found out that I was reasonably proficient in both, and that it was for the lack of proficiency in these two qualities that some of my friends, whom I considered highly imaginative and creative, were not doing so well in school.

My father did not believe in 'positive feedback' and would not praise me for doing quite well in the various exams in school (and later in college)—he used to tell my mother that all the praise might go to my head—instead, he'd ask me why the gap in my marks (those days marks were in absolute numbers) from the student who was ranked second had not improved compared to last time!

Looking back, I think this lack of positive feedback served one good purpose later in life. It has helped me in trying not to overestimate myself in any capacity. Even when other people have gushed with praise for me on various occasions in my professional career, while that has been pleasant, it was for myself largely water off a duck's back (in a symmetric way, facing attacks and criticisms has not usually dislodged my footing). I usually tell myself that I more or less know what I am worth—nothing more, nothing less. I think I am not prone to false modesty, but I remember what Winston Churchill reportedly said, in his usual pompous, haughty way, about Clement Attlee. When someone praised Attlee as a modest man, Churchill (reportedly) said, 'He has much to be modest about.' I know very well I have much to be modest about.

One major difference between the world of school and my home-schooling (plus playing with neighbourhood kids) is that it makes you aware of how important social skills are, in cultivating diverse friendships and particularly in interacting with students coming from vastly different social backgrounds. Coming from a low-middle-class background in Kolkata, I had, until then, no idea how different the lifestyle of rich kids was (these were days when there was no TV to give you voyeuristic insights into the life of the rich). So when one rich classmate invited me to his birthday party, and asked me to give him a 'tinkle' so that he could give our driver directions about how to reach his home, I could not easily tell him that our family possessed neither a phone to 'tinkle' with nor a car. My phone-less car-less status persisted all through my youth in Kolkata.

At the other end of the spectrum, I had some difficulty with the lower-middle-class attitudes to poverty that I found among friends and relatives. Some of them were a bit sanctimonious. The famous lines of one Bengali poet say: 'O Poverty, you've made me noble/ Given me the dignity of Christ'. But when you look at poverty from close quarters, as I did in the extremely poor families of the children I used to play with, and later in the many village surveys I have carried out as an economist, one can see how utterly degrading poverty often is. At the same time, I have also seen how valiant the fight against poverty (particularly by women who are at the front line of this battle) can be. This fight is not always very noble or dignifying; one can see (and even appreciate) how canny and devilishly resourceful you have to be.

In general, in the popular culture all around me, canniness was implicitly or explicitly highly valued. Even in the children's fables full of anthropomorphic animals, I often noticed how the clever fox outwits everybody and often wins at the end, and is a kind of role model. As a child, I also used to ponder about the oft-repeated dictum, 'honesty is the best policy'; we were being asked to be honest, not because it was morally the right thing to do, but, all things considered, and maybe as a long-term strategy, one should opt for honesty. I found out later that this is very much akin to the way economists are trained to think.

There are some other aspects of the culture of poverty that I observed with great interest in my neighbourhood in Kolkata. One is the obsession with personal cleanliness and rites of purification (say, the baths you take after touching the wrong things) merrily coexisting with complete indifference to public squalor just a few steps outside the house. Later in my life, I read some cultural-anthropological studies of the sharp distinction Indic culture makes between the private and the public, the home and the outside world. Looking at the squalor, disarray and the shabbiness, some of which could be substantially corrected and repaired with some amount of community effort, I often reflected, even as a boy, why it is so difficult for the community to get its act together.

In a way, this has been a running theme in my subsequent work in economics, both theoretical and empirical—trying to understand the difficulties of collective action, both at the micro-level (why do farmers resolve their water conflicts with other farmers more easily in some villages, but not in others) and at the macro-level (why do some countries in, say, northeast Asia and north-west Europe, seem to succeed better in collectively organizing short-run sacrifices for long-run betterment). The particular question of the impact of heterogeneity and inequality, both social and economic, on success in such collective action has always interested me. The early 1990s was when I came to know Elinor Ostrom (she, later, was the first woman to get the Nobel Prize in economics, although her field was political science); she told me that I was one of the very few economists she had met until then who was keen on issues of collective action in the local commons (her preoccupation). I told her that it all went back to the dingy neighbourhood in Kolkata where I grew up.

In 1983, I was invited by All Souls College, Oxford, to give one of their endowed set of lectures. In three lectures, I reflected on the problems of collective action being at the heart of the political-economic problems of India, an extremely unequal and heterogeneous country. These lectures were published as a short book in Oxford the next year, and since then I have noticed a peculiar asymmetry in its reception among economists and other social scientists. This book got a kind of benign neglect from most economists, but among other social scientists it is my most-cited book. This, I think, is partly because I did not publish in the book the background technical-theoretical notes I had which would have interested economists, but also partly because it was mainly about some general speculations on India. Mancur Olson, a pioneer in the economics of collective action, showed much interest in that book when his attention turned to developing countries. Though by then my own interest had gone beyond his concentration on macro-level freeriding problems (about sharing costs of collective action in a situation of self-interested calculation).

In my Kolkata neighbourhood, there was one kind of collective action that was unusually successful—this related to religious festivals. Every autumn there was a tremendous collective mobilization of neighbourhood resources and youthful energy in organizing the local pujas for one deity or another, and, on these occasions, almost the whole community participated with devout dedication and considerable ingenuity (including openly pilfering from the public electricity grid for the holy cause—this art locally known as 'hooking').

These festivals had both religious and cultural dimensions, and with Bengali society being highly politicized, politics was not far behind. In my childhood, politics in my neighbourhood was dominated by the Communist Party, and contrary to what you would expect, the communists were often enthusiastic participants in those religious festivals. The main difference between the pujas of non-communist and communist localities was in the brochures they produced on these occasions (in our neighbourhood, they would, for example, invoke the goddess Kali, the fierce deity of destruction, to come and slay the forces of the evil demon of capitalism) and in the list of celebrity artists they'd invite for their cultural soirées, containing mainly those of leftist persuasion.

Many years later, when my Italian classmates in England used to discuss Catholic Marxism in their country—on one occasion, I even participated in a vigorous discussion with them on the famous film by the Marxist poet-director Pier Paolo Pasolini titled *Gospel According to St. Matthew*—I told them about the communist Kali worshippers of my neighbourhood in Kolkata. I also told them of a communist activist Brahmin neighbour who combined, with touching sincerity, his daily activities as a mantra-chanting family priest in several households with his indefatigable party propaganda work every morning at the street crossing near our house, trying to catch hold of passers-by and apprising them of the evildoings of the ruling capitalist-lackey party and his marching in the streets in his lunch break from office work, shouting slogans against American imperialism.

This fluidity of ideology and practice only adds, as I told my Italian friends, to a long list of common characteristics India shares with Italy: A culturally rich civilizational legacy, great cuisine, good-looking women (with liquid eyes), dysfunctional bureaucracy, mafia-controlled localities, widespread corruption, chaotic traffic, messy politics (John Kenneth Galbraith's widely cited description of India as a 'functioning anarchy' is equally applicable to parts of Italy), and a general sense of triumph in evading laws (Italians have an expression: *'Fatta la legge, trovato l'inganno'*—no sooner is a law passed than someone finds a way to dodge it). One may now add to this list the ominous rise of right-wing populism in both countries.

In my graduate student days, when an Italian friend was showing me around Napoli, he first took me to the university where he was teaching. In the large faculty common room, I saw several old men dozing; he pointed to them and said that until these geezers died there was no vacancy and so no promotion—a phenomenon not unfamiliar in the Indian universities, at least in those days. Walking the backstreets of Napoli reminded me of my neighbourhood in Kolkata (now the widely acclaimed novels of Elena Ferrante evoke some similar images). I also remembered watching in Kolkata the many, mostly black-and-white, Italian films based in such cities. In some of them, there was Sophia Loren walking the cobbled streets in majestic defiance of the lewd comments and proposals thrown at her by the neighbourhood loafers, and her dismissive scattering of repartees in dubbed English (but with soft 't' and 'd'), 'Do that to your mother, do that to your sister ...', as she went on her hip-swinging trot.

In our Kolkata neighbourhood, there was a large, corpulent man, who was a bailiff or some such official in the municipal office. It was whispered that his illicit income at the office far exceeded his salary. Every morning before he went to office in his car, he donned his white suit in the sweltering heat, and a hand-pulled rickshaw would come to his door to take him to the four or five temples in the locality (his car could not navigate all the narrow lanes). In front of those temples, he'd stand and silently say his prayers, and then he'd start, first slowly, then ferociously, twisting his ears for several minutes, pre-atonement one presumed for his daily sins. Some people think that Hinduism, like Catholicism, offers many ways of pacifying deities or buying off pardons for sins.

The case of this corpulent man was first pointed out to me by my father, a close observer of religious hypocrisies all around. When I was young, I had many conversations with him on religion. He always took the hard line and quoted Marx on religion as the opium of the people. Much later, I found out that in the line just before that famous quote, Marx was actually much softer on religion; he called it 'the sigh of the oppressed creature, the heart of a heartless world'. Even though I have never been religious myself, my attitude to the personal religion or spirituality of others has been softer. I have, however, a visceral dislike for most organized religions—particularly if they are in the business of harmfully polarizing or misinforming people.

I have accompanied some friends and relatives to visit temples and mosques in India, admired their architecture from outside, but usually did not enter them. I often ended up with the duty to guard my companions' shoes outside, as losing good shoes at the doors of temples and mosques is a common mishap. Some families even adopt the practice of leaving one shoe at one side and the other far from there. (I am reminded of the story an Italian friend told me of a Neapolitan mayoral election when the candidate distributed left shoes among his electorate, with the promise of giving them the right shoe on being elected.) In cathedrals in Europe, if they are not crowded (which is impossible in Indian religious places), I have often entered, and liked to sit there quietly, just as I have enjoyed devotional music either in Western or Indian classicals, or in some Tagore songs.

In old age, with the indignity of deteriorating health and of losing his control over most things, with friends mostly dead or incapacitated, my father was quite miserable and, unlike other Indian old people, did not have religion to turn to. He then partly lost his mind, and took to ranting loudly alone in his room—all his frustrations and regrets of life came out like streams of lava. He did not go gently into the night. Dylan Thomas goes on to say: 'Old age should burn and rave at close of day/Rage, rage at the dying of the light'.

In the midst of all this rage and rant, my father, always the teacher, would sometimes suddenly stop if the commentator in the radio set nearby made a grammatical mistake and he'd loudly correct them. In America, when a plane is about to land, the captain usually announces that we'd arrive 'momentarily'. This use of the word is in a long list of 'no-nos' that my father had taught me, so I remember him every time I'm on a plane negotiating its way down.

When my father used to rant alone in his room, we did not enter it nor try to talk to him; we just let him be himself. With my mother, for a period, we had the opposite problem; we wanted to talk to her, but could not because of her medical condition. She had a massive brain haemorrhage, and was in a coma for nearly two months. I flew from California to be at her bedside in the Kolkata hospital. The doctor said that she might come out of coma any day, and it might be of help if she saw me when she woke up; so I used to be on a whole-day vigil. Some people said that patients in a coma could even faintly hear you, so you should keep on talking, which might stimulate them regaining consciousness. But I did not try, I just sat beside her for several weeks. Many years later, I saw a Spanish film, *Talk to Her*, written and directed by Pedro Almodóvar, where two women in separate incidents become comatose and are in the same hospital. There, one man continuously talks to the woman as if she were awake, and even advises the man with the other woman to do the same. In particular, he says even when in a coma, women understand men's problems.

2
Life in Kolkata's By-lanes and College Street

The gully cricket I played in my neighbourhood also had a tournament, where different localities of north Kolkata competed. I once played in such a tournament which was being held in the far north of the city, some distance from where I lived. I don't remember the game now, but I met a savvy boy there, somewhat older than me, who opened my eyes about Kolkata politics. When he asked me which locality I was from, he stopped me when I started answering with a geographic description. He was really interested in knowing which particular mafia leader my neighbourhood fell under. Finding me rather ignorant, he went on to an elaborate explanation of how the whole city was divided up into different mafia fiefdoms, and their hierarchical network and different specializations in different income-earning sources (protection rackets for traders, prostitution, smuggling, railway wagon hijacking, etc.), and their nexus with the hierarchy of political leaders as patrons at different levels. After he figured out the coordinates of my locality, he told me which particular mafia don my neighbourhood hoodlums (the local term is 'mastan') paid allegiance to. I recognized the name; this man's family had a meat shop in the area.

Since that day, my whole outlook to local politics changed, and soon after, I saw a newspaper photo where this mafia don was sharing the dais in a political rally with the chief minister. This was the beginning of my academic interest in gangster politics and its role in the power relationships in different parts of the world. Later, when I read Mario Puzo's *The Godfather* (before the movies based on it came out), I realized that this was a feature of metropolitan politics in rich countries as well. Now, of course, there is a whole industry on this, in literature, movies and TV—in India, the Mumbai underworld, for example, in the novel *Sacred Games* by my Berkeley English department colleague, the writer Vikram Chandra, has been oft depicted, but not so much Kolkata's.

I soon started closely observing the methods of operation of the local mastans, how they work out their demarcation of the business of extortion (sometimes the system broke down, and violent turf wars took place, like when we heard loud booms of explosions coming from the street where the brothels were), how they mesh their organization with that of the political and cultural mobilization by the local politicians. Two of their characteristics immediately struck me as a young observer.

One is about how they start. In the neighbourhood, many young men start bodybuilding (some in gyms, called akharas, and some outside). Soon, these musclemen go for the job-entry tests for the lower ranks of the police. Those who pass the tests become policemen, and those who fail turn to apprenticeship with the mastans. This, in general, is probably true in most parts of the world, as the line between the police and criminals at the lower level is usually rather thin. Max Weber is known to have described the state as having the 'monopoly of violence'. In most such neighbourhoods, there is actually an oligopoly of violence, but with some structure.

Furthermore, I used to see in the mastans a peculiar mixture of cruelty and almost sentimental loyalty. They can be quite brutal in their crimes elsewhere, but in the immediate locality they can have touchingly sentimental relationships with whom they consider as their extended family (including those who have established family-like relationships with them). They'd have no scruples in assaulting women elsewhere, but they'd give their lives to protect women in the locality who have established some 'fictive-kinship' relationship with them as 'aunts' or 'sisters'. Mario Puzo's book also emphasizes the special role in the mafia of loyalty to family and other close relations in the locality.

Talking of violence, I should mention that my earliest memory of violence is from the immediate pre-Partition Hindu–Muslim riots in Kolkata. I was too young to comprehend what really was going on, but from overheard snatches of grown-up conversations about the killings (usually of innocent people like the old Muslim umbrella repairman in our neighbourhood whom my father knew), the oppressive grip of tension and fear all around, and whispers of rumours (often about horrific rapes committed by villains always from the 'other' community), I could form a ghastly picture in my mind. Then, at night, there were these screams of 'Allah hu Akbar' (God is Great) from Muslim neighbourhoods and rival screams of 'Vande Mataram' (We Worship the Mother) from Hindu neighbourhoods, the aggressiveness of each shout barely concealing the fear and desperation underneath. I saw how under that unrelenting pressure even ordinary people with ordinary feelings of humanity turned into ferocious beasts with fangs and claws.

One day, the news came that Muslim mastans of a nearby slum were massing to destroy a Shiva temple in the gateway to our neighbourhood, and then maybe attack all of us. The local elders asked all the households to get ready (for example, by boiling large amounts of water which we were to pour on the invaders from rooftops). At the end of our street lived a group of sturdy young men who were sweepers and latrine-cleaners by occupation. The mastans in our street mobilized them to defend the temple—watching all this from our window, my father wryly commented that these latrine-cleaners in normal times would not be allowed entry into the temple that they were now being herded to defend. After some agonizing time, an 'all-clear' notice came. I was not sure if the battle was won or did not take place at all.

I still remember the day the army was mobilized to pacify the disturbed neighbourhoods of Kolkata. As they were marching in the lane in front of our house, as a frightened but curious little boy, I opened the front door to watch them. A Gurkha soldier pointed his bayonet and screamed at me to get back into the house. Many years later, I remembered that day when I read a poem by Charles Simic, the American poet laureate, about a day in his childhood in Serbia:

… remember the Germans marching
Past our house in 1944.
The way everybody stood on the sidewalk
Watching them out of the corner of the eye,
The earth trembling, death going by …

A little white dog ran into the street
And got entangled with the soldiers' feet.
A kick made him fly as if he had wings.
That's what I keep seeing!

I have always noted how, in normal times, Hindus and Muslims participate in one another's religious/cultural festivals, how Hindus in thousands go on pilgrimage to visit Muslim shrines, for generations they live together in relative amity (though intermarriage is uncommon), how there is so much cultural integration in classical music, art, architecture and cuisine, how much of the beautiful rural folk music of both communities embodies deep syncretic values (which Mahatma Gandhi, Tagore and Nehru used to exhort us about), and yet, at times, and at the provocation of interested parties, it all turns out to be so fragile.

A couple of years after the Partition of India, a destitute refugee widow once came and pleaded with my mother to hire her as a live-in domestic maid. After some hesitation, my mother hired her; when we asked what her name was, she said, 'Just call me Gauranga's mother.' The whole day she used to work quietly, and, at night, for lack of space in that cramped house, she'd sleep in the kitchen. In the next room was my study table, where I worked until quite late. One night, long after everyone else in the house fell asleep, I heard, coming from the kitchen, first a groan, then a prolonged high-pitched wail. I rushed there and found the woman wailing in her sleep—the same thing happened almost every night. When, in the morning, we asked her about it, after a long silence the story came out. In her village home, where she lived with her son, Gauranga, and her husband, one day a mob came. They all ran and hid in the nearby pond. But the killers found them, and even as she managed to swim away, she saw her husband and son being decapitated, and the water in that part of the pond turning a dark red. To this day, I cannot forget that piercing wail, rending the night-time sky—the wail of a wounded subcontinent.

One remarkable redeeming feature of my dingy neighbourhood was that within half a mile or so there was my historically distinctive school, and across the street from it was Presidency College, one of the very best undergraduate colleges in India at that time (my school and that college were actually part of the same institution for the first thirty-seven years until 1854), adjacent was an intellectually vibrant coffee house, and the whole surrounding area had the largest book district of India—and, as I grew up, I made full use of all of these.

College life was a big and refreshing change for me in many ways. There was a lot of independence, opportunity to think in new ways and participate in a great deal of vigorous discussion on a whole range of discourse—including radical thoughts and risqué topics. Interaction with so many bright young minds all around was scintillating. Also, the proximity of so many women (this was my first experience of a co-educational institution) added to the excitement. There was, of course, a lot of one-upmanship, intellectual pretensions, and showing off. But, in general, the discussion both in college and in the coffee house (which was really an extension of the college) mostly rose above all that. There were invidious class distinctions among students, many of them coming from far richer households than mine, thus with more access to not just material goods—some of them came in cars and they were much less shabbily dressed than I was, for example—but cultural artefacts and networks, the superior sense of what was 'cool' (to use today's language) and what was not, and the inevitable name-dropping. But soon, I figured out that I was not any less well read or politically less aware or informed than some of the rich or culturally snobbish students, and that, to my giddy delight, even some women were prepared to listen to what I had to say. Slowly, I developed an intellectual confidence to overcome some, though clearly not all, of the class barriers.

The college had inspiring teachers in many fields. At the beginning, my most favourite fields were history and literature. I was an avid reader of literature; in college I had regular interactions with students both in English and Bengali literature. One of my maternal uncles who stayed with us accumulated a large number of cheap-edition books which the USSR used to distribute in India at throwaway prices. My uncle's collection had the works of Karl Marx, Friedrich Engels, Vladimir Lenin and Joseph Stalin, but also of Ivan Turgenev, Leo Tolstoy and Maxim Gorky. In high school, I found the prose in the former set too dense to do more than leafing through; but the latter set of literature books I gorged on. Earlier, apart from bits of Shakespeare to Charles Dickens to Graham Greene, I remember having a special liking for Aldous Huxley's dry novel *Point Counter Point*. In college, after reading Simone de Beauvoir's novel *The Mandarins* about the intellectual milieu in Paris, I was so fascinated that I thought (unrealistically) about writing a similar novel on the Kolkata milieu. In the long break between high school and college, I had systematically gone through many of the classic novels and short-story collections in the treasure house of Bengali literature. Each afternoon, I used to go out for long walks with a school friend who was also a literature freak, and we used to discuss our previous day's readings in a frenzied, intoxicated way.

Among my contemporaries in college in Bengali literature were Arun Sen, later a noted Marxist literary critic, and Prasanta Pal, the famous Tagore biographer. I was close to Prasanta for many years (I was the first to take him to Santiniketan, as he used to remind me). He was planning the Tagore multi-volume biography all the way to Tagore's death year, 1941. After his terminal cancer was diagnosed, I have seen how heroic and indefatigable his attempt was to get all the material to write as much as he could. He ruefully commented to me: 'It's a race between my death and that of the "old man" (Tagore).' Prasanta's end came too soon, and he could finish only the ninth volume (taking Tagore to 1926).

In college, among my contemporaries in English literature Gayatri Chakravorty (later Spivak) is now the most well-known in the world of literary theory, feminism and postcolonial studies. But I also used to interact with the poet and writer Ketaki Kushari (later Dyson) and with Samik Banerjee, now one of Kolkata's distinguished theatre and cinema critics. I remember Ketaki, who, as the editor of the college magazine, made me write an English essay on the literature of the then 'angry young men' in Britain (playwrights and novelists including John Osborne, Kingsley Amis and John Wain), as well as a Bengali short story, a rather sentimental one. Gayatri, Samik and I had represented the college in debating teams in English; Samik and I also participated in debates in Bengali. In recent years, Samik has been my unfailing guide in the world of theatre and cinema in Kolkata, taking me to many performances, and introducing me to some of the notable actors and directors. Samik also once took a long interview with me for a magazine in film criticism on how, as a social scientist, I looked at the last few decades of Bengali cinema.

The experience of debating in college helped me in many ways. First, it removed any stage fright I felt before speaking, which has helped in my later career of giving lectures in public fora to large audiences. Also, in many of the debate competitions, we were told only at the last minute what the topic was, or we did not know if we were to speak for or against the main proposition. This gave us the practice of thinking on our feet, and of carefully considering both the pros and cons on a given topic. The latter was consistent with my general mode of thinking: on many issues, I can see both sides to some extent and often take a middle position. This displeases passionate partisan people. After a lecture in England many years ago, where I pointed to both sides on the state vs market debate, a veteran British development economist came up to me and said that it seemed to him that I was 'running with the hare and hunting with the hounds'. As Ambrose Bierce, a nineteenth-century American writer, said, 'We know what happens to people who stay in the middle of the road, they get run over.' Throughout my professional life, I have been a little sceptical of certitude, and more comfortable with ambiguity and complexity. Václav Havel is reported to have said, 'Keep the company of those who seek the truth; run from those who have found it.'

But in college debates in English, the style at my time was a certain British Council–encouraged light, frothy style—where the topic did not really matter, the main purpose was to keep the audience entertained through sharp repartees, jokes and putdowns. (I knew some debaters who collected jokes and used them whatever the topic was.) This did not quite agree with me, even apart from my disabilities in those years in light English conversation as opposed to bookish talks. Later in my life, I was twice invited to the Oxford Union, the Mecca of such British-style debate. Both times, I had some other engagements, so I declined. Somehow, it also did not seem worthwhile for me to fly from California for such a short flashy performance.

In Kolkata, the best debater I knew in this British style was a college alumni and lawyer friend much senior to me, Sudhangshu Dasgupta, who in his time off ran a debating society. If he ever had the chance, I believe he could have given stiff competition to even the best of the Oxford Union debaters. Let me narrate here one of the many anecdotes of his debating that I remember. Once, in a public debate in a big hall, he arrived late. By the time he arrived, the proposition to be debated as well as which speaker was to speak on which side had already been announced. He was designated to be the first speaker to speak against the proposition. As he was entering the hall, the first speaker in favour had just finished, and Sudhangshu heard the chairman calling upon him to come to the dais and speak. He slowly walked to the dais, wiped the sweat on his brow, looked at the board where the proposition was written, and started speaking in favour, without checking what side he was on. After a few minutes, the audience caught on to his mistake, and titters and snickers were rippling through the hall. Sudhangshu paused for just a second, quickly guessed his error, and resumed: 'Ladies and gentlemen, in the last few minutes I was trying out an experiment. I was trying to defend this proposition on the board, and you were all giggling. That shows how ridiculous this proposition is.' And then he proceeded with the usual torrential flow of his speech delivery, but now against the proposition.

In spite of my abiding interest in literature when I came to college, I was vaguely inclined to major in history. In the long break between school and college, I chanced upon two books of Marxist history which opened me up to a new vista of looking at history. The first was Maurice Dobb's *Studies in the Development of Capitalism*. This book showed me that there was a discernible pattern in the jumble of facts in history, which attracted me. Soon after, I read a lesser Marxist history book, A.L. Morton's *A People's History of England*, which showed me how recasting the old widely known history of England from the people's perspective gave you new insights. These books whetted my appetite to read more of Marxist history.

In Presidency College, there was a thriving tradition of Marxist history; the doyen of the historians was the Marxist historian Susobhan Sarkar, who had inspired generations of history students there (I managed to attend a couple of his lectures as a sit-in student, but soon he was to leave Presidency after a long career there). Sarkar's son, Sumit, also a famous historian now, was a contemporary of mine in college. All around me, in college and in the coffee house, the dominant intellectual current was that of Marxists.

In College Street, the main thoroughfare in front of Presidency, and the road which I walked every day between my home and college, was a-throb with energetic leftist movements—the most important of which were the protracted agitations in demand for adequate food at affordable prices for the poor. Loud processions, barricades, blocking of streets, tear gas, police chasing students, and the occasional police shooting became part of my daily excitement.

But, on the intellectual level, doubts slowly gathered in my mind—not so much about Marx, but more about some of the Marxists around me. Many of them were unreconstructed Stalinists; they would dismiss the by-then well-documented atrocities of Stalin as mere American propaganda, and go on repeating the usual Party line and cant, to which I became allergic. They also dismissed, too easily, the value of what they described as 'bourgeois democracy'. In general, I found the official Marxist schema much too neat to fit in many of the complexities of social relations around. Actually reading Marx, particularly his late works, I found him much more open than the Marxists I met— no wonder, faced with so-called Marxists around him, Marx reportedly told his son-in-law that he was not a Marxist.

There were furious debates among several of us at the coffee house tables. In order to fortify my arguments, I started reading up particularly on the writings of anti-Stalinist European leftists. Every Friday, the local British Council library would get its latest copy of the *New Statesman*. As soon as the day's classes were over, a friend (Premen Addy, a historian and also the captain of the college cricket team) and I would take the bus and rush to that library. The magazine column we breathlessly read first was that of Isaac Deutscher, the Polish Marxist writer, famous for his three-volume biography of Leon Trotsky. (After his death in 1967, Premen later in London told me that he came to know and become a friend of his wife and collaborator, Tamara Deutscher.)

The coffee house those days attracted all kinds of characters. One table had several budding poets smoking away and, short of money, would sometimes be found sharing one cup of coffee among themselves (Allen Ginsberg, the American Beat poet, in what I believe was his last poem, was nostalgic about his Kolkata days in the early 1960s, referring wistfully to the 'young coffee house poets'); another table would noisily be discussing their literary preferences as signifiers of political partisanship (Jean-Paul Sartre vs Albert Camus, Bengali poets Buddhadeb Bose vs Bishnu De, etc.); at a corner table, two lovebirds could be found cooing to each other, ignoring the din and bustle around; at another table, a rising film star and poet (Soumitra Chatterjee) and a friend (Nirmalya Acharya) would be busy editing the latest issue of the leading intellectual Bengali magazine *Ekshan*; in another, some students would loudly be discussing the student union elections or the latest soccer game results; at one table, a young man would be holding the open palms of two women making a pretence of reading them; another table housed some famous Bengali writers on their way back from visiting their publishers in the neighbouring book district; at a corner table, a lonely, bearded, once-famous poet, now mentally unbalanced, could be found staring into the middle distance ...

Life in Kolkata's By-lanes and College Street

For a time, I also edited an (English) political-literary magazine from the coffee house titled *ISM* (Indian Students' Magazine), which was started and funded by a young businessman, a regular at the coffee house, whom I did not know well, but who wanted to be associated with intellectual activities. In the beginning, before others' contributions started coming in, I wrote the editorial and one of the main essays inside, and, just to show that a sufficient number of people were reading it, once I even wrote, under a false name, one of the letters to the editor, criticizing my own editorial of the previous month.

Another regular at the coffee house was an economics professor (not at the college), Amlan Datta, whom my communist friends loved to hate. When I first went to college, he had recently published a book titled *For Democracy*, which was essentially a short tract giving the usual liberal arguments against Stalinism in a cool-headed, logical way. When I read it, I did not consider it a great book, nor did I find anything particularly objectionable in it. The abusive words I heard about him made me curious, and one day I walked across to his table and introduced myself. Very soon, we became good friends, in spite of our large age and status difference—he a university professor and a leading public intellectual; I, a callow student recently out of high school. What I immediately liked about him, even though I disagreed with him on many points, was that he'd give me a patient hearing and honoured my arguments by giving a respectful, point-by-point rebuttal. After some time, when we knew where we agreed to disagree on politics, we moved to other subjects like literature. I also found out that of all my acquaintances he had the largest collection of Western classical music records and glossy books of Western art reproductions. So, by arrangement, I used to go to his home on Sunday afternoons when I'd listen to the music and look at the art prints for hours. He also introduced me to Chinese cuisine, an appreciation of which has lasted all these years.

Although I remained an admirer of Marxist history (over time, with a growing list of important qualifications), I soon realized that to delve into the materialist interpretation of history, I needed to understand the intricacies of economics—so this was how I gravitated to that subject. Looking back, I think my first exposure to Marxist history through Maurice Dobb's book may have inclined me in that direction, since Dobb himself was an economist (whom I met several years later in Cambridge, England). There is a story that when he was first offered the job in Cambridge by the conservative economist Dennis Robertson, he wanted to come clear that he was a member of the British Communist Party, to which Robertson replied, 'So long as you give us a fortnight's notice before blowing up the chapel, it'd be all right.'

Even though I arrived at economics with the aim of interpreting history, it soon gave me a more general perspective. First, it showed me the value of precision and empirical testing in thinking about socially important issues. This immediately appealed to me, as two of the first courses I liked in college were on deductive and inductive logic. More importantly, economics gave me a deeper understanding of the incentive mechanisms that motivate people and sustain social institutions. It made me think why some of the glib solutions suggested by my leftist friends were difficult to sustain in the real world, unless based on motivations/norms and constraints of people in that world. Why are cooperatives and nationalized industries, suggested as substitutes for private enterprise, often (not always) dysfunctional? Economics asks the question: If there is a social problem, why does it not get resolved by the people on their own, and if your answer is that it is the 'system' that is to blame—which was the main message of many leftist stories I read and plays/movies I watched—economics teaches us to go beyond and look into the underlying mechanism through which that 'system' is perpetuated or occasionally broken.

Fortunately for me, in Presidency College those days, economics was combined with political science, as I have always looked at the two subjects as intertwined. I found that classical economists of the eighteenth and nineteenth centuries looked at economics as political-economy, and analysed some of the major questions of distributive politics. Aristotle in his book *Politics* (which was one of our textbooks) describes man as a 'political animal'. In some sense, I have been a political animal ever since my childhood. My mother told me that by age five I was a regular newspaper reader; nowadays, I read about ten newspapers (including news websites) of different countries every day.

Looking back, my early interest in politics might have something to do with one of my maternal uncles, who was a political prisoner of the British. He was a member of a revolutionary group that tried (without success) to assassinate a notorious British Governor of Bengal. After arrest, the leader of his group Bhabani Bhattacharya (now Kolkata's Bhabani Bhavan is named after him) was hanged in 1935, and my uncle got life imprisonment, which he served until shortly before Indian Independence in 1947. He had served his sentence in several jails (including in the jail in the Andaman Islands), and one time, when he was transferred to a jail near Kolkata, my parents took me to visit him. My father lifted me up on his lap and, even then, I remember, it took me a while to find the small hole through which he was barely visible. I think he loomed quite large in my thoughts as a boy; as an adolescent, I wrote a Bengali novella (for a magazine brought out by some friends) with its beginning loosely based on what I'd heard about him from my mother and grandmother.

After release from prison, he used to visit us almost every day and told me many stories of his prison life (including torture and beatings)—not in a complaining way, but in what-else-do-you-expect-from-the-imperial-authorities way—but most of the time, we discussed current politics. He continued political activities with the socialist group led by Ram Manohar Lohia (when I was in college, he even made me write an article for the Lohia-edited magazine, *Mankind*). Around that time, he once took a trip with a non-violent resistance group to protest against Portuguese rule in Goa. The Portuguese police, instead of imprisoning them, took them up a hill and threw them down back into Indian territory. I still remember the morning in our house, my mother dressing his several horrible-looking wounds, while he, undeterred, kept on talking to me about the political situation in Goa.

Not surprisingly, in the early part of my youth, my politics was full of patriotic zeal. A big change happened in my thinking when I borrowed from the college library and read Tagore's book *Nationalism*, his 1916 lectures in Japan. In it, Tagore was trenchant in his criticism of the Western idea of the nation state, 'with all its paraphernalia of power and prosperity, its flags and pious hymns, … its mock thunders of patriotic bragging', and of how it stokes a national conceit that makes society lose its moral balance. The date being 1916 amazed me; he was going against the current in India's freedom struggle (although later I realized that Gandhi had a not-dissimilar view of the nation state). It also made me understand better Tagore's three novels on related themes (*Gora*, *Ghare Baire*—on which the Satyajit Ray film *The Home and the World* is based, and *Char Adhyay*) which I had already read in high school. This book led me to Tagore's other essays (until then, I had read mostly his fiction and poems). I started thinking of the complexities in the issues of nation, state and society, and their interrelationships—themes which have preoccupied me ever since. It's an irony of history that given Tagore's above-mentioned view on nationalistic 'pious hymns', today, whenever Tagore's song—adopted after his death as the Indian national anthem—is played, if you don't stand up, you may be arrested by the Indian police or harassed by the over-zealous nationalists.

My early views on left politics have been shaped by my coffee house days of discussion and readings (and College Street agitations), and also by two of my father's classmates from Dhaka University who influenced me. One was Binod Chaudhuri (my father's closest friend since their schooldays), and the other was Sachin Chaudhuri, the legendary editor of *Economic Weekly (EW)* and later *Economic and Political Weekly (EPW)*. Both Chaudhuris—no relation—were tall, graceful and handsome elderly gentlemen who took me under their wings.

Binod uncle lived near us, came with his family penniless from East Bengal, found a low-paying clerical job and, towards the end of each month, had to borrow money from my father even for his groceries. Transcending the sweaty struggles and pettiness of daily life, he had the amazing capacity to switch off to a world of intellectual wonder, curiosity and learning. Many mornings he'd come and sit down with me, and get involved in an intense discussion on some books we had both read, some op-ed article in the newspaper that morning or some other political issue, always on equal terms with this teenager, never condescending. One time, we were rapt in arguments on the matter of some Soviet intervention in Eastern Europe; I was strongly criticizing it and he somewhat defending it referring to various Central Intelligence Industry (CIA) machinations—suddenly, he asked me what time it was (he could not afford a watch). When I gave him the time, he jumped and realized that it was long past what he had promised his wife about returning from his shopping, and then going to his office. He referred to his wife with a sweet pronoun in his Comilla district dialect; the nearest equivalent term I can think of is what much later I heard in the British TV series 'Rumpole of the Bailey', where Rumpole, the elderly barrister, used to refer to his wife as 'she who must be obeyed'.

Sachin Chaudhuri, who lived in Bombay, came to know, I think from Binod Chaudhuri, about my teenage forays into writing political pieces, and he asked me to share them with him, and sent back detailed (handwritten) comments on them. A little later, he started encouraging me to write for *EW* (copies of which he got sent to me every week). But I was too diffident; I was a neophyte economics student, and I knew of *EW*'s sky-high reputation (Prime Minister Nehru had given a standing instruction to his assistants that as soon as the weekly came out it should immediately be at his desk). Many years later, in my days at the Massachusetts Institute of Technology (MIT), when I met Paul Samuelson, the great American economist, he once told me that he thought *EW* was a unique magazine, having topical columns on every week's events and, at the same time, publishing specialized analytical articles, some quite technical. I found out that he, like many stalwart economists and other social scientists in the world at that time, had himself written for *EW*—this was partly a tribute to the magnetic personality of Sachin Chaudhuri which attracted some of the finest minds and created a rich intellectual aura around the magazine.

Finally I yielded, and my first *EW* article (it was a review on a book by the Chicago economist Bert Hoselitz, the founding editor of the journal *Economic Development and Cultural Change*) came out while I was still at Presidency College. Since then, over many decades, I have lost count of the number of pieces I have contributed to *EW* and its successor *EPW*—some articles on quantitative analysis, some others straightforward opinion pieces. (Every time I have felt like paying a small part of my debt to Sachin Chaudhuri.)

In my interactions with him, I was struck by two of his special qualities. One was that he argued with me at equal level. I remember, when Milovan Djilas, a former vice president of then Yugoslavia, came out with his book, *The New Class: An Analysis of the Communist System*—referring to the party bureaucracy under such a system having the characteristics of a dominant class—it caused quite a stir, and the communists were, of course, scathing in their criticism. I wrote a review article on the book, finding some elements where I agreed, and found it belonging to the tradition of disillusioned communists who had seen the system from inside, like Trotsky, who in his 1937 book *The Revolution Betrayed* analysed the impact of what he called a 'bureaucratic caste' in the communist system. Sachin Chaudhuri told me that while he partly agreed with me, he thought I was going too far in the other direction. We argued back and forth in (handwritten) letters, but he was always very fair and decent even in disagreement. The other attribute of his that impressed me was the catholicity of his views. Amlan Datta once described him to me as 'the most liberal among leftists, the most leftist among liberals'. It was his broad-mindedness and openness to all kinds of intellectual discourse that attracted to the pages of *EW* and *EPW* intellectuals from the whole range of the political spectrum.

When I was a student at Cambridge, England, Sachin Chaudhuri visited there for a term. Since he was less busy there than he was in Bombay, I had a great opportunity to have long conversations with him on wide-ranging topics, including, of course, the Indian economy and polity. Cambridge, at that time, had some fans of Mao Zedong both among students and faculty—observing them, he privately expressed to me his scepticism about the fad.

He was also very generous as a person. I have been told that in Bombay it was widely known that his large apartment (which he shared with his brother Hiten Chaudhuri, a film producer and businessman) was open at all hours to guests. There was apparently a standing instruction to their live-in helper/caretaker that when any guest came, he was to make arrangements for their comfortable stay. Once, a gentleman whom neither of the Chaudhuri brothers knew was looking for a place to stay in Bombay, and was unsuccessful in his search. Then someone asked him to try the Chaudhuri apartment. When he arrived at the apartment neither brother was around, and the helper followed his instruction of arranging for the new guest's food and lodging. In the next few days, each brother casually greeted the guest, assuming that he must be an invitee of the other brother. One day, in the morning Hiten Chaudhuri was having his tea and reading his newspaper, while in another part of the room this guest was doing the same. At one point the guest, just to strike up a conversation, told Hiten that the arrangement at this place was nice indeed; he assumed that Hiten must also be a casual guest like him. Hiten said, 'What do you mean?' You can imagine the rest of the conversation.

The first time I met Sachin Chaudhuri in Kolkata was at the apartment of another of his brothers, when I was still in college. One time, he came to visit our house, and commented on the number of sweet shops in the neighbourhood; I said Kolkata was unrivalled in the number of rosogollas (a favourite Bengali sweet) and poets per square mile. I last met him when I was on my way from Kolkata to my teaching job at MIT, and he had asked me to stop on the way and stay with him at his apartment in Bombay. He threw a dinner party for me, and afterwards, took me to his study and insisted that I wrote an *EPW* editorial for the next issue, and kept on plying me with my favourite after-dinner liqueurs. It was quite late when I finished, and then, half-drunk, I overslept and almost missed my morning flight. A few weeks later, my MIT colleague Paul Rosenstein-Rodan walked into my office and grimly said, 'Sachin is no more.'

When the three people who were most influential in my intellectual development in early youth—my father and his two classmates—passed away, apart from grief, I also felt desolate that I had lot more things left to discuss with them. In my father's case, I was actually expecting to see him as part of my regular periodic visit; I was on an India-bound plane for this visit, but, by the time I arrived after the long journey from California, he was suddenly gone—a cousin had just completed the cremation. A long time ago, my father had instructed me not to follow any after-death rituals, so I did not. But soon, a priest appeared from nowhere and kept insisting that at least some basic Hindu rites must be performed. When I stubbornly refused, he became angry and started cursing me that my father's 'unpropitiated soul' was going to haunt me and the house, at which point I showed him the door.

I remembered a story attributed to Voltaire who was opposed to most established religions. On his deathbed, a priest arrived to give him one last chance of redemption and asked him to disown the Devil. At this, Voltaire is reported to have whispered: 'Father, this is not the time to make new enemies'.

Presidency College had a good department of economics and political science. I'd say that the teaching standard at my time there would compare quite favourably with the standard I found later when teaching undergraduate classes in Berkeley. I remember in my first lecture in Berkeley in a large undergraduate class I was using some bit of calculus. After my class, a student came to see me to complain about the use of calculus in class. I told her that I was not using any advanced calculus, so if she brushed up her high school-level calculus she should have no difficulty in following the class. She said that in her high-school in Carmel, a coastal town in California, there was the option to take either calculus or yoga, and she had chosen the latter. I told her, unhelpfully, that this was a choice unheard of in the land of yoga, India, and, I thought to myself, certainly in Presidency College.

One outstanding teacher I had there was Bhabatosh Datta. I can say that if I have to count four or five of the best undergraduate economics teachers anywhere in the world in my experience, I'd include him in the list. He did not merely have an excellent expository style, more importantly, he inspired us, even as undergraduates, to aspire to reach the frontier of the subject. I remember once rushing to the library to take out a front-ranking research journal (*Quarterly Journal of Economics*) to read up some new article that he had referred to in class. This is somewhat rare at the undergraduate level in most parts of the world. Of course, I did not understand half the article without taking his help. As the poet Robert Browning said, a man's reach should exceed his grasp; by pushing us this way, Datta wanted to see us achieve more.

While he was teaching us abstract economic theory in class, we used to read in newspapers (and in the pages of *EW*) his frequent writings on Indian economic policy. While most of these were in English, we hardly knew that he was at that time also editing a large set of economic essays as part of the massive enterprise to bring out a Bengali encyclopaedia—undertaken by the Bangiya Sahitya Parishad (Bengali Literary Society). Shortly after my graduation, he invited me to write essays for that encyclopaedia. A couple of decades later, he invited me to write a book in the economics book series in Bengali for the common reader that he was co-editing. All in all, he was a great inspiration for me in many ways.

On several occasions in my later years, in different parts of the world, people have asked me why there are so many Bengalis among the prominent Indian economists. I have usually responded jocularly that Bengalis are notoriously bad in business, so they tell the world how difficult it is to make money, and thus they all become experts in the economics of poverty. But the real answer has partly to do with the high standards of undergraduate economics teaching in Presidency College for some post-war decades, begun by professors like Bhabatosh Datta; the other part of the answer, I suppose, has to do with role models—when Amartya Sen and his Presidency contemporary Sukhamoy Chakravarty published several research articles in top international economic journals, it inspired generations that came later to the college.

Another legendary teacher in college was Dipak Banerjee (many people now hear about him as the father of the Nobel-laureate economist Abhijit Banerjee); he has inspired generations of students, including Abhijit. Unfortunately for me, he joined the college only a few months before I left it. In those few months, he taught us a course on the rather dry subject of methodology, but later, students have experienced the whole range of his teaching in diverse fields of economics.

But I had the good fortune to know him personally outside and beyond college. He was fond of me, and it was a pleasure to know this attractive person—a man of versatile interests, great style, and charming conversational wit. Over the years, whenever I have been in Kolkata, I have never missed an opportunity to visit him (and his wife, Nirmala, a noted economist, and Abhijit) and bask in the warm glow of the Banerjee household. He was a great connoisseur of classical music and Bengali food. When invited to lunch or dinner at his home, and overfed, I'd be told that I'd not be allowed to leave the table without partaking of some varieties of Bengali sweetmeats that he had gone many miles that morning to procure from the only speciality shop in the city where they were made. I have known Abhijit since when he was quite young and, to this day, treat him like a younger brother. When Abhijit and Nirmala invited me to give the first Dipak Banerjee Memorial Lecture in Presidency College, after his untimely death, I remembered how he had encouraged me to keep on writing in Bengali, and, on an impulse, I gave the lecture in Bengali (although the prepared slides I had were in English).

Dipak Banerjee fought a valiant, but losing, battle in protecting the high standards of economics teaching at Presidency College against interference by the Left government in West Bengal in the name of anti-elitism. Of course, such interference in government-funded educational institutions is not the monopoly of the Left; it continued with successive governments as part of their political patronage distribution. Now the right-wing government in Delhi with their pernicious ideological agenda is systematically decimating educational institutions that they consider as full of liberals and lefties, and taking every opportunity to stack them with loyalists. I shall later discuss this, as I have seen from the inside how a public university like the University of California, Berkeley, tries to maintain institutional insulation from the political process and preserves world-class academic excellence.

In my Presidency College economics class, I was particularly close to three students: Manish Nandy, Kamal Mitra and Kalpana Bose. Manish, an accomplished debater, was the first to encourage me to participate in college debates. He and I were both interested in literature, and in writing both in English and Bengali. Both of us were somewhat allergic to the typical Bengali inclination for over-sentimentality and verbosity; in reaction we were somewhat reticent/condensed in our expressions both in talking and writing. Through Manish I got to know his remarkable family, particularly his elder brother, the social psychologist Ashis Nandy (on whom more later).

Kamal had a distinctive style, with curiosity tuned more into human-interest stories than intellectual ones. He used to stay with his grandfather, Satyen Bose, the famous physicist—the subatomic particle Boson, that follows what is called Bose–Einstein statistics, is named after him. There is a story that once he was being felicitated in a big Kolkata public gathering, and suddenly in the middle of it he said, 'What am I doing here?' and promptly left. He was a great promoter of Bengali writing in science (Tagore dedicated his science book, *Vishwa Parichay*, to him). We regularly visited Kamal at his house. At home, Bose often played the Indian stringed instrument esraj and, while playing it alone in his room, sometimes tears would stream down his cheeks. We heard the music, but never dared going near his room.

Kalpana and I started going out together while in college. We did not have the resources to go to any clubs or posh lounges. So we mostly went to public parks, saw movies together, and took long walks in the streets of Kolkata, miles and miles, quite a feat of what the French call '*flânerie*'. After four years or so, we married.

3
A Foreign Student in Cambridge, UK

At age twenty-three, after a brief stint of teaching at Calcutta University, I, accompanied by Kalpana, proceeded to Britain on a Commonwealth Scholarship. The scholars from different parts of India were asked to assemble in Delhi, from where we were to take the flight to the UK. The only experience I had of an any flights before that was when I flew from Kolkata to Guwahati in Assam, representing Calcutta University in an inter-university debating competition. That flight experience had not been good, as our propeller-driven Dakota plane had hit a supposed 'air pocket'. So I had some unnecessary trepidation for the long Delhi–London flight.

A few months before I went to Delhi, Jagdish Bhagwati, already a star economist, had written an article in *EW* advocating the case for devaluation of the Indian rupee, to which I wrote a kind of counter, arguing for a more general policy. When Jagdish read it, he enquired with Sachin Chaudhuri about who I was. I got a message from Chaudhuri that as I was soon to be in Delhi, Jagdish wanted to see me there. In Delhi, he (and his colleague and partner, Padma Desai) took me to the Delhi School of Economics (DSE). This was a good opportunity for me to get to know Jagdish particularly, as his expertise was in international trade theory—an area I was planning to specialize in, and Jagdish gave me appropriate encouragement. I also met there K.N. Raj (more on him later), the doyen of Indian economists at that time. Many years later, when Paul Samuelson at MIT put me on the spot by challenging me if I knew any low-caste Indian economist, after a frantic mental search Raj's name came handy.

In the administration of Commonwealth Scholarships those days, the host country (in my case, Britain) was to decide which university the student would be assigned to, and they were inclined to send students to British universities that were less in demand. They had initially chosen the University of Glasgow for me, but when Amartya Sen (whom I had not yet met, but had correspondence with) came to know about this, he persuaded the administrators to switch my scholarship to Cambridge University. In the university, a college then had to be chosen. Amartya-da, who was a Fellow at Trinity College, told me that all the seats in the college that year were already taken; he introduced me to a Fellow at Pembroke College (Michael Posner), who then arranged for my admission there. Kalpana got admission at Newnham College (as a foreign student, her tuition fees, which we had to pay, were far above that for regular British students).

The day we arrived at Cambridge, the British Council put us up in a hotel for three days, and asked us to find some accommodation ourselves in that period. We went to a housing office which gave us a list of rental vacancies. We took that list and went to several places, but all of them said that there was no vacancy. We went back to the housing office, and they were (apparently) puzzled, as their office was supposed to be notified whenever a vacancy was filled. After a couple of days' futile search, it suddenly dawned on me that the landladies simply did not like how we looked.

On the third day of search, we gave up on the housing office lists. Someone in the economics department advised me to look into the rental ads in the local evening newspaper, *Cambridge News*. After a couple of failed searches from the ads there, I chanced upon an ad, which, at the end, added a significant expression, one I have not forgotten to this day: It said, 'No petty restrictions'. We rushed there even though it was a bit far from the campus, and immediately got a bedsitter for us to stay in. The house was a bit dingy and, on weekends, there were loud parties and splashes of vomit in some crannies, but for us 'No petty restrictions' was a great relief. We needed lots of coins to feed into the machines for gas fire in our room and for heating the water to take a shower. Several times in the middle of the shower, money ran out and cold water started coming out relentlessly, and we had to jump out. There was a common kitchen with a stove to share with the other tenants on the floor. I remember a Nigerian co-tenant took hours to get his meat 'properly' cooked; while waiting for him to finish, I'd be regaled with stories about Nigeria (including how his Igbo community people were 'superior' to the northern Nigerians—this, incidentally, was the time just before the Igbos in Biafra seceded from Nigeria and a devastating civil war ensued).

Another co-tenant, a sweet French girl named Claudine, once got me into trouble. One day, she frantically came to me asking for help in kicking out a 'guest' in her room, who was obviously overstaying his welcome. Since my childhood, I have always, I think prudently, tried to avoid situations where there was a possibility of fights—particularly with bigger fellows—but here I was with a 'damsel in distress' appealing for help. So very gingerly I went to her room (imagining to myself the scenes where Charlie Chaplin fought with big men in some of his films). To my good fortune, the man in her room, quite drunk, eyed me closely, grabbed a bottle and left the room cursing both of us all the while.

Cambridge is a beautiful city, so the outside made up for much of the drabness of our living arrangements. In any case, to save on heating costs we both spent much of the day and the evening in libraries and other university spaces where there was central heating. Later, I found out how some other people, financially constrained like us, saved on heating costs.

In some of the Cambridge cinema halls, they'd often have film retrospectives of various important European directors, which I had missed in Kolkata. Twice or thrice every week I used to steal away from my desk in the library to watch movies in the matinee show, which was cheaper than the regular shows. The halls at that hour were largely empty, except for some old people who had found out that given the senior discounts for the matinee show, they were a much cheaper source of warmth than heating their own homes in the damp cold of Cambridge. Thus, many an afternoon in those dark halls, amidst a symphony of snoring pensioners, I undauntedly concentrated on the sublime films.

In Kolkata, various film societies often showed more easily available East European films, usually involving grim, but occasionally gripping, stories of heroic life struggles under Nazi occupation. (I realized much later that some of these stories were also indirect protests of the directors against the then Soviet domination in their countries. This was the case, for example, in some of the films of the great Polish director Andrzej Wajda; his father was among the thousands of Polish officers killed in the Katyn forest by Stalin's secret police.)

So in Cambridge I came upon what can be called an 'abundanza' of European art films. To borrow the words of the Irish writer John Banville, for me it was an 'opulent pleasure garden where I sipped and sucked, dazed as a bumblebee in full-blown summer' (though Banville's context was exploring a lover's body).

I knew that Cambridge was by the river Cam, but the first day when I looked for it I could not find it. From the map, I knew that on my way to the economics department I had to cross it; I stopped and looked around, but I could not see anything like a river. Then I asked a passer-by, and he pointed to what I had thought was a small ditch or a canal I had just crossed. It was difficult to take it as a river, as, in India, I was used to much bigger rivers. Over time, however, I saw the serene beauty of this mini-river, with its placid water by the weeping willows, the swans, gliding boats and all.

There was a time when the Cambridge economics department was one of the most famous in the world. By the time I went as a student, its relative rank had declined somewhat—particularly compared to a few American universities—but it was still very high. As I was going to specialize in international trade theory, the professor who was assigned to supervise me was James Meade (later to get the Nobel Prize in that field). He was an extremely decent, soft-spoken and modest man (he declined a knighthood). I was told that he was a superb musician (I occasionally heard him humming inside when I knocked at his door) and an excellent carpenter.

He was also an austere man. He usually gave me appointments at 8 a.m.; on wintry mornings, when I arrived shivering from the long walk from my bed-sitter, I'd find that he had switched off the heating in his office (he, of course, asked me if I minded, but how could I say I did?). He was the most conscientious supervisor imaginable. He'd promptly and meticulously read all the writings

I inflicted on him, write detailed comments in the margin, mark a few lines on some pages saying that he had not vetted those lines as the mathematics used there was somewhat beyond him, which I should get checked by someone else (at his urging, I had soon a joint supervisor appointed: Frank Hahn).

Looking back, the one regret I have about James Meade is that preoccupied as I was with my dissertation on international trade, I mostly talked with him on that subject. Much later, I started working on a different subject, when I found out he had worked on it for many years—the subject of combining democracy, liberty, equality and economic efficiency, involving sub-topics like worker-managed firms, firm-level partnership between capital and labour, market socialism and universal basic income (what he called 'social dividend'). By the time I read his work on these topics, he was already too old, and died shortly after. I had missed a golden opportunity to benefit from interacting with him on those topics.

It is also unfortunate that this gentlest of men had to suffer the bitter partisan battles the economics department went through shortly after I left. It had originally started with respectable intellectual disputes about the concept and measurement of capital and its role in capitalist production systems, linked with some issues of income distribution. There were healthy debates on these issues between economists at Cambridge, Massachusetts, and those at Cambridge, England. This intellectual issue was, in a way, hijacked by some far-left economists in the latter place as part of their partisan political battles within the department in faculty appointments and direction of research. Unhappy with these squabbles, some of the big names in the faculty, including Meade, left Cambridge, leading to a decline in the department's standing in the world. History has repeatedly shown that, in academia as in the world of politics, such doctrinal differences between the far left and the social democrats can lead to irreversible damage—even though their substantive difference is really not that large in the ultimate analysis. It has been said that academic politics can be nasty 'because the stakes involved are so small'.

It was also unfortunate that one far-left economist whom I have greatly admired, Joan Robinson, let herself be used in these partisan battles. I have always thought that her contributions to economics—both in the 1930s, on Keynesian economics and the economics of imperfect competition, and in the 1950s, on the intricate questions she raised on capital theory—easily deserved a Nobel Prize, which she never got. We students were actually a bit afraid of her; she was brusque in her manners and did not care for social pleasantries. I used to see her taking long walks in Cambridge, always dressed in an Indian salwar kameez, with her white hair pulled back in a bun. (I was advised by other Indian students not to greet her casually when I met her walking. Apparently, one Indian student had greeted her with an innocent but formal, 'Good morning, Mrs Robinson!' and she sharply retorted: 'So what?') She, however, had a special affinity with India and used to spend a few weeks there (mainly in Kerala) every Christmas (she told us that she was there escaping from the commercial 'hell' of England during Christmas).

In seminars, she'd sit in front and quickly fall asleep, and then at the end the clapping for the speaker would wake her up, and she'd ask sharp questions. Amartya Sen has described her as 'totally brilliant, but vigorously intolerant'. I also found her a bit politically naïve, the way she repeated the then Chinese government rhetoric eulogizing the 'great Cultural Revolution', or the way, once after a visit to North Korea, she gave us a lecture, all gaga about the splendid achievements of the North Korean government.

There are alternative speculations about why she did not get the Nobel Prize. I don't think it was necessarily the misogyny of the Nobel selectors at that time. More likely, they were afraid that she might have rudely refused it, or even on acceptance, might have behaved 'improperly' in front of the Swedish monarch during the elaborate prize-giving ceremony (something the Swedes care a lot about).

Frank Hahn, who became my joint supervisor with Meade, was—personality-wise—quite the opposite of Meade. He was a boisterous man given to coarse remarks, took childish pleasure in outraging you and, if you looked offended by his remarks, he'd try to be even more outrageous. Once, when I told him that in the vacation I was going to India, he said: 'I see you and Amartya always going to India. What's there for you? People there are defecating all around and, without electricity, the peasants just copulate, as the only entertainment in the dark they can have.' I knew if I acted aggrieved at this, he'd go farther. So just to stop him, I said: 'Frank, you have a Eurocentric idea of the time of copulation. Indian peasants don't copulate at night. The peasant works the whole morning, then the wife brings their lunch to the field. After lunch in the shade of a tree and some hookah smoke, they make love in the lonely serenity of the afternoon.' He gave me an impish smile appreciating my invention. Another time, he illustrated how hierarchical Indian academia was. He was sitting in the office of the chairman of an economics department in India, when he asked for a glass of water. He said, 'All the chairman then did was to clap his hands, and in came a Reader in economics, holding a glass of water.'

But as a supervisor, he helped me with his sharp mind and sage advice. I last saw him in Siena, Italy, ill with an incurable degenerative disease. He came to my lecture in a wheelchair and at the end told me: 'My dear boy, good lecture, but A-, you need to work on it a bit more.' Then he turned to the students around and said, 'Who among you wants to have the privilege of pushing my wheelchair back to my office?'

Shortly after my arrival at Cambridge I struck up a warm friendship with a very bright young faculty member, Jim Mirrlees (who was to get the Nobel Prize later), recently returned from a stint of research in India. (Although he was a high-powered theoretical economist, he had what seemed to me an almost religious/moral fervour for doing something to help poor countries.) Much more than Frank Hahn, he got involved in the theoretical analysis in my dissertation, and helped me in making some of the proofs of my propositions simpler and less inelegant.

One time, I had found an error in the proof of a proposition in a widely read article on growth theory recently published by Hahn (jointly with Robin Matthews). I was pretty sure that their proposition was correct, but not the way they proved it. The morning I showed this to Hahn in a department common room, he and several others got busy on the blackboard with constructing an alternative proof, but all of them failed. At one point, Mirrlees entered the room and asked what was going on. He looked from a distance for a few minutes at the futile attempts on the board, and then proceeded to another part of the board and wrote down a neat proof. Everyone in the room clapped. His method of proof also gave me an idea in proving some propositions later in my dissertation.

In Cambridge, your supervisor cannot be your examiner; the dissertation has to be approved by two examiners—one internal (to the university), the other external. Mirrlees eventually was appointed my internal examiner. Incidentally, he also became the internal examiner on Kalpana's dissertation later, even though her work was not on theory, but on Indian agriculture. I used to tell Jim that while other people had a family doctor, we had in him a family thesis examiner. Whenever he and his first wife, Gill (who I think was a schoolteacher), went to a dinner party, and economists there indulged in their bad habit of talking technical economics, I used to notice Jim's sweet gesture in valiantly trying to whisper into Gill's ears translations of those technical arguments in more comprehensible language. (He later lost Gill to cancer.)

Even though Amartya-da was instrumental in my going to Cambridge, and we often chatted in the evenings, and he gave me a lot of advice about negotiating life in Cambridge, I was never his student nor was my research at that time related to his on social choice theory. Later, when his (and my) research moved more to specific policy areas in economic development, we interacted a lot more. Also, he left Cambridge for DSE shortly afterward.

I benefited in my dissertation from interaction also with Christopher Bliss (an English–Catholic fellow graduate student) and Christian von Weizsäcker (a visiting economist from Heidelberg, belonging to the famous Weizsäcker family, which included several distinguished academics and statesmen, including a President of Germany). For use in my work on growth theory I audited some courses (on non-linear differential equations) in the mathematics department; I was generously helped by an English graduate student there in catching up. Kalpana rewarded him with an Indian dinner at our home, which he relished.

Since I was working on the interface of international trade and growth theory, it was my good fortune that at the time Cambridge was at the frontline of growth theory, with its own faculty plus some eminent year-long visitors. The most distinguished among the latter were Kenneth Arrow and Robert Solow. I was in awe of both of them, and found out how decent and approachable they were.

If there was any economist who deserved more than one Nobel Prize, it was Arrow, whom I have always regarded as the greatest economist of the twentieth century (in the company of only John Maynard Keynes, and possibly Paul Samuelson). There is hardly any branch of economics which has not been enriched by him and, in addition, he opened up new branches. He was a man of infinite intellectual curiosity. He gave me comments on my papers (two of them grew out of his work on growth theory), and put me in touch with some people in the US who were working in related areas. In view of my work being at a later stage than theirs, he advised me to quickly publish some of my papers, which I then did, even before I finished my dissertation. He and Hahn were jointly writing a book on general equilibrium theory, which Hahn grandiosely described as 'the last nail in the coffin of capitalism', to which Arrow added: 'And my job is to make sure that nail is golden.'

Arrow was such a fast thinker that in class we sometimes had difficulty in keeping up with him. In the midst of his exposition of a particular idea, he'd pause and move over to some new idea that had just crossed his mind, before we could fully grasp the original idea. He was also a man of charming simplicity. I had often seen him bicycling across the campus (both in Cambridge, and later in Stanford). Once, after a seminar, we all went out for a drink and he joined us; I saw a bulging bag strapped across his chest while seated. I offered to relieve him of it and put the bag next to his seat. He declined my offer, telling me that as he often lost his bag, he was under strict instruction from his wife to keep it firmly strapped to his body.

Robert Solow was (still is, at ninety-eight as I write this book) a stylish, witty man, and bore his brilliance very lightly. In Cambridge, he took a particular interest in my work and soon became a mentor. He gave the Marshall Lectures in Cambridge on the basis of a paper he was jointly writing with Arrow and von Weizsäcker. In this paper, he was rising up to a challenge posed by Joan Robinson—how to theoretically cope with heterogeneous capital, with machines produced at different dates having different productivity, newer machines being more productive than old ones (which are scrapped in the process of growth). This started a new set of theoretical models in growth theory called 'vintage capital' models. Inspired by Solow's lectures, in some of my dissertation chapters I used the idea that low productivity in poor countries might be due to old machines being scrapped later. I published several other papers with such models in top journals. Solow liked these papers and, one day, before going back to MIT, he asked me if I'd like to join the faculty there, which threw me off balance (more on this later).

He used to stay in a house next to Fenner's Cricket Ground in Cambridge. He asked me to explain to him the strange game they were playing there. He saw some family resemblance of the game to baseball, but found it mysteriously slow, and said the strangest thing was that for a period nothing seemed to have happened, and yet people clapped in appreciation—I had to explain the 'maiden over' to him. I gave him a short account of the game rules, and ended by saying: 'Bob, think of it as baseball on valium.' (These were days long before the invention, to me rather unwelcome, of twenty-over or one-day cricket games.)

Among other members in the economics faculty at Cambridge, there was the great Italian scholar Piero Sraffa. He was administratively the professor-in-charge of us, the graduate students. So I met him a few times in that connection, but never quite intellectually engaged with him—partly because, by that time, he was a bit reclusive and did not teach classes or attend seminars, but also because I was so much in awe of his reputation in areas where I had little expertise. His work in economics was path-breaking in taking price theory to its classical roots, he had an influence on Ludwig Wittgenstein's philosophy (which the latter acknowledged), and he was a close friend of the Italian Marxist thinker Antonio Gramsci (when the latter was jailed by Mussolini in 1926, Sraffa used to regularly supply him with books and even pen and paper, with which Gramsci wrote his famous *Prison Notebooks*, procured by Sraffa from the prison authorities after Gramsci's death in 1937).

Other faculty members with whom I wish I had more interaction were Nicholas Kaldor, Maurice Dobb (I did tell him that his book had helped me come to economics) and Luigi Pasinetti—many years later, when I gave the first Luca d'Agliano Lecture in Development Economics in Turin, Luigi called me from Milan, which was a pleasant surprise, and we had a long talk. Both Kalpana and I saw quite a bit of two young faculty members, one was Geoff Harcourt (the friendly Australian) and Ajit Singh, an astute Marxist academic and organizer (the leftists, including some gorgeous upper-class British women, doted on him).

Among students, I knew quite a few Italians, including Michele and Bianca Salvati (Michele later became a member of the Italian Parliament and a major 'theoretician' for the Democratic Party of the Left), Giorgio La Malfa (he once took me around Napoli and the beautiful island of Capri, later a leader in the Italian Republican Party and twice a minister in the Italian government) and Marcello de Cecco (when he was in the University of Rome, every time I passed through, he'd take me to dinner at superb Italian restaurants and talk in his world-weary, savvy way). We had a South African fellow student, Francis Wilson, who later was a professor at the University of Cape Town. When, in 2000, the International Labour Organization in Geneva invited me to give their Nobel Peace Prize Lecture in South Africa, I jumped at the opportunity to make my first visit to the country. After my lectures were over, Francis took me and Kalpana on a long trip to the north, almost to the border of Namibia, and it was that (brief) time of the year when the nearby deserts were all in bloom—a feast for the eyes. His wife, Lindy, a noted documentary filmmaker, showed us her remarkable film *The Guguletu Seven*.

The South Asian friends with whom we were close included Aziz Khan and Swadesh Bose of Bangladesh, and Uswatte Arachchi and Nalini de Silva of Sri Lanka. Nalini, a no-nonsense Sinhalese woman, decided to marry a fellow student from Sri Lanka, who was Tamil, and all hell broke loose with her family back home, with whom she finally decided to break relations. Until then, I had underestimated the intensity of hatred for Tamils among some Sinhalese, about which I knew only vaguely. (This was almost two decades before the ethnic civil war broke out in Sri Lanka.) Much later, Uswatte invited me to give lectures to graduate students in Colombo, and I saw the elaborate military security arrangements all around the city amidst ethnic hatred run amok in a beautiful, lush green island.

We kept up with Aziz and Swadesh and their families in their later professional careers (particularly when Aziz was teaching at the University of California, Riverside, and Swadesh was at the World Bank). At Cambridge, Aziz had introduced us to the songs of Paul Robeson, Pete Seeger and Joan Baez. Aziz also shared my avidity for Bengali literature. Swadesh had a past life of leftist party work and imprisonment in East Pakistan days; he had quite an acute sense of current politics, which is what I mostly discussed with him.

In our last year in Cambridge, one of the retired teachers of Kalpana's Newnham College rented us a large room, into which we moved. This was in a quiet, verdant area of Cambridge, and a short walking distance from the economics department. Soon, our room became the meeting place of several of our Indian friends almost every evening. Some like the historian Premen Addy (friend from my Presidency College days) would often come early in the evening, and announce to Kalpana that the food at the college dining hall was particularly 'inedible' and politely ask her to feed him.

Shortly thereafter, others—Kalyan Mukherjea, a mathematics student (in later life, a professor at UCLA and then at Indian Statistical Institute (ISI), but also, importantly, a professional player of the Indian stringed instrument sarod), Prabir Roy, a physics student (later to be professor at the Tata Institute of Fundamental Research in Mumbai), Suhas Chakravarty, a history student (later taught at Delhi University) and Partha Dasgupta, an economics student (later a professor at Cambridge) would arrive. Quite intense discussion, after a point, in a somewhat hushed tone (as the Newnham teacher retired to bed rather early), fuelled by drinks, followed until late into the night. Then, after midnight, all would depart, with the frequent exception of a drunk Kalyan, who would declare with half-closed eyes that he'd like to spend the night there, and promptly fall asleep. But then his loud snoring kept us awake much of the rest of the night.

Before the Newnham lady went to bed, Kalyan would often lustily sing for us and occasionally entertain us with his musical spoofs. Sometimes, along with him an effervescent Telugu woman, another mathematics student, Sucharita Desiraju, would arrive. She was the granddaughter of the philosopher and the President of India, S. Radhakrishnan. I was told that the son of Pakistan's then military ruler Ayub Khan, who was a student at Cambridge, once propositioned Sucharita and said that between the two of them the India–Pakistan problems could be resolved, but Sucharita rebuffed him, obviously not mindful enough of those problems.

A Foreign Student in Cambridge, UK 59

Talking of progeny of country leaders, Nehru's grandson Rajiv Gandhi was also then a student at Cambridge, often seen together with an Italian woman named Sonia, but I did not know them. (I met Sonia Gandhi later in 2010, when she invited me to a conference in Delhi at the Nehru Museum. When the invitation originally came to my email, I was at the point of deleting it, which I usually did with the frequent invitations I used to get those days from the widows of various African dictators eager to share their wealth with me, and I thought here was another such email from another political widow.) Rajiv's brother, Sanjay, was also sometimes in the area, though not a student. Some say that he was into fancy cars, and that if he saw one he liked parked in the street, he'd take it for a joyride, with or often without the owner's permission. His penchant for cars and taking liberty with other people were both quite evident in his later life.

My Presidency College friend Premen was always a voracious reader, particularly of political, social and military history. He often told me of new books in those areas and sometimes persuaded me to read them. But, by the time I saw him again in Cambridge, I could see his slow turn from his fascination with Trotsky to Mao. This was in line with a general movement among the young in the European left around that time. Jean-Luc Godard's 1967 film *La Chinoise* captured the restless energy of politically activist students in contemporary France, foreshadowing the student rebellions in a year or so.

A Chinese student in Premen's hostel provided him with copies of official publications from Beijing, which Premen read with interest, but I saw mainly propaganda in them. He and I used to go to China-centric evening talks, say, by Joan Robinson (praising the new anti-bureaucratic directions for the world's left being shown by the Cultural Revolution) or by Joseph Needham (on the great strides in Chinese history in science and technology). Premen directed me to Needham's multi-volume magnum opus *Science and Civilization in China*, but I could manage only a partial skimming. I was, however, attracted by what is now known as the 'Needham Question': Why has the West overtaken China (and also India) in science and technology, despite their earlier successes? By now there have been several attempts to answer this question by historians and economists, but none of which I have found fully satisfactory.

Through Premen, I met one of his friends—a cheerful bohemian fellow from Bombay whom everyone called by his last name, Hamied (many years later, I found out that he belonged to the business family that started the international pharmaceutical company Cipla). He usually spoke to us in a charming mixture of English and Urdu. He was not doing well as a student in Cambridge. One day, Premen unexpectedly got a letter from him from Paris, saying that he had decided to seek his fortune in France, and asked him and me to pay him a visit. After a few weeks, another letter informed us that he was soon going to give up his lodgings, and this was our last chance for free accommodation in Paris. (He also warned that I should not bring Kalpana as his was a rather spartan single-room bachelor's pad not at all suitable for women.)

For Premen and me, both poor students who had never been to Paris before, this was some opportunity—so we decided to take him up on his offer. In the last minute, something happened so that Premen had to cancel his visit, and so I ended up alone at Hamied's place, which turned out to be even more spartan than I had anticipated. The common toilet was a couple of floors below in a huge, ramshackle building. Hamied also told me that in many such buildings in the area there was no arrangement for taking a bath; most people went once in several weeks to the public

('Turkish') baths some distance away. I had a clue then to the origin of the French perfume industry. (Later, I read stories about how badly the Royal Court at Versailles under Louis XIV stank.) Some even say that Europe slowly learned proper bathing from its colonies.

I also realized that Hamied was soon going to give up this accommodation mainly because he was running out of money and was desperately looking for a job, but one hurdle was that he did not speak French and hardly understood it. He told me a story about how in the previous week he had seen a sign in a store saying 'vacances', which he took to mean as 'vacancies'. So he entered the store and asked in English for job openings. It so happened that the man in that small travel agency did not understand English at all and proceeded to show Hamied brochures for beautiful places for taking a vacation. Hamied, at the beginning, thought those were the places where the vacancies were and got excited. Soon, both realized what the problem was, and the man got furious for his wasted time. Hamied told me he did not understand what the man was saying, but his firm guess was that he was being cursed at. As a hot-blooded man, Hamied had to curse right back, but he realized that if he cursed in English the man would not understand, while he himself would remain dissatisfied as his command over Urdu curse words was much better than English ones—so he hurled some choice Urdu epithets at the man and came out of the store.

Over the next few days, while Hamied went searching for a job, I went to the usual museums and tourist spots in Paris. And, in the evenings, I would meet up with Hamied and an Algerian friend of his at a café, and then go to an Algerian place for couscous with meat. One problem of being with this nice Algerian was that when we were seated outside, if a pretty woman was passing by, he'd immediately stand up and greet her with a warm 'salut', which the women usually ignored and went forward. He'd then sit down and shake his head in awed appreciation of female beauty, and say, 'Formidable', 'formidable'!

Back in Cambridge, late afternoons in the summer had a particular ethereal beauty. The daylight would be there until quite late, streets were relatively empty, soft sunlight bathing the houses and the trees where the birds were back and twittering. You could see an eccentric professor riding a unicycle, some boys walking wearily back from the day's cricket game, a young woman, with braids swinging, running late for her tryst, elderly people going into college chapels for evensong, distant voices from the students' acting a scene out of '*A Midsummer Night's Dream*' at the back of a college …

Cambridge was a great place to see theatre performances by students. Apart from plays done at the college backs, we occasionally went to the Cambridge Arts Theatre (founded by Keynes in 1936), say, for some performance of Chekov plays. I always thought, as with the writing of detective stories, the British have a particular flair for drama performance, and the standard of even young amateur theatre is quite high.

The building where this Arts Theatre was had a canteen on the rooftop, where I'd often go for lunch, walking through the King's College grounds. Sometimes, I'd see there the stooped figure of E.M. Forster from that college, already in his mid-eighties, seated at a table surrounded by admiring students. I did not go talk to him, but looking at him from my lunch table, I used to remember the first piece of his I had read in college—long before reading his *Passage to India* or *Howard's End*. This was an essay where the famous lines are:

> I do not believe in Belief … Tolerance, good temper and sympathy are no longer enough in a world which is rent by

religious and racial persecution, in a world where ignorance rules ... if I had to choose between betraying my country and betraying my friend I hope I should have the guts to betray my country.

In the world today of rampant, rabid nationalism, I often remember words like these of Forster (and Tagore).

4

A Young Faculty in Cambridge, Massachusetts

When Robert Solow asked me in Cambridge if I'd like to join the faculty at MIT in the other Cambridge, I was taken aback, and asked for some time to think about it. Until then, I never imagined living in the US—a country I had never visited before and what I saw in Hollywood films was not always attractive. I was planning to go back to India, where my ageing parents, younger siblings and the majority of my friends were.

There was also a mental block. Growing up in the leftist environment of Bengal, I had developed a visceral distaste for the American political regime in general, its imperial hegemony and its support of oppressive regimes all over the world in the name of fighting the Cold War. The ongoing Vietnam War was obviously a major irritant. At the same time, I knew that in the world of new ideas, entrepreneurial innovations and academic excellence, American pre-eminence was undeniable. In particular, the MIT economics department was then, as it is now, one of the top two or three departments in the world.

Most of my friends told me that it was silly of me not to give an immediate positive response to Solow. When I asked about what it was like living in the US, most of them were not very helpful. Only Kalyan, the mathematics student, who had some experience of living there, told me that it should be fine, except that I had to be mindful about two things: (a) whenever there was a policeman around, I should keep my hands out of my pockets; otherwise I'd be shot on suspicion of hiding a gun; and (b) I should minimize visits to doctors, not just for the expense involved (particularly compared to the National Health Service in the UK), but also because American doctors were supposedly 'knife-happy'—on the slightest pretext, they'd cut out a limb or two, as the fees they got from surgery were high!

After about two months of dilly-dallying, I accepted Solow's offer. The process of getting a visa at the London embassy was highly bureaucratic (and included questions like if I ever was a communist, if I ever felt like committing suicide, etc.; strangely, the next time I went for an American visa, these questions were not asked—presumably once you've seen Disneyland, you'd no longer have communist or suicidal propensities).

Through a local friend, I rented an apartment just a few steps away from Harvard Square, which was a boon as it was only two subway stops from my department at MIT, apart from the various delights of Harvard Square (two or three cinema halls, a variety of restaurants, bookstores—with one of them open twenty-four hours—walking access to seminars and talks at Harvard, etc.). I did not have a car (or a driver's licence) in

Kolkata or Cambridge, England; I barely managed with the same in Cambridge, Mass. This was possible because of the tolerably good public transportation connections from Harvard Square, and also because an MIT economics student from Kolkata, Sanjit Bose, and his wife, Uttara, became close friends, and often took us around to various long-distance places. For instance, thanks to them, a drive through northern areas like New Hampshire during the 'fall colours' season was a dazzling experience.

Along with me, several other young economists were hired at MIT that year, including Joe Stiglitz (a future Nobel laureate), Duncan Foley (from a Quaker family, later a Marxist professor at the New School for Social Research), Miguel Sidrauski (cancer claimed this Argentinian friend in a couple of years) and Michael Piore (later a well-known labour economist). Duncan and his wife, Helene (a classics scholar), became our good friends; we often met and went to movies together (including, I remember, two landmark movies, *Bonnie and Clyde* and *The Graduate*, which represented turning points for Hollywood movies).

Both Joe Stiglitz and I worked until quite late at night in our offices, which were close together. Late evenings, the janitors would come to sweep the floors and clean the bins. Sometimes, they'd sit down in our rooms and chat about the latest in sports, weather or politics. To Joe, this was routine, but he did not realize how pleasantly out of the ordinary it was for me, coming from India. To this day, in India, I have never seen a sweeper or toilet cleaner daring to sit and chat with professors (or students). This level of social equality (even allowing for all the dark history of racial discrimination and oppression) had been a distinctive characteristic of the US, even compared to Europe (I remember Gramsci writing about Italian society some day aspiring to reach the American level of social equality). When the janitor at our apartment building found out that I was an economist, he said he'd try to be my 'buddy', so that he could get tips about how to make money (little did he know that I had no clue). Arriving in the US, some changes in my daily life compared to that in India or England struck me (of course, these were days long before globalization and internet rendering the American experience almost universal—the German filmmaker Wim Wenders once said that America had even colonized his subconscious). One big change was the relentless assault of commercials throughout the day, either on TV, the radio or in the streets crowded with billboards. The second was an excessively cheerful way of people greeting one another and stating how 'awesome' or 'amazing' or 'fantastic' things were. It was difficult for me to match such ebullience. Third, in shops and elsewhere, there was an exasperating number of choices to be made at every point. I went to an ice-cream shop, and was immediately asked to choose from the thirty-two flavours displayed on the board. After a lot of effort, when I chose one, more choices were thrust on me—cone or cup, plain cone or sugar cone, single scoop or double scoop, and so on. I commented to a friend that such abundance of choice in the ice-cream shop was in sharp contrast with the limited choices in political candidates one faced. Fourth, I was not at all prepared for the clock changing in the fall and in spring—I became suddenly aware of the relativity of time. Fifth, compared to England, the heating and bathing facilities (including the mixing of hot and cold water in the same tap) were usually much more satisfactory. Sixth, I did not realize how bone-chillingly cold Boston winters were.

One obvious change in our daily life was, of course, that from an impecunious student I had now become a salaried professor. This, of course, was relative. Shortly afterwards, when I went to Chicago for a seminar, my seatmate on the plane, a businessman, asked me what I did for a living. When I said I was teaching at

MIT, I thought he'd be impressed; instead, he gave me a pitiful look and said, 'Don't you mind being poor?' I remembered someone once telling me that matrimonial ads in Indian newspapers, after spelling out the desired lucrative occupations of the groom (company executives or government jobs, like income tax officers whose non-salary sources of income could be significant) sometimes added, considerately, that 'professors will do'.

At MIT, I had my initiation into a breathless pace of academic activity that was quite different from the pace I had seen elsewhere until then. The whole place was a dynamo of research activity; you could almost hear the hum and feel the energetic throb of multiple high-powered brains at work. While teaching was an important part of daily activity and it often fed into research, it was research where the main action was. Later, I found out this was more or less the case in other top departments in the country, but it was here that I had my first experience. There was the thrill of thriving at the frontier of your subject—you could see the frontier visibly moving from one seminar to another, from one widely cited journal article to another; you had to run fast even to remain at the same place, and while the competition and the race were invigorating, you could also see the jostling and the occasional hustle.

I was amazed by how well-informed people were about who was doing what in which department in the country, who was pushing the (research) boundary where, which young faculty you had to attract before others could grab them, what was the going market rate for a particular 'hotshot' scholar, who was having an offer from which top department, and so on. (This reminds me of a phone conversation I had with the dean of a top east coast university much later, when I joined Berkeley. This dean wanted to know if I'd be interested in joining his university. Before he went any further, I told him that I had only recently settled down in Berkeley, both my wife and I liked the place, we had just bought a house, and so I'd not be interested in moving. He talked for a while and then gave up. But before ending the conversation, I think he took pity on me and gave me a bit of 'personal advice'. He said he could see that I was not yet used to the system in the American academic market. 'When somebody offers you a job,' he said, 'you don't say no even before I tell you the salary I was going to offer you, which I am sure is much higher than what Berkeley is paying you. Even if you are ultimately not really interested, you try to get all the information, take the time, bargain with your department, and get a raise for yourself.')

At the MIT department in those days, the most revered leader clearly was Paul Samuelson, who, every day at noon, would preside over the lunch table at the Faculty Club in the top floor of the building. At the table, he'd often entertain us drawing upon his spectacular collection of stories and gossip, not just about economists, but often about physicists and mathematicians. To Paul, there was a clear hierarchy of disciplines. It was visibly demonstrated to me one day when we took a visiting English friend who wanted to meet Paul. We told Paul that he'd be interested to know that this friend had done his degree in astrophysics, but now he was thinking of moving to economics. At this, Paul immediately said, putting his hand above his head, 'Astrophysics, then economics (he lowered his hand to his chest level)? What next? Theology (moving his hand to the knee level)?'

I have the greatest respect for Paul's many fundamental contributions, both to shaping the methods and tools of economics and to its substantive content. Yet, I have sometimes felt that he has pushed the subject more towards an application of physics and classical mechanics and equilibrium systems than it may have been completely healthy for the subject. Fortunately, there is now a greater appreciation in economics of biological-type processes and even non-equilibrium systems of complexity theory, not to speak of cultural processes familiar in anthropology.

Paul's clearly was one of the sharpest minds I have come across anywhere. His mastery over different branches of economics was phenomenal. Also, unlike many economists of his, and certainly later, generations—particularly in the US—he was deeply interested in the history of economic thought (something that is now hardly taught in most major economics departments). Even on Marx, he had some thoughtful papers. I am told that once asked by a radical MIT student what, in his opinion, was valid in Marx but not taught in any MIT course, his brief answer was: 'Class struggle.' That shows a breadth of vision missing in many contemporary technical economists. In his evaluation of Joan Robinson, he showed unrequited generosity. In 1970 (at the peak of the controversies between the two Cambridges) he called her 'one of the greatest analytical economists of our era'.

The other thing that struck me was how hard-working he was, even after reaching the peak of his discipline, both in academic research and in the world of policy advice, including writing a regular column for the *Newsweek* magazine. (I have been told that even at age ninety he used to come regularly to office, and was very active). I found the doors to his office always open; he'd stop work and cheerfully swap stories with most people who visited him.

I started teaching the graduate class on international trade, jointly with the famous trade economist and economic historian Charles Kindleberger. He was a delightful person to work and interact with; he was an enthusiastic old-style gentleman with lots of funny stories in his bag.

One time, Paul, who liked to try teaching different graduate courses in different years, told me that he'd like to teach the international finance class next term jointly with me. I had never taught that subject before, and yet how could I say no to him? Later, I realized that I should have never agreed to that. First, he always took his classes at 8 a.m., which was too early for me. I barely function at that hour. More than that, even when it was not my turn to teach, some mornings I'd be woken up by a call from him at 6 a.m., telling me that he had some unexpected summons from Washington, D.C., and had to catch a flight immediately and so, could I substitute for him that morning. I did not enjoy those occasions.

At the lunch table, whenever the names of two stalwart economists of his generation came up, Paul would never miss an opportunity to take good-natured potshots at them: one was politically to his right (Milton Friedman) and the other to his left (John Kenneth Galbraith), though with the latter he shared some proximity to the Kennedy administration.

He was also remarkably well informed about details of other countries. When a Bengali student with the surname Bose introduced himself to Paul, he said, 'Bose? Any relation to the scientist Bose (Satyen Bose, the physicist), or the fascist Bose (Subhas Chandra Bose—who was actually quite opposed to fascist ideas, but the Jewish world never forgot his meeting with Hitler in 1942), or the communist Bose (Jyoti Bose, then communist chief minister of West Bengal)?' He missed the name of his MIT engineer-colleague, Amar Bose, who built the Bose sound system and may be the only Bose now the younger generations have heard of.

Of the senior professors at MIT, other than Samuelson and Solow, I had a somewhat close relationship with Paul Rosenstein-Rodan, a pioneer in development economics. He had grown up in Vienna and taught in England before reaching MIT. He had advised governments in many countries and was full of stories. In India, he knew Nehru and Sachin Chaudhuri well. He had an excited, omniscient way of talking about various things. At the beginning of our many long conversations, he asked me what my politics was like. I said, 'Left of centre, though many Americans may consider it too far left, while several of my Marxist friends in India do not consider it left enough.' As someone from 'old Europe', he understood, and immediately put his hand on his heart and said: 'My heart too is located slightly left of centre.'

One of his many stories involved his trip to rural Egypt. He told that once he was travelling in the countryside in a car in the early evening. He saw a big field in one village where people were gathering for a cinema show; he stopped there, and as he walked closer, he saw that the large screen was made of rather thin paper. So he asked his Egyptian companion why it was paper, not the usual cloth screen, the latter asked him to wait; he'd soon know why. The film started, and sure enough it was a Bombay film, where, at the beginning, the villain was winning both in the fight scenes with the hero and also in the love scenes with the heroine. As this went on for some time, the viewers were getting angrier and angrier; at one point, they couldn't take it any more. They all stood up and, with great fury, started throwing their little knives at the screen, which soon got badly perforated. The projector was then stopped, and another paper screen was installed before the film could continue to its ultimate crowd-satisfying end.

Among other MIT faculty, apart from the other assistant professors, I got to know reasonably well Peter Diamond (in public economics), Karl Shell (a growth theorist), Richard Eckaus (a development economist) and Peter Temin (an economic historian). But I became particularly friendly with some of the graduate students who had either just finished their dissertation or were soon going to. In the former group were George Akerlof (who would go on to win the Nobel Prize in economics in 2001) and Mrinal Datta Chaudhuri (a Santiniketan classmate

A Young Faculty in Cambridge, Massachusetts 73

of Amartya-da, doing his dissertation a bit late in his academic life—Samuelson, for fun, used to call him 'Chatta-Daduri').

Mrinal soon became one of the best friends I ever had (more on him later). George is one of the most imaginative and creative economists around, his Woody Allen-esque anxiety-prone and easily frazzled manners hide his powerful mind. He also became a good friend whom I saw a lot more later as a colleague at Berkeley. At MIT, I was often together with Joe Stiglitz, George and Mrinal—this was the most sparkling set of companions I could imagine. (Through them I also got to meet the distinguished growth theorist Hirofumi Uzawa—more on him later.) Among all of us, Joe was then in a phase of spectacular productivity, publishing numerous first-rate papers.

Among the students nearing the end of their dissertation, I knew Avinash Dixit and Martin Weitzman well. Avinash brought from his mathematics background (in Cambridge, England) an elegance of analysis to economic-theoretical problems that was impressive. Apart from his many original contributions, his unifying overviews on different topics have been a valuable guide for many. He used to be a bit of an Anglophile, but racial issues in England were partly responsible for his moving to the US.

Marty Weitzman was in many ways a striking character. When I first met him, the first thing I noticed about him was his accent—it sounded like a deep New York street drawl, which, at first, I had some difficulty in following. (I don't know if his early years in a New York orphanage were responsible for this; Weitzman was actually the surname of his foster parents.) But soon I got used to his accent and his charming informality. At that time, he was a leftist, fresh from his formative student years in the tumultuous 1960s. He was a technically sophisticated economist, but, unlike many others of his ilk, he grappled with big systemic issues, which particularly attracted me. We spent several afternoons discussing those issues, but, unlike many on the left, he was a maverick, spurning clichés and always thinking out of the box.

Over the years, his economics became somewhat less radical. He once told me that in a visit to his parents' summer cottage, he discovered on a shelf his heavily marked old copy of Friedrich Hayek's book *Road to Serfdom*. In his youthful radical days, he had marked many of Hayek's passages with loud, dismissive comments like 'BS-BS-BS'. But now, he told me, he was surprised to find how some of the issues raised in the book were important, and he felt compelled to erase those profane markings. When in the early 1990s, I wrote an article about how the old idea of market socialism (using the market mechanism to achieve objectives of social justice) needed to be reformulated to take into account many of the incentive and information issues raised by Hayek, Marty was a particularly appreciative reader.

After making path-breaking contributions in the field of comparative economic systems, he gradually moved to the field of environmental economics, soon becoming a leader in it, challenging some of the standard cost-benefit calculations, when we cannot ignore the small but not entirely negligible probability of catastrophic risk in the matter of climate change from greenhouse gas emissions. So his pleading for control of those emissions became particularly urgent and influential. (I grieve personally and for the world that such a brilliant man recently took his own life.)

Two other MIT students I knew well were Stan Fischer (he was my student at the international trade class, later taught at MIT, and held top positions at the International Monetary Fund [IMF], the World Bank and at the Federal Reserve) and Robert Merton (later a Harvard professor and a Nobel laureate). I moved from our Harvard Square apartment to a campus apartment

A Young Faculty in Cambridge, Massachusetts 75

at MIT, and both Stan and Robert also lived in the same tall apartment building.

We all worked until very late at night at the department, and, for occasional breaks, we used to play table tennis. I remember one night when Robert and I were playing, a piece of paper fell out of his pocket. When I pointed his attention to that, he thanked me profusely because on that piece of paper he had written out the formula for option pricing in stock markets with the intricate proof of the relevant theorem that he had recently worked out (presumably he had not kept copies), which ultimately got him the Nobel Prize. Robert's father, also with a similar name, was famous as the founder of modern sociology. Robert told me that in his early youth almost every night at the family dinner table there were distinguished scholars whose conversations he could hardly fathom. His Nobel Prize may have elevated his position later at that table.

There was another well-known economist who later claimed that he was my student at MIT, but, for some reason, I cannot remember him from those days: Larry Summers, later treasury secretary and Harvard president. Once, I was invited to give a keynote lecture at the Pakistan Institute of Development Economics at Islamabad, and on the day of my lecture they told me that Summers (then vice president at the World Bank) was in town, and so they had invited him to be a discussant at my lecture. After my lecture, when Larry rose to speak he said, 'I am going to be critical of Professor Bardhan for several reasons, one of them being personal: he may not remember, when I was a student in his class at MIT, he gave me the only B+ grade I have ever received in my life.' When it came to my turn to reply to his criticisms of my talk, I said, 'I don't remember giving him a B+ at MIT, but today after listening to him I can tell you that he has improved a little; his grade now is A-,' and then proceeded to explain why it was not an A. The Pakistani audience seemed to lap it up, particularly because until then everybody there was deferential to Larry.

Later, when I asked Stan Fischer if Larry was really my student, he told me that he might have taken my undergraduate class. The undergraduate classes were larger than graduate classes, and I do not remember many of those students (one very bright MIT undergraduate I do remember teaching was Hal Varian, who later became my colleague at Berkeley, and has been the chief economist at Google for some years).

In my undergraduate classes at MIT, I noticed that many of the students were ready with the class textbook and their yellow markers, waiting to highlight parts of the text as I lectured. But, in my lectures, I usually talked about my thoughts on the subject, not following any particular textbook, which confused these students. They seemed to be bright, but a bit more like high-school kids. This was somewhat different from the undergraduates I had seen in Cambridge, England. This could be because the English students started college about a year later and so were a bit more mature; and also there could be differences in the general level of school education.

Shortly after my arrival at MIT, a petition protesting the American bombing of North Vietnam was circulated among the faculty, which I immediately signed. The next week, the signed petition came out as a full-page ad in the *New York Times*, but I was disappointed to see that most of the senior professors at MIT did not sign it.

Around that time, I remember Kalpana and I joined an anti-war protest march, that started at the Cambridge Common near Harvard Square and proceeded across the Charles river, all the way to Boston Common. (Some people, over-cautiously, had advised me against it, saying that this might put at risk my then tentative immigration status in the eerily exotic category called 'resident alien'.) During this march, one feature of American political life became clear to me. Most of the protesters were students, faculty and other liberal, educated professional people. In some areas, blue-collar workers from the sidelines were jeering at us, and, at one place, they became rather hostile and started throwing garbage bins at us. I think many blue-collar workers thought that these privileged, educated people were being unpatriotic and disrespectful of their boys who were fighting and dying in the jungles of Vietnam. The gulf between the working classes and the liberal elite in the US has widened much further in recent years. To me, this was (and is) a major organizational failure of the liberals and the left, in not approaching workers with more empathy and attempting to convince them how vested interests use their boys as mere cannon fodder.

In about two to three years, I noticed a big change in the mindset of the MIT faculty. On another petition protesting the Vietnam War, most of the senior professors did sign. Around that time, I remember some heated discussion at the lunch table at the Faculty Club. One senior professor, who still refused to sign, kept saying, 'I'd like to keep my mind open.' To this, Robert Solow made a cutting remark; he said, 'If you keep your mind that open, stuff's going to ooze out.'

On one issue of international politics, however, I learned over the years not to open my mouth in the faculty discussions—actions and policies of the Israeli government. I have seen the same distinguished faculty member who'd loudly deprecate violent killings of civilians or suppression of human rights by the American authorities in Vietnam or elsewhere will be blind to similar actions by the Israeli government against Palestinians. I have been astounded by the facile labelling of any criticism of Israeli government action as anti-Semitism or prejudice against the Jewish people—a confusion made by otherwise brilliant people. Over the years, I also found out that my friends in Israel (particularly those who used to be active in the Peace Now movement) were much less likely to indulge in this confusion than my Jewish friends in New York and Boston.

On this matter, I was quite naïve at the beginning when I joined MIT. One day, when people at lunch were discussing that morning's newspaper headline and deploring American action in Vietnam or Cambodia, I pointed out that the other headline in the same day's newspaper was about similar Israeli action against Palestinians. At this I noticed a resounding silence around the lunch table. After some interval of embarrassing silence, somebody started discussing house prices in Lexington. I took the hint and fell silent. But my neighbour at the table, Joe Stiglitz, suddenly interrupted the Lexington house price conversation, and said he thought I was right and that we should seriously discuss the Israeli issue. But nobody else showed any interest, and people at the table soon dispersed. I also stood up, but Joe kept going. As he and I were slowly walking down the stairs to our second-floor office, Joe went on talking, still agitatedly. Moments later, I saw a senior professor at the department hurriedly running down the stairs, but not before muttering something when he was passing Joe. I did not fully hear what he said, but I think I heard something about what 'self-hating Jews' do.

Over the years, very slowly, this has changed somewhat. An increasing number of liberal Jewish people in the US have started being somewhat critical of Israeli government actions. (On the other hand, Christian evangelicals have now become dedicated supporters of the latter.) One major public intellectual I used to read avidly in the *New York Review of Books* was Tony Judt, who wrote both on Europe and Israel. On his latter writings, he often earned the epithet of 'self-hating Jew'. In 2003, he wrote a piece where he argued that Israel was on its way to becoming a 'belligerently intolerant, faith-driven ethno-state'. In two decades since then, no one has convincingly shown that Israel has definitely changed course. Unfortunately, now India seems headed that way too.

When I first attended the occasional Harvard–MIT joint faculty seminar, I was dazzled by the number of luminaries in the gathering and the very high quality of discussion. Among the younger participants, Joe Stiglitz was quite active and his intensity was evident when I saw him chewing on his shirt collar, a frequent absent-minded habit of his in those days. Sometimes, one saw the speaker incessantly interrupted by questions, say, from one of the big-name Harvard professors, Wassily Leontief. At Solow's prodding, I agreed to present a paper at that seminar, with a lot of trepidation, but fortunately Leontief was not present that day.

At Harvard, the economist I knew best was Steve Marglin whom my friends, George Akerlof and Mrinal, had introduced me to. He was, at that time, regarded as a whizz-kid and was one of the youngest tenured professors at Harvard. He had earlier spent some time in India and became an admiring friend of Punjab's strongman chief minister Partap Singh Kairon. He was very friendly with me and Kalpana (Steve gave her useful comments on her ongoing dissertation), but I had seen him behaving somewhat abrasively with others, including senior professors.

Steve's early work was on investment and evaluation of development projects. Then, in the late 1960s, his research and politics took a major turn in a heterodox, radical direction. When he gave me the first draft of his later widely known paper titled 'What Do Bosses Do?'—arguing that the Industrial Revolution was less a technological advance and more an organizational restructuring, with capitalists getting dominant control of the labour process—I was quite impressed.

But I was less impressed a few years later—by that time I was in India—when he turned to more sociological themes, sometimes praising traditional Indian joint families and community life as an exemplar for individualistic Western society that banishes old people to lonely exile in nursing homes and allows market transactions to destroy community life. I remember having a long correspondence back and forth with him on this. I asked him to check with the young people and the daughters-in-law in Indian joint families about how they felt on this matter, and pointed to how oppressive communities in India could be for some individuals/castes. He later went a step further and published an article titled 'Development as Poison: Rethinking the Western Model of Modernity'.

Around that time, I met in Delhi his then wife, Frédérique, a cultural anthropologist, who expressed a similar view. I remember once getting into a tense argument with her when she spoke against vaccinations (for smallpox and cholera) in Indian villages that 'Westernized' intellectuals like me supported. She thought villagers' turning to superstitious worshipping of goddesses that would ward off diseases—instead of vaccinations—was also how community bonds got strengthened. Another American cultural anthropologist I know had approvingly termed such phenomena as 'calamity is community'.

Later, Steve turned from such sociological themes to post-Keynesian macroeconomics, where I found his contributions more plausible. I think from this work of his and that of another friend, Lance Taylor (at MIT and then at New School of Social Research), I became more aware of the link between inequality and deficiency in demand from poor people, hurting economic growth, which, in my earlier involvement in growth theory, I did not pay enough attention to. Lance had in mind the Latin American countries he was familiar with, but I increasingly see a Latin American-type 'conclave economy' in today's highly unequal India, where a limited sector caters to an affluent elite demanding relatively capital-intensive and skill-intensive goods (fancy cars, high-end medicine and care, software), whereas much of the general economy suffers from insufficient demand and underutilization of capacity, and thus low aggregate investment and employment.

A senior professor at Harvard I came to know reasonably well was Gottfried Haberler, who, in his early years, was a product of the Austrian School of Economics. As he was a leading international trade economist, and since he found out that I had specialized in that area and was teaching the course at MIT, he'd often invite me to his seminars and to lunches at one of the residential 'houses' of Harvard undergraduates with which he was associated. I found him very decent, but rather conservative in his views.

At a different end of the political spectrum was another senior Harvard economist, John Kenneth Galbraith, whom I met but did not really know. (By the way, to meet this man of 6 feet 9 inches height was to feel crushingly 'vertically challenged'— someone once vividly described the sight of Galbraith getting out of a car 'one limb at a time'.) I read his bestseller book *The Affluent Society* when I was in Presidency College. I have heard that when someone told him that on the basis of this book he was then the second-largest-selling economist author ever, the first being Karl Marx, he immediately said, 'But the purchases of my book are all voluntary.' I think his economics belonged to the distinctive American tradition of Thorstein Veblen and other institutional economists, but I found most technical economists dismissing him mainly as a popular writer. He was a master of English prose and, in the latter part of his life, he was invited to give lectures in campuses more often to the literature departments than in economics.

In the days of Vietnam War protests, in a campus rally, Galbraith called on Harvard students to boycott the classes of professors engaged in 'classified' research. At MIT, I also noticed the close relation between some technology-related academic researchers and parts of the US Department of Defense. Of course, there were different kinds of such research (after all, the internet was the outcome of defence-related research, which has transformed civilian life). Much depended on the nature of the contract between the government agency and the research team, and how much freedom the academics retained in their independent pursuit of such research. The boundary between the need for secrecy on grounds of national security, and the need for transparency and integrity of academic involvement can be rather tenuous or ambiguous. Also, research priorities tend to be defined and dominated by government funding oriented to immediate military and geopolitical interests. In such a context, the independence of public research funding organizations like the National Science Foundation or the National Institute of Health in the US become particularly important.

Sometime before I joined MIT, the *New York Times* came out with a report which found that the MIT Center for International Studies (where some of the development economists had research projects) was partly funded by the CIA, and some of these projects were also in India, which gave rise to considerable tension in the relationship between the Centre and the Indian Planning Commission, and the relationship was soon terminated.

I also found out that in MIT, private commercial enterprises often funded research. I remember once somebody from the Campbell Soup Company walking into my office and telling me that he had found out that I worked on growth theory, and the Campbell Soup Company was indeed acutely interested in growth, so he'd like to know if we could come to a mutually helpful arrangement. It took me some time to persuade this man that my work was completely useless for making soup or increasing its sales, and to get him out the door.

But this relationship between university research and commercial innovations (which I later saw in a public university like Berkeley as well) is a serious issue on which the US may be more advanced than other countries. Subject to the issue of academic freedom and research independence on which vigilance by academic committees is, of course, crucial, this give and take between the academic and business community is something on which there is much to learn for countries like India. In India, public research is highly bureaucratized, and the link between university research and commercial enterprises is extremely weak. There was one serious case I myself observed in West Bengal some decades back. The district of Howrah, adjacent to Kolkata, used to be a thriving centre of small-scale light engineering goods industry. But it declined as it could not adapt to the changing market needs and technological competition. The technological adaptation needed was not very complex and could easily be achieved if there were any link between the Howrah business firms and a reputed engineering school (what used to be known as BE College of Shibpur) which happened to be located in the same district. In the absence of this link, hundreds of thousands of people lost their jobs and the area became blighted.

The aforementioned the *New York Times* report also happened to show that the CIA had funded the widely known Congress for Cultural Freedom (CCF). I remember in my student days I was an avid reader of the British literary magazine *Encounter* of which the poet Stephen Spender was a founding editor; in Kolkata, my teacher/friend Amlan Datta and the philosopher-writer Abu Sayeed Ayyub used to edit a similar magazine, *Quest*—both of these magazines were publications of the CCF. As I myself have contributed some essays to *Quest*, I was initially shocked when I read about the CIA funding, but I did not feel particularly guilty, even though my contempt for the CIA had remained unabated. The only trouble was that this could give a handle to those who'd like to deprecate you anyway. But, sometimes, I even thought that the CIA money that went into bringing out good magazines, like *Encounter* and *Quest* (and Boris Pasternak's novel *Doctor Zhivago* some years before) meant there was less money for it to spend on nefarious purposes.

At MIT, outside the economics department, there was one scholar whose several lectures I have attended: Noam Chomsky. I knew of him as a pioneer in modern linguistic theory, but his fame in the outside world is as America's topmost dissenter (his position is somewhat like what used to be that of Bertrand Russell in Britain—a towering figure in his own subject philosophy, but his fame outside was that of Britain's leading dissenter).

Chomsky in his lectures used to tirelessly blast the framework of American imperial policy, the capitalist military–industrial complex, the corporate-controlled media machinery for manufacturing consent and the near-complete lack of control of common people over economic policy. I often agreed with the main thrust of his lectures, but the question that nagged me and never could ask him in the surging crowd of his admirers around, was about the feasibility of the positive socio-political alternatives he might have in mind.

In some of his writings, his constructive ideas seem close to old-style left-libertarian or anarcho-syndicalist views; in one place, he describes his ideological position as revolving around 'nourishing the libertarian and creative character of the human being'. What little I have read of this positive side of his ideological position has left me somewhat unconvinced; I have wondered if he has fully applied his mind to the various problems that arise in the real world beyond the anarchist or left-libertarian utopia.

Of the various social science writings in this area, I have found the work of the semi-anarchist political scientist James Scott more thoughtful than those of Chomsky. In his book *Two Cheers for Anarchism*, Scott endorses many of the ideas of great anarchist thinkers of the past (like Pierre-Joseph Proudhon or Mikhail Bakunin) on the independent self-organizing power of individuals and small communities for informal coordination without hierarchy. However, he also recognizes that the state is not always the enemy of freedom and that the state has an important role in safeguarding the relative equality that is necessary for small-group coordination and mutuality.

My life outside MIT included my ever-enthusiastic search for different kinds of films. This required keeping track not just of both American and international films in the art cinema halls of Harvard Square and downtown Boston, but also special shows of rare, non-commercial films shown at specialized venues and occasions. At one point, I became a member of the Boston Experimental Film Society. Their shows were at a remote place; yet, I used to go there, changing buses more than once.

But soon I realized that the objective of this Society was different from what I was looking for. Their purpose was to show not necessarily good films, but films that experimentally transgressed the restrictive boundaries and conventional norms of that time. For example, as gay rights were still banned in Massachusetts, many of the films there were trying to push the boundary in this respect. With all my sympathy for liberal causes, I was not mainly looking for advocacy or defiance-oriented films. I was looking for good cinema. One evening, they were screening a film, the focus of which turned out to be on motorbike subcultures, bordering on neo-Nazi style, vivid homosexuality and the occult. Halfway through, I was toying with the idea of leaving, when suddenly the film was stopped, lights came on, and the organizers came in front to announce that we should not be alarmed, but the Boston police had surrounded the hall. They said the police might arrest them, but not the viewers, so if we quietly walked out without provoking the cops then there should not be any problem. That was the last time I went to their shows.

At MIT, in the next two or three years, my research productivity went on at a frenzied speed. I published in all the top five journals, even twice in some of them within a fairly short span of time and was getting occasional job-exploratory phone calls from other departments in the country (including, incidentally, from Berkeley), but all through a vague dissatisfaction was slowly growing in me. I realized that the pyrotechnics of publishing at the frontier of a very narrowly specialized subject, however ego boosting, was not ultimately satisfying to me. I saw all around me, not just at MIT, several young economists, who, after mastering a fancy technique of analysis, were looking for a problem to apply it to and thus get a publishable paper, somewhat like a hammer in search of nails or, to put it more grandly, like in Luigi Pirandello's play, *Six Characters in Search of an Author*.

Also, most of my papers then were theoretical (using low- to middle-brow mathematics), none dealing with data from the lives of real people. My work related to international trade and to economic growth, while my interest started shifting to understanding processes of economic development, where I found out that most of the existing data—at least available then in the US—were reports on aggregative statistics of different countries, which were hardly useful in understanding what was going on at the ground level. I also started having qualms about the preoccupation of economics with issues that are quantifiable and measurable, leaving out other topics, even though the latter could be more important. I was aware that other social sciences, say, sociology or anthropology, while generating powerful insights on important topics, sometimes indulged in a lot of grandstanding and a kind of 'anything goes' looseness, without any clear criterion of falsifiability that economists look for. But the cliché about economists often searching for the 'lost keys' in an area where there is some pre-fixed light, rather than in the dark area where the keys were actually lost, seemed more often true than false. Besides, I thought, with our methods of precise analysis, we might be missing on a lot of ambiguity and complexity in the larger picture, particularly at our current state of empirical knowledge. It might sometimes even be the case like what Ansel Adams said about photography: 'There is nothing worse than a sharp image of a fuzzy concept.'

So I started thinking of going back to India, to observe and analyse the lives of the poor from a closer angle, though I never had the illusion that I'd be anything but an onlooker even there. My homeward thinking was shared by Kalpana, and also somewhat pushed by the severity of Boston winters.

I had a long discussion on my thinking with Amartya-da. He did not discourage me, but he wanted to make sure that I was aware of the big academic gamble I was taking—going to India and working with field data was likely to get me branded as an 'area-studies' person, which, at least in those days, was like going on exile, away from the frontier of economics (and a topmost department like MIT). Unlike today, those were days when field research in remote places was mostly unheard of in economics, and, in any case, this kind of development economics was definitely considered as backwaters, unworthy of smart economists.

I still decided to go back to India, after three years of teaching at MIT. When I told the chairman of my department, he said with some (not quite accurate) pride, 'Nobody leaves MIT voluntarily.' What I told him by way of explanation amounted to what lovers usually say when breaking up, 'It's not you, it's me.'

5
Grappling with Life in Delhi and with Data

Though I decided to go back to India, which institution I'd join there took some more time to determine. I had a standing invitation from K.N. Raj at the DSE. Even before I left MIT, he asked me to teach a course in Delhi during MIT's summer vacation period. I went and taught part of a course, which had good students (including Amitava Bose, who in his later professional life became close to me, served as a director of the Indian Institute of Management Calcutta, and finally lost his long battle against cancer). But I soon found out that the only job Raj could offer me was that of a Readership (associate professorship), as a full Professorship was not yet vacant. Amartya-da advised me against accepting a Readership, since in Indian universities there could be 'many a slip' even when a Professorship became vacant. I went back to MIT after the vacation, and soon after I got a message from T.N. Srinivasan of the ISI in Delhi, offering a full Professorship there, which I accepted.

I was somewhat familiar with the Kolkata headquarters of ISI, a world-class centre for statistics those days—with a leafy campus—but I did not know much about the Planning Unit of ISI in Delhi where I was to work. It did not have a campus at that time as it was originally linked to the Planning Commission, which was housed in a large government building called Yojana Bhavan. When P.C. Mahalanobis, the distinguished statistician and founder-director of ISI, was a member of the Planning Commission, from 1955 to 1967, he wanted this unit to provide research input to the planning process. By the time I joined ISI, Mahalanobis had left the Planning Commission, and this unit turned itself into a general research outfit—though later some teaching of post graduate students started. It continued being housed in that government building until a new campus for the Delhi branch of ISI was completed.

My main attraction to this place was T.N. Srinivasan. (Everybody, including his son, used to call him 'TN'—once, the Danish economist Bent Hansen, who later was my colleague at Berkeley, told me that he wondered if, when TN was a baby, his mother, while putting him to sleep on her lap, also called him 'TN'!) He did his dissertation (at Yale) and immediate post-dissertation work on economic theory, and yet, after returning to India, he immersed himself in detailed applied empirical work on the Indian economy, which is what I now intended to do, after my primarily theoretical work in the two Cambridges. For the next few years, it was with TN's meticulous guidance that I plunged into the murky waters of Indian data, and also co-authored with him several papers and books, analysing those data.

Shortly after I joined ISI, TN told me that it was customary for a newly appointed professor at ISI to go and talk to Mahalanobis for an hour or two. The latter, usually in Kolkata, was soon going to be in Delhi for a visit and would give me an appointment. I asked TN if this was an 'interview'; TN said that it was not quite that, but he might ask me a few questions. At the appointed hour, I went to see him on a very hot afternoon at the place where he was staying. I remember he wore khaki shorts.

Let me first give a brief background for Mahalanobis for those who do not know much about him. He was a major figure in Bengal's cultural and intellectual life. His family belonged to the reformist Brahmo sect, closely involved with the Tagore family, which also belonged to the same sect. He was an advisor and confidant of Rabindranath Tagore, served as his personal assistant particularly during his international travels, and was the general secretary of the university at Santiniketan for ten years. During his student days at Cambridge University, he became a friend of the mathematical genius Srinivasa Ramanujan. On his return to India, he was teaching physics at Presidency College, but became interested in the relatively new subject of statistics, and the idea of ISI was born in his Presidency College office. He made many contributions to the field of statistics, but his major public service included setting up the framework of Indian statistical systems, like the National Sample Survey (NSS). When Nehru involved him in India's economic planning, he provided not merely its statistical base but also a theoretical framework (called the Mahalanobis model).

It so happened that I had met Mahalanobis a few years before that hot afternoon of the 'interview' in Delhi. When at MIT, I was once invited by Harry Johnson, the famed international trade economist, to give a talk in his seminar at the University of Chicago. When I was a graduate student, Harry had helped me a lot by giving detailed comments on my papers in correspondence, long before I met him. Harry was a large man, a Henry VIII lookalike, and a big eater and drinker. Even when he was listening to someone, his hands would be busy chiselling a piece of wood to make small figures (his office shelf was full of these figures he made, some of well-known people, including one, as he pointed out to me, of his Chicago colleague, Milton Friedman).

After my talk, Harry told me that there was a gala dinner that night at the university for a visiting Bengali professor, Mahalanobis, and he'd like to take me there. There, at the large dinner table, I found that Harry had arranged for me to sit next to Mahalanobis. I introduced myself to him and said in Bengali that I did not imagine having the good fortune of meeting him there in Chicago. He quietly listened to me and then continued regaling the whole table about his travels in China (including his meeting with the premier, Zhou Enlai) just before coming to Chicago. At some interval, he turned to me and whispered in Bengali, 'You said it was a good fortune to meet me—are you interested in a job at ISI?'

I was taken aback, and slightly annoyed; I told him no, I had a good job at MIT. He said I should not misunderstand him, he was a man of clear-cut words, not given to beating around the bush. He had heard good things about me from Harry, and if I so wanted it, I could have a job at ISI the next day. I said no to him once again. After the dinner, maybe to assuage me, he said he was proceeding to the home of the famous Indian astrophysicist S. Chandrasekhar and insisted that I join him. At Chandrasekhar's place, he introduced me, but I did not have any further opportunity to talk to Mahalanobis. Little did I know at that time that I'd end up at ISI in a few years.

At the 'interview', I realized that he did not remember our encounter in Chicago, nor did I remind him of it. He started by asking me what my dissertation was on. In the first half sentence I could utter in reply, somehow the word 'model' was there. He immediately assumed it must have been the 'Mahalanobis model' of planning; I didn't have the heart to tell him that the models in my dissertation had nothing whatsoever to do with his. Then he went on and on about various things, full of his sparkling intelligence and, of course, his self-absorption. In the one and a half hours of my 'interview', I doubt if I uttered more than a couple of half sentences.

Over the years, I have heard many stories about Mahalanobis. One relates to his youth. He and Sukumar Ray (Satyajit Ray's father, a pioneer in Bengali literature, known for his nonsense rhymes and gibberish) were the two contemporary Brahmo whizz-kids active in literati circles. They used to arrange regular meetings at someone's home for serious discussion. But as usually happens in such Bengali middle-class gatherings, much time was taken up in the serving and enjoyment of food delicacies. Mahalanobis objected to this and said this was leaving too little time for discussion. So he sternly announced that from then on no food should be served in the meeting. For the next couple of times, people morosely accepted the rule. But Sukumar subverted it, by one time arriving a little early and persuading the food-preparers in the household (usually the women) that for the sake of the morale in the meeting, food-serving should be resumed. By the time Mahalanobis arrived, everybody was relishing the delicacies, which infuriated him, but he gave up.

His sternness was evident also in the way he ran ISI in Kolkata. Those days, most people there had as office space only a cubicle with adjustable wooden partitions. I have heard that Mahalanobis used to express his satisfaction or dissatisfaction with your work by adjusting those partitions overnight. In the morning, if you arrived to find your cubicle had shrunk, you understood that the director was unhappy with your work. I used to know a very decent, soft-spoken artist, B.N. Parashar, who, at one time, worked at ISI. One morning, when he saw his cubicle had shrunk, he was found quietly sobbing. (When I met Parashar later, he was a renowned artist in Kolkata. He presented me with some of his charcoal sketches on the theme of poverty. This generous, unassuming man was very popular with the street children near his hostel. He trained a poor village woman, Shakila, to do montage art and she excelled in it, and later had several exhibitions both in India and abroad.)

When I was in high school I had read a Bengali novel about a research institution run by a revered authoritarian director—later, I came to know that the author was an ex-employee of ISI. Once, when the ISI workers' union was restive with the director's rule, I am told that Mahalanobis summoned the union leaders and warned them that if they gave him trouble, he was going to wind up ISI. He apparently added that he and his wife had stored a large number of letters that Tagore had written to them; they could manage the rest of their lives by selling the publishing rights to those valuable letters—but if ISI closed down what would these workers eat? (I later had an occasion to read those letters as his wife serially published them in a Bengali magazine.)

At the same time, it is a singular achievement on his part that he got together and stimulated the work of a large number of excellent Indian statisticians at ISI and, for a time, made it one of the leading institutions of statistical research in the world. He also attracted some of the world's most renowned statisticians and scientists (and some economists) to come and visit ISI during its heyday.

One of the distinguished people who came to ISI and stayed on and became an Indian citizen was J.B.S. Haldane, possibly the twentieth century's most accomplished biologist. I remember when I was a student in Kolkata, we often went to the ISI library, as it had the best journal collection in Kolkata. In that library, we often saw this large Englishman in an Indian tunic, with a fat unlit cigar in hand, reading *Biometrika*. I now wish I had the courage to go and talk to this formidable-looking man. Later, I read a lot about his eccentric personality. As a Marxist, he once claimed that reading Lenin cured his gastritis. He said political dissent led him to leave England for India, but another reason was that he'd not have to wear socks—'sixty years in socks is enough,' he said.

He often experimented on himself. In one of his self-experiments, he suffered perforated eardrums. He later said, 'The drum generally heals up; and if a hole remains in it, although one is somewhat deaf, one can blow tobacco smoke out of the ear in question, which is a social accomplishment.' Once in Trinity College, Cambridge, he was going to be appointed a Fellow, but he ruined his chances when he brought along a large jar of urine from his laboratory to the college dining table.

When he was asked by some theologians what he'd tell God if he met Him after his death, he replied that he'd ask why He had a partiality for beetles—there are apparently 4,00,000 known species of beetles in the world. (Another atheist, Bertrand Russell, when asked the same question, was reported to have said that he'd ask Him why He made the proof of His existence so hard.)

The day I joined ISI at Yojana Bhavan, one of the first things TN told me was about the state of the toilets. The ISI offices were located on the sixth floor, and those days, in all government buildings, the higher in the building the worse were the facilities, due to water-pressure problems and more people. So he recommended that I should go down to the second floor, where the offices of the exalted members of the Planning Commission were located, for the toilets there were better. Thus, during my days at ISI, I mainly went to the Planning Commission area to relieve myself. In that area, I also noted that all the offices were air-conditioned (while our offices on the sixth floor were not), and each air-conditioned office had an attendant at the members' beck and call seated just outside the closed doors, stewing in the heat. Our offices at least had ceiling fans.

I remember my friend George Akerlof, from MIT and later Berkeley, on a one-year visit to ISI had a sixth-floor office, but he'd not switch on the ceiling fan above him. I asked him why, and he said all his loose papers would fly, which drove him crazy. I told him about paperweights, but he found that was too arduous, and so, while at work in his office, he was bathing in streams of sweat. Another time, I visited George in his apartment. I found half of his living room taken by stacks of V8 juice cans. He said his stomach could not stand spicy Indian food, so he mainly subsisted on V8 juice, which he procured from the American embassy where a large supply came at the beginning of every month. Yet, here was George, busy finishing that path-breaking paper of his, which was later to get him the Nobel Prize. (Most Western readers are surprised by the first few pages in that paper, which are full of Indian examples.)

Yojana Bhavan, being a government building, had a liveried gateman who'd check your ID card for entry. Every day, I undertook a long bus journey to reach my office. The bus stop was near the gate and every day, the guard took some minutes to scrutinize my ID card. One day, I was called in office by an American friend who was visiting Delhi and he offered to take me to lunch. After lunch, he dropped me at the gate of Yojana Bhavan in his large American car. The gateman saw me coming out of that car. He not only did not ask for my ID card, as a bonus I also got an ostentatious salute.

Growing up in India, I knew how hierarchical and status-oriented Indian society was, but the city of New Delhi took it to a bureaucratic extreme. I was told that in those days, if you told anyone the address of your government quarters, people would immediately know your approximate salary scale. The city's residential pattern, inherited from its colonial rulers, was highly structured. If you are a top secretary in a ministry, your assigned quarters will be a large bungalow with acres of gardens in prime real estate in the city centre, often a short distance from your office which you traverse in a chauffeur-driven official car. But if you are a lowly clerk or an orderly/peon in the same office building, you'll come in a crowded bus from many miles away, often from outside the city.

Since I used to go to office by bus (until a colleague started giving me a ride in his car), I also noticed a peculiar pattern in the plying of Delhi state buses compared to the buses I was familiar with in Kolkata. You are waiting at a bus stop along with dozens of other people of different age groups and with different amounts of baggage on them, and you'll see bus after bus skipping your stop—particularly if they don't have to unload any passengers at that stop. (Economists, of course, will point out that the bus driver and conductor, on fixed pay, have no incentive to take more passengers.) And if the bus does have someone getting off at that stop, it will stop some distance away and, by the time all the waiting passengers with their baggage run to reach there, the bus is likely to have sped off.

What particularly amazed me was the attitude of both the passengers, who were already in the bus, and those who were haplessly left behind—the former highly amused at the pitiful failure of so many in the catch-me-if-you-can game, and the latter disappointed, but not particularly agitated. (If this continued for some time in the streets of Kolkata I was familiar with, large numbers of people would have barricaded the road and stopped the next bus, and probably vandalized it.) Standing at the Delhi bus stop, I had often pondered the lack of empathy among one set of people and the lack of anger among the other, particularly when, the next day, the people in these two sets could be interchanged. The social scientist in me speculated if the long history of invasions in this north-western part of the subcontinent, and the attendant brutalities, had left a social legacy that made many common people in the area both deficient in empathy and prone to resignation to their fate.

Another bureaucratic aspect of life in Delhi those days was that even for many daily necessities you needed 'connections' with some official to smooth your way. The year after we settled in Delhi, our son, Titash, was born. Kalpana asked me to look into the possibility of getting a Delhi Milk Scheme 'token', which you needed for getting good-quality public supply of milk bottles at a reasonable price. When I asked around about how to get such a 'token', I was told that I had to go and get the approval of the local MP (member of Parliament), which meant jostling with a large crowd of supplicants at the MP's office or house, or get someone who was friendly with the MP to give the latter a call to ease my way; I was quite reluctant to do either. (For similar reasons, I remained on the perpetual waiting list for a telephone connection at home.)

I realized that the previous years of picking up a milk carton from the supermarket shelf abroad had spoilt me. Before that, in Kolkata, my father, who was a stickler for the purity of our milk supply, had arranged with a local milkman to bring his cow and milk it right in front of us, so that there was no chance for him to adulterate the milk. I remember as a child talking to that Bihari milkman, who told me an amazing story about his two cows. They were let loose after all the milking was done every morning to go and graze in the grassy fields outside the city, many miles away from his house. Every evening, the cows would by themselves negotiate unerringly the various streets and labyrinthine lanes and by-lanes of north Kolkata and come back to the milkman.

So one day, at my ISI office, while I was still preoccupied with the thought of procuring milk, there was a knock at my door and in came a life insurance agent eager to sell me a government-provided life insurance policy. As usually happens with young people, life insurance was not uppermost in my mind, and I thought of dismissing this man as soon as he was finished with his sales pitch. But before he finished, he added that as my loyal insurance agent he could also help me out in other matters relating to public services. I asked him if he could procure Milk Scheme 'tokens'? He asked, 'How many do you want?' So I asked him to get a 'token' by the next day and then I'd be prepared to talk to him about life insurance. The next day, he delivered a token to me and became my life insurance agent. (By the way, as a child, I remember when I first heard the expression 'life insurance', I wondered how someone could miraculously insure a life against death.)

One quite positive aspect of my Delhi experience was that, for the first time, I felt I was in an all-India city. In office or in after-hour gatherings, I had never before met so many people from different parts of the country, speaking different languages, dressed in different attire, eating different foods, and yet sharing a difficult-to-define all-Indian identity. In the middle and upper classes, of course, the commonalities were often defined by English as a bridge language, their interest in Bombay films

(I detest the word 'Bollywood') and cricket, and, of course, by a politically manipulated enmity towards Pakistan.

I have often wondered for the vast masses of the poor in India, with so many different languages, cultures, religions, castes and foods, which common things they all shared (particularly in those days prior to the internet and social media, even TV had not yet come in a big way in their lives)—surely the epics (but even those were different in different regions, the Ramayana, for example, in the South can be quite different from that in the North particularly at the folk level), and perhaps pilgrimages. I read an article by the cultural anthropologist Nirmal Bose (teacher of my sociologist friend André Béteille), where he says that contrary to the idea of the British unifying India, for many centuries, the people going on pilgrimages from different parts of India met, interacted and shared in a common multifaceted cultural identity.

I remember my sister once told me that when she used to live in Kerala, my mother visiting her, had long sessions with a neighbour, a woman her age, neither understanding a word of the other's language, and yet continuing in their own languages for hours to communicate with each other their joys and sorrows! I suppose the pilgrims interacted similarly.

At my ISI office, there were several good economists. Apart from TN, there were B.S. Minhas, Kirit Parikh, Suresh Tendulkar, Sanjit Bose (my friend from MIT days), V.K. Chetty, Dipankar Dasgupta and others. Of these, in many ways, the most colourful character was Minhas. A shaved, un-turbaned Sikh, he used to tell us about his growing-up years in a poor farmer family in a Punjab village. He was the first in his family to go to school. He went to Stanford for his doctorate, before returning to India. He relished—a bit too much—his role as the man who spoke the blunt truth to everyone, including politicians, policymakers and academics. He illustrated his Punjabi style by telling the Bengalis that he had heard that in Bengal when a man had a tiff with his wife, he'd go without food rather than eat the food his wife had cooked; he said at home he did quite the opposite: 'I go to the fridge, take out my food and eat it; then, if I am still upset, I go to the fridge again and take out my wife's food and eat it all up—serves her right!'

At ISI, Bose, Dasgupta and Chetty were theorists; Minhas, TN, Parikh and Tendulkar did multi-sector planning models as well as quantitative studies of particular sectors like agriculture, water, energy, etc. TN, as probably India's most versatile economist ever, did both theory and empirical quantitative work. (He and I started editing a new journal on quantitative economics, which later became the journal of the Indian Econometric Society). To my great benefit, TN was also most knowledgeable about Indian data. Without his guiding hand at the beginning, I'd have felt completely out of my depth in the data world. These were days when data were stored in boxes of computer punch cards. Data storage was often in awful condition—I used to jokingly ask how we could be sure that some of the data in the form of holes in the punch cards were not made by the insects that infested the storerooms.

I particularly delved deep into data collected by the NSS, which, as I have noted, was one of the great contributions of Mahalanobis to the Indian statistical system. He brought Indian data and survey design to the world frontier—I have heard that when, in the 1950s, Zhou Enlai first visited India, he was impressed by the advanced stage of Indian survey data collection, compared to China. I also learned a great deal in my discussion with bright statisticians like Nikhilesh Bhattacharyya and others at the Kolkata ISI, who were immersed in survey design and meticulous analysis of NSS data. In addition, there were many veterans of field-level data collection in the NSS office, long chats with whom made me aware both of the high-quality parts of the data and the pitfalls to avoid, which a simple crunching of the punch card data would never have brought out. After several years abroad of mostly manipulating equations in my theoretical research, this was a big change for me—dirtying my hands with massive amounts of data, which brought me often a lot of exasperation and frustration, but also occasional spurts of exhilaration.

Every day at lunch-time, we used to gather at the office of Minhas—some people brought food from home and shared (giving me a taste of regional food variety). Amid chit-chat and gossip, there was occasional useful information. Once, from the director of ISI, C.R. Rao, I came to know that the royalty cheques from his New York publisher were being stolen by someone in the publisher's office by opening a fake account in his name. I realized that I had not received any royalty from the same publisher for my first book either, which I had attributed to no one buying my book. On enquiry with the publisher, it turned out that there was a fake account in my name as well.

Some days there would be visitors at lunch, usually high-level officers from different policy circles. In India those days, a great deal of data was mostly confined to some obscure offices of the different ministries in New Delhi and, without personal access, the data would be out of bounds for most researchers. The lunch connections with some of these high-level officers were useful for me in opening those doors. Also, the lunch discussions made me knowledgeable about the kind of policy issues that were uppermost in the minds of the Delhi policy elite, and the intense political intrigues and haggling that were behind many important policy decisions of the government.

Largely because of TN's international fame, many important economists from abroad visiting Delhi would agree to give seminars at ISI. One problem was that the number of faculty we had was rather small (and our students were also not that many), and famous people giving seminars with a very small number of attendees was a bit embarrassing. So TN issued an office order to all clerical staff to attend the seminars. This resulted in an immensely bored audience doing their office duty, but at least the room was full. I remember one lady, whom I used to see knitting wool much of the time at her office desk, now brought her knitting to the seminar addressed by some international luminary.

There was, however, a remarkable exception to the largely passive staff: one Mr Verma. Many years ago, when Mahalanobis was hobnobbing with Soviet-type planning, Verma, who claimed to know Russian, was hired to translate or interpret Russian planning documents. But when Mahalanobis left, there was no one there who had use for Russian documents, so Verma had nothing to do. Every morning, at the start of office time, he'd come, sign the registry of attendance, and then start perambulating the corridors of Yojana Bhavan. The whole day you'd see Verma—a small, dark man—slowly walking the long quadrangular corridors of the sixth floor of that building, always anti-clockwise—others called him 'anti-clockwise Verma'. Sometimes, he'd pause and enter a faculty office, as he once did with mine, and chat. He asked me if I was interested in the universal common language, Esperanto. I politely told him yes, and that opened the floodgates of his long lecture on that language, and how it could serve the cause of international harmony and peace. The next day, he came again and gifted me with several short pamphlets he had written extending the frontiers of Esperanto.

Verma used to sit at the front of the seminars given by visiting dignitaries and would always ask questions. One time, in the middle of a highly abstract mathematical presentation by a visitor, he raised his hand and demanded to know how all this was going to solve the problem of the rising price of rice that he faced in the market. I don't think the speaker quite recovered in the rest of his talk. There was also a story that in the early 1960s, when the great Russian mathematician Andrey Kolmogorov visited ISI and gave a talk, Verma, at the end, stood up and made a long comment in Russian. Kolmogorov patiently heard him out and then said, 'You see, my English is not good. Could you please say it again?' Verma's claim of knowing Russian got a bit dented that day among his colleagues.

At ISI, we were assigned statistical assistants who'd take our large data analysis jobs to the IBM computer at the Planning Commission, but for relatively small jobs, they'd do the calculations themselves by furiously rotating the handles of the small Facit mechanical calculator they each had—you could literally hear the noise of 'data crunching'. This was before electronic desk calculators came to Indian institutions. I remember buying a small Texas Instruments calculator in a short trip abroad and was quite impressed by its capacity; I told TN that I did not need to learn the operation of Facit machines, which I saw him cranking all the time. (This reminds me of a British economist, Ivor Pearce, who told me that just before the Second World War he used to work for an accounting firm, where they had not yet heard of log tables; he said he finished the whole day's work in just an hour by using the log table and read books in his office the rest of the time.) Of course, I am told today that our tiny laptops/smartphones contain computing capacity million times larger than the biggest IBM machines in India at that time.

The statistical assistants at ISI were literally called 'computers'. (I was a bit taken aback when, on the first day, a man came to see me and said, 'I am your computer, sir.') One day, when I was chatting with this human 'computer', I asked him who else he had worked with. He said that some years back he had worked with a famous foreign professor who was rather short-tempered and used to scream at him for the slightest delay or lapse. (It so happened that I knew this professor.) I said he should have protested if the professor was unnecessarily rude. He gave me a sneaky smile and said that he and the other 'computers' had taken their 'revenge' on that guy. When I asked how, he said they used to mess up his calculations without the professor knowing about it. I was aghast (and also made a mental note not to trust his data analysis of that period). This was an example of what Jim Scott, the political scientist, has called 'weapons of the weak' in his eponymous book; many decades earlier, the famous Czech novel *The Good Soldier Švejk* had satirical accounts of passive-subversive resistance of military authorities by the soldier.

I have myself faced such subversive behaviour on the part of lower officials in Delhi in a somewhat different context. Once, I went to the office of a particular ministry in search of some data which I knew they had, but officer in-charge openly said that he could not show me the data, though he did not give me any good justification. I told him that these data were collected using taxpayers' money, and since no national security issue was involved, he was duty-bound to release the data. He just smiled dismissively.

Back in office, TN told me that in India when I wanted something in a ministry I should not go to the lower officials; I should instead work my way from the top down (this was called 'proper channel' in official parlance). TN gave me the contact of the higher-level officer in the same ministry, who, when I told him what I needed, immediately called the lower official and asked him to share the data. The next day, I went to the same official who had refused me before. He was now full of oily politeness and said that it was the great fortune of the ministry that a professor like me was going to make good use of the data. But for the next few months, on one excuse or another, he made it very difficult for me to lay my hands on the data. After a lot of running around, I finally got the data, but I tried to fathom the reason behind his delaying tactics. Was it his resentment that I went to his boss instead of buttering him up? Was it his way of asserting his passive-obstructive power (the weapon of the weak)? Or did he expect some bribe from me? (In general, on bribery in Indian offices, apart from the ethical problem, practical problems abound: How to know whom, when and how much? Sometimes touts are there to help in this matter.)

Occasionally, there are even more unpredictable barriers to research with data in India. A few years later, when I was at the DSE, for big data analysis, I used to send my research assistant to the IBM 360 mainframe computer located at a different part of the campus, where, after you submit your job on the long queue, you'd get back the results after three or four days. For small jobs, there was an antique IBM 1620 machine in the basement of the DSE building. One time, I had a relatively small job and I needed the results quickly. So I asked my assistant to take it to the basement and get it done on the smaller machine. She soon came back and said the computer was 'down'. After a few hours, I sent her again, but it was still 'down'. I decided to check myself what was going on and went downstairs. Usually professors themselves did not go there, so when I was there the officer-in-charge rushed to greet me. When I asked what was wrong with the computer that it was down for so long, he said that nothing was wrong with the computer, but they were not to run it when the air conditioner was not running, and he did not know why that was.

I then went and found the man who was in charge of the air conditioner; he said there was nothing wrong with the air conditioner, but he'd not run it as the water tank at the back of the air conditioner was empty. I presumed he was referring to the water-cooled condenser in a large commercial air conditioner that was connected to a water tank at the back; in hot climate, that could be important. Of course, he did not know why there was no water in the tank. By that time, I was desperate. So I went to the garden at the back of the building where the tank was supposed to be and indeed found the tank empty. As soon as the gardener, who lived in a small cottage nearby, saw me, he ran to come and greet me. When I asked him why there was no water in the tank there, he sheepishly mumbled something in Hindi that I could not catch. By that time, a small crowd of peons and others had gathered around me. They told me that in connection with some religious festival, the gardener had village relatives visiting him and given the water shortage in his cottage, they had come and used up the tank water to take their bath. I was dumbfounded contemplating the chain of events. The gardener's rural family, through the simple action of bathing, had made a university department's computer system dysfunctional and disabled my analysis of data (which, incidentally, was about the problems of rural households in India). Is this what they call the 'butterfly effect' in chaos theory?

At ISI, one day, the American economist Daniel Thorner walked into my office and engaged me in a lively conversation, with his dancing eyebrows and unbounded enthusiasm. I had, of course, read his many substantive papers in *EW* on Indian agriculture and economic history. I also knew how, in the early 1950s, in the McCarthy era, he had lost his job at the University of Pennsylvania for refusing to give information on his leftist friends, and then went on to live in India with his wife, Alice (a fellow India scholar), for a decade, before taking up a position in Paris. Now, when he came to see me, he had just read my *EPW* paper showing—on the basis of NSS data—that poverty had increased through the 1960s in rural India. He asked me not to put so much trust on NSS data (he jokingly said that increasing poverty estimates by NSS data might be a reflection more of the increasing sense of misery on the part of the underpaid NSS workers). He encouraged me to accompany him in his next trip to Punjab villages, where he promised to introduce me to beer-drinking, tractor-driving women farmers, the harbingers of the future of agricultural capitalism in India. Much of what he said was, of course, tongue-in-cheek, and we became good friends. But this friendship was to be a 'brief candle', as cancer soon cut his life short.

There were two ways Daniel had unwittingly nudged me in a direction that I was already contemplating for my next line of research with data analysis. One was to probe deeper into the quality of survey data in India (particularly NSS data), and the other was to attempt collecting my own data on many interesting questions that NSS data did not cover. On the first, TN was a great guide, as throughout his professional career, he had repeatedly probed Indian data quality issues, more in depth than most other Indian economists. (In 2019, after TN passed away, when I was invited by the India Policy Forum in Delhi to give the first annual lecture in his memory, I chose Indian data quality as my theme.) At ISI, both of us found some problems with NSS data, but, on the whole, we remained impressed by the survey design as originally envisaged by Mahalanobis. I remember the statistician Nikhilesh Bhattacharyya, in response to the usual charge that field investigators were now lazy and unscrupulous, and prone to data manipulation, told me that NSS data manipulation was not impossible, but Mahalanobis had built in so many checks and cross-checks in the survey design that to be an effective data manipulator, the field investigator had to be a PhD in statistics! (In recent years, however, the bureaucratization of the NSS organization and running the surveys with casual, insufficiently trained workers and paltry resources have significantly diminished its quality, leave alone the indecent attempts at discrediting and suppression by the current government of survey results that were not to its liking.)

In 1974 (incidentally, the year of Daniel's death), TN and I co-edited a volume of essays by several researchers called *Poverty and Income Distribution in India*, in which some essays, including mine, probed the quality of NSS data. (At Abhijit Banerjee's initiative, a new edition of the book with some additional essays came out in 2017.) C.R. Rao, the great statistician and then Director of ISI, decided to celebrate the original volume's publication by inviting Prime Minister Indira Gandhi to formally release the book.

I had strongly objected, saying that I was in general against politicians releasing academic books, and I was particularly against this specific politician (already there was a country-wide resistance movement led by the widely respected J.P. Narayan against her leadership, which would culminate in her declaring the Emergency the next year, thereby suppressing all political opposition and dissent). C.R. Rao blithely ignored me, went ahead, and, on the day of the event, ordered four chairs to be on the dais in front of a large and distinguished gathering of academics and officials from different parts of Delhi. I refused to be on the dais with the Prime Minister and stood at the back of the gathering. I knew I had put TN in some trouble; I think he understood the nature of my objection, but he also had unflinching loyalty to Rao, his guru. Before the Prime Minister arrived, Rao sent TN to me on a last attempt at persuasion, but I still refused. So, at the last minute, my chair was removed from the dais.

On the second direction towards which Daniel had nudged me—going beyond NSS data and collecting my own—my major guide and collaborator was another senior statistician–economist, but at the Kolkata office of ISI, Ashok Rudra. I had met Rudra before, but we really hit it off in one long train journey from Delhi to Kolkata when we found ourselves, unplanned, on the same train. Rudra was an unorthodox Marxist, with a doctorate in statistics, a prolific writer, both in English and Bengali, on diverse subjects (history, economic planning, radical politics, literature), fluent in French (by then separated from a French wife), a Tagore scholar, a biographer of Mahalanobis and a top public intellectual of Bengal.

In that train journey, when we started talking, we found out, with the increasing exhilaration of discovery, that on many cultural and political matters we had similar views. For example, even though he was a Marxist and I was not (though I was intensely interested in the questions Marx raised), our criticisms of orthodox Marxist dogma and of the Marxists in Bengal turned out to be remarkably similar. After a point, he proposed that we should write a joint article spelling out these criticisms, and I agreed. It was already late night and other passengers were preparing to sleep, but we kept on talking—discussing the structure and arguments to be developed in that paper. We decided that I'd write the first draft in the following week. This was the first of our many future joint papers. In a few weeks, it was published in *EPW* with the tell-tale title 'Totems and Taboos in Left Mythology'. Needless to say, the article brought forth severe criticism, even vitriol, in left circles, but at least it was spared the label of being 'reactionary' with which leftists usually branded most criticisms, since Rudra's Marxist credentials were difficult to doubt.

As the train was hurtling through the night, we kept on talking. At one point, I told him that I was keenly interested in what Marxists call 'relations of production' and the nature of interrelationships in villages between landlords and tenants, employers and employees, lenders and borrowers, but the data, including surveys like the NSS, hardly scratched the surface. So we needed to carry out some detailed surveys of those interrelationships on a large enough scale so that we could reliably generalize about whole regions. This required new forms of sample designing. He, as a statistician and a Marxist, got excited, and we planned to pursue this. This was the origin of the many village surveys we carried out over the next decade, and the many articles we published both in India and abroad. Such large-scale, data-intensive granular work on agrarian relations was, at that time, quite rare in development economics, so we were in somewhat uncharted territory. But it sure was exciting.

6
The Social and Intellectual Milieu in Delhi and Kolkata

Sometime before Ashok Rudra and I started on our large-scale village data collection, I was already doing some theoretical and conceptual work on agrarian relations. My first, mainly theoretical, paper on sharecropping (jointly with TN) came out in the *American Economic Review* in 1971. That paper was unsatisfactory and had quite a few loose strands, but it was one of the first papers to look theoretically into an economic-institutional arrangement of a developing country at the micro level. This was a time when development economics was preoccupied with macro issues like the structural transformation of the whole economy, involving transition from agriculture to industrialization, or problems of its aggregate interaction with more developed economies.

In a short trip abroad, I presented my work on sharecropping in a seminar at Yale where my friend Martin Weitzman, who was teaching there, was present. He later told me that it made him start thinking of a more general context, that sharing profits or revenues with workers in a modern firm might resolve some macroeconomic problems like unemployment—he later came out with a book on this titled *The Share Economy*.

Joe Stiglitz by that time had also moved to Yale, and asked me to stay overnight with him after my talk. That night, at his home kitchen, as he was washing the dishes after our dinner, we kept on talking about various aspects of sharecropping. I told him that to me sharecropping was clearly an inefficient institution in agriculture, and yet it had been around for millennia in different parts of the world. We were both wondering why. Joe started looking at it from his point of view of imperfect information (the landlord being unable to monitor how much effort the peasant put in). That led to his chain of thinking which ultimately produced his classic paper on sharecropping in 1974.

The other theoretical agrarian-relations issue I wrote about was how the landlord (sometimes also the employer and moneylender) used his interlinked transactions with the sharecropper-employee-borrower to entrench his position, even as he provides some otherwise unavailable services to the latter. But many people around me in India interpreted such interlinked relations as what they called 'semi-feudal' or debtbondage relations. Even if we ignore that the term 'feudal' in the European sense is somewhat inappropriate in the Indian context—reading the Marxist historian Perry Anderson's work on Europe had convinced me on this—my hunch was that bondage relations were not quantitatively the most important aspect of Indian agriculture, contrary to repeated assertions in leftist academic or party documents. When I said this to Ashok Rudra in our train journey, he immediately agreed and we made this one main focus of our village surveys.

We took a random sample of 110 villages in West Bengal, and collected detailed data on the typical relations in land, labour and credit markets in these villages, so that we could generalize about the whole of West Bengal. Among other things, we indeed found out that debt bondage was a relatively marginal phenomenon in Bengal agriculture (outside of localized pockets in remote areas), and we documented large varieties of effectively commercial though informal, voluntary though unequal, relations between landlords and peasants in the state.

This was a matter of some importance in West Bengal politics. By the end of the 1960s, a militant movement, defying the two main communist parties, had started. Because of its origin in an armed peasant revolt in an area in north Bengal called Naxalbari, such movements are often called 'Naxalite' both in Bengal and the rest of India. The usual description of the rural economy by students and intellectuals who were sympathetic with this movement largely followed the above-described 'semi-feudal' debt bondage line.

The leaders of the movement declared 'the decade of the 70s as the decade of liberation'. In rural areas, some land grabbing and assassinations of 'class enemies' were carried out, and urban areas saw a great deal of terror and selective, though sometimes purposeless, killings. The government of the day then launched an operation of brutal repression, imprisonment, torture and killing. (I joined Rudra in donating money for the legal defence of Naxalite prisoners.) By the middle of the 1970s, the movement was largely snuffed out in West Bengal (though embers of the fire still burn in the jungles of central India).

In my Kolkata neighbourhood, I saw the movement also as a generational revolt. In some left families, while the elderly or middle-aged members had their allegiance to the traditional communist parties, the younger members (sometimes even teenagers) expressed their defiance of the older generations by being active in or sympathetic to the Naxalite movement. And, like young people elsewhere, they had a partly romantic, partly hot-headed view of the potential for revolution.

I had a peculiar experience of meeting a group of urban youth who described themselves as Naxalites in Delhi. In the early 1970s, the eminent historian Ranajit Guha often visited us in the evenings. In the 1950s, he had left the communist party and became a major scholar of intellectual history, and, in his later life, was a pioneer in looking at Indian history from the subaltern point of view—history from the bottom or marginalized sections of society. When I met him, he was sympathetic with the Naxalite movement, and had connections with some of the active youths in Delhi who were then underground. He once challenged me and asked if I'd dare meet these youths, and get acquainted with their 'ground-level experience' on land relations in India. He said that this could be a 'learning opportunity' for professors like me. I immediately agreed.

So a few other academics and I were instructed to come one evening to a 'secret' place in Delhi. At the appointed hour, we gathered in a darkened room with windows tightly curtained and only a couple of candles lit. Soon we saw about ten or twelve young men marching into the room, chanting the hushed greeting of 'Red Salute'. (To me, they looked like earnest young men of affluent families, possibly ex-students of St Stephen's College.) Guha, presiding over the occasion, said that we'd have first a statement of the current land and the village revolutionary situation from those youths as they saw it. Then I, as someone who had researched on the agrarian relations in India, would make a statement and later, if the other academics had anything to add they could. After that the youths would respond and then the meeting would end.

It started with the group leader putting up a tiny map of India on the wall and pinning a little red paper flag at each of the places where 'action' was currently going on. Even though India has more than half a million villages, the map was so small that ten or so red flags were enough to make the whole map look red. The leader pointed to the map as obvious proof that India was 'ripe' for revolution. Then he gave his understanding of the ground reality of land and peasants. All I heard was a collection of clichés, as if he was just regurgitating rhetoric he had learned from some cheap pamphlet. I had actually expected much better from these intelligent-looking young men. Then, when my turn came, I said I agreed with them that the condition of the landless peasants of India was indeed atrocious, but the nature of exploitation and the type of agrarian relations in different areas were quite complex and diverse. I then cited some simple data from my research to illustrate my points. I ended by saying that not being aware of the complexities might actually hurt their revolutionary cause. Then, after some brief comments from the other academics, Guha invited the youth leader to respond to our comments. I braced myself for being called 'reactionary', 'bourgeois', a 'class enemy', etc., but what happened next left me aghast. The leader just repeated his initial statement in toto, and nothing whatsoever in response to our points. It seemed to me that he had learned one statement by rote and used it for all occasions. Then they all stood up and left the room, marching and chanting 'Red Salute'. That was indeed a learning experience for me!

The Naxalite phase in Bengal was a short, tragic chapter in politics, but in Bengal's cultural-emotional life, its implications were deeper and reflected in its literature—most poignantly yet forcefully captured by the writer Mahasweta Devi, one of Bengal's

The Social and Intellectual Milieu in Delhi and Kolkata 117

most powerful political novelists. Among the film directors I knew reasonably well, both Mrinal Sen and Buddhadeb Dasgupta intensively grappled with the theme, in the films *Calcutta 71* and *Padatik* (*The Guerrilla Fighter*) for the former, and *Dooratva* (*Distance*) and *Grihajuddha* (*The War at Home*) for the latter. Again and again in the twentieth century, some Bengali youth have been fascinated by the romanticism of revolutionary violence—as was the case in the early decades in the freedom struggle against the British (I have earlier mentioned about my maternal uncle caught in its vortex), then again in the 1940s when the sharecroppers' movement (called 'tebhaga') was soon followed by a period of communist insurgency in 1948–50, and then in the Naxalite movement of the late 1960s and early 1970s.

In the early literature, Tagore often engaged with this theme (something already familiar in nineteenth-century Russian literary imagination, reflected in several novels). By temperament and political judgement, Tagore was opposed to revolutionary violence and the unthinking passions associated with it, and yet, he had a soft corner for the young people involved. This theme is dominant, for example, in his novel *Char Adhyay* (*Four Chapters*) and, in its preface, he writes about his once close friend Brahmabandhab Upadhyay, who, parting company with Tagore, joined the revolutionary movement. In this preface, Tagore recalls the brief touching moment one evening when he came back after some years as a disillusioned man to see Tagore. (In the 1862 Russian novel *Fathers and Sons*, Ivan Turgenev had a similar ambivalent attitude to the radical character Yevgeny Bazarov.) In much of the profuse literature generated by the Naxalite period, while the repressive state is in the background, there is a pining over the wastage of the lives of so many idealistic youths for a brave social justice cause—a cause that was, in my judgement, an insufficiently thought-out one.

With Ashok Rudra (who was much senior to me and yet, my most frequent co-author in this period) I shared a great deal of common interest in economic, political, literary and cultural matters, but we had some serious differences as well. One of them was on this issue of revolutionary violence. He did not quite agree with my belief that however just the cause may be, violence inevitably creates a monster that can easily spin out of control and devour the cause itself, apart from triggering the brutal counter-force of the state. Ashok Rudra had introduced me to the illustrious poet and journalist Samar Sen, who also nursed a similar penchant for the idea of revolutionary violence. I did not argue with him as I did with Rudra, but I made my views clear to him, though at his invitation I contributed some articles to the radical magazine *Frontier* that Sen was the founder-editor of. Many years after his death, I gave the Samar Sen Memorial Lecture in Kolkata in Bengali.

Another issue of my difference with Ashok Rudra was on market reforms. He did not care much for the efficiency arguments that preoccupy reform-mongering economists; the primacy for him was social justice plus the vulgarity and alienating effects of crass commercialization that capitalism brings. I could not persuade him that the alternative to market reform is often a state monopoly, which itself generates injustice (particularly as the state-favoured bureaucrats and oligarchs can exploit small people) and that in India's structured society, a low-caste person may sometimes prefer the anonymity of the market to supplicating patrician state officials.

Ashok Rudra once had a public falling-out with Satyajit Ray on the latter's deviations from the original Tagore story in his marvellous film *Charulata*. On the substantive matter of the film director's autonomy in adaptation of literature, I was mainly on Ray's side, but I did not like the director's arrogant and harsh words against Rudra in the Bengali magazine where the discussion took place. Ray no doubt was a great filmmaker, though I was not a fan of some of his late films. I had met him once when someone took me to his home in Kolkata, but also when he came to Berkeley to screen his film *Shatranj Ke Khilari* (released internationally as *The Chess Players*) at the Pacific Film Archive in the Berkeley campus. When the Archive people requested Ray to say something before the screening started, I found it rather odd that Ray said that he had nothing to say except that viewers should note that everything used in the film (meaning the furniture, costume, etc.) was 'authentic' (to the period and the characters involved). In my judgement, the importance of this kind of authenticity could be a bit overplayed in a work of art. Later, at a party after the screening, I had an opportunity to talk to him about types of Bengali fiction that were worth considering for film adaptation.

Rudra would often give me the manuscripts of his literary output (including that of a Bengali novel and a play that he wrote) and his various journalistic writings for my comments before publishing them. On his literary pieces, I often told him that I found some of them a bit too romantic for my taste, and that I also found him rather conservative (not uncommon in the Brahmo sect background he came from) in his outlook to sexuality. He'd keep on arguing, but we never had a falling-out, which he had aplenty with fellow scholars. He was a very bright if difficult person—but I found ways of negotiating his rough edges. Whenever we met, we spent hours discussing all kinds of things, until I last saw him at his home in Santiniketan, when he said he was feeling out of sorts and, on my return to California, I heard about his heart attack and death following some medical bungling. In 2019, I gave the Ashok Rudra Memorial Lecture at Santiniketan, also in Bengali.

My village surveys jointly with Rudra were more economic-anthropological than the usual statistical surveys, and yet different from anthropological studies which were usually on a small scale. This got me thinking about the methodological differences between economists and social anthropologists. The latter would often go to a village and even live there for a time, closely observing the villagers' behaviour, their ways of making sense of their life and of participating in the community—all this yields rich ethnographic accounts, which sometimes (not always) suggest some generalizations about a society. But such generalizations are often hampered by 'my village vs. your village'-type differences, and the difficulty of defining standards of comparability of findings across villages. Besides, the ethnographic approach sometimes is prone to give too much attention to striking but not too typical events or characteristics—'outliers' in statistical parlance.

On the other hand, economists in order to be policy relevant have to generalize over very large numbers of villages, and so pay particular attention to sampling designs and the validity of statistical inference. The largeness of sample size necessarily leads them to use standardized, coarse, lowest-common-denominator categories to describe what are essentially delicate, nuanced, complex, ambiguous and fine-grained features of a society or economy. Economists find it particularly difficult to capture in their data processes and relations rather than their outcomes. My work with Rudra to capture those agrarian 'relations' thus had to go beyond standard economic surveys; we had to design special statistical methods for this purpose.

Carrying out field surveys is now more common among economists than they used to be, but I think they can benefit if, *before* launching large-scale surveys, they talk to anthropologists, sociologists (and social workers) who have intimate knowledge of the area. This may help in deciphering what are the important questions to ask and what is the appropriate local way of framing the same generic question. And *after* the survey, such talks may help in understanding the mechanism or the process through which the observed/measured data generate a particular finding.

In 1984, with support from the Social Science Research Council, New York, I organized an international conference in Bengaluru (then known as Bangalore), where some economists, statisticians and anthropologists were invited to thrash out the methodological differences between the disciplines when they try to configure changes in the rural economy. One ultimate outcome of that conference was a volume that I edited titled *Conversations between Economists and Anthropologists*. Later, in 2003, supported by the Ford Foundation office in New Delhi, a Berkeley colleague, Isha Ray, and I organized a kind of follow-up interdisciplinary international conference in Goa; this time, the focus was on how the different disciplines look at the problem of cooperation in the local village commons. This also resulted in a volume titled *The Contested Commons*, a sort of 'Conversations II' that we jointly edited.

Economists and anthropologists do not usually talk to one another, and even in the rare case that they do, there is a tendency to talk past one another. We tried our best to minimize this by keeping the focus on somewhat narrow topics, and I think in this we were moderately successful.

In academic conversations, my experience in American universities has been that people talk mostly to others in their own discipline (or even in a narrow sub-field within the discipline). There is a contrasting pattern in Oxford–Cambridge colleges. There, at dinner, one day next to you is a physicist, and another day a postmodern literary critic, and you have to carry on intelligent conversation—this, of course, gives rise to a lot of clever dilettantism. Throughout my professional life, I have been a specialist in some things and a dabbler in various things, so I want a bit of both kinds of conversations.

Even though my ISI office was in the Planning Commission building in New Delhi, I was living in an apartment complex far away in 'Old' Delhi, nearer Delhi University. The main attraction of staying there was the number of academic friends who lived in the same complex, apart from its being in a rather open, leafy, quieter part of the city (the hilly walkway at the back—called 'the ridge'—was full of parrots and monkeys). My MIT friend, Mrinal, who stayed there, arranged with the landlord for our rented accommodation. Mrinal was then a popular teacher at the DSE. His wife, Eva, was a feisty and resourceful Italian woman, coming from a political family—her father was an active anti-fascist, killed in Rome in 1944 by a Nazi ambush; her maternal uncle was the famous development economist Albert Hirschman (whom I admired for his sparkling insights and particularly for what he called his 'essays in trespassing' in a variety of disciplines; we met a few times at Princeton). Eva, coming for the first time to India, quickly figured out the tricks of negotiating the daily complications of life in Delhi, and by the time we arrived she, a savvy foreigner, helped us settle in the city. It used to be quite a spectacle to see a sari-clad Eva haggling in street Hindi with the wily shopkeepers of Delhi and relishing it.

Hardly any day went without my long chats with Mrinal. We shared a great deal in our interests. His wacky sense of humour was combined with a serious thoughtfulness on many issues. On political issues in particular, he was one of the wisest and shrewdest observers I have known. When Eva later left him and went with (and married) his best friend since their boyhood in Santiniketan, Amartya Sen, I saw a different side of Mrinal—that of pained

The Social and Intellectual Milieu in Delhi and Kolkata 123

dignity and graceful fortitude. (I last saw Eva in her apartment in London a few months before her death from terminal cancer; I found her busy writing a long letter to her young daughter to be left as a kind of legacy.)

There was a large number of other academics in different apartments in that Delhi complex—Ashis Nandy (the social psychologist, one of India's leading social thinkers, whom I knew from my Kolkata college days) and his musician wife, Uma; a historian couple, Sumit (my classmate from Presidency College) and Tanika Sarkar; R. Rajaraman, a prominent physicist, and his wife, Indira, a notable economist; Veena Das, a remarkable sociologist, and her husband the economist, Ranen; my ISI colleague Sanjit Bose and his wife, Uttara; two economist couples, Arjun and Jayashree Sengupta, and Badal and Swapna Mukherji. There was even a time when some of these academics took on the responsibility of getting the children in the complex together and taking informal/fun afternoon teaching sessions for them. But much of the time, the neighbours had lively chat sessions in one another's apartments. This was probably the finest experience in my life where so many bright academics lived vibrantly together and yet respected each other's privacy. Apart from Mrinal, in my later life, I kept up mostly with the Nandys and the Sarkars, and with Indira Rajaraman (whom I saw often in Delhi conferences).

I used to spend many evenings either in Mrinal's or Ashis's apartment. Mrinal often had get-togethers with his DSE economist colleagues like Amartya Sen, Sukhamoy Chakravarty, and Dharma Kumar, historian Tapan Raychaudhuri, and the sociologist André Beteille, or government economic advisors like V.K. Ramaswami and P.N. Dhar. Of these, the most erudite and serious was Chakravarty, the best collection of amusing stories was with Raychaudhuri (an Oxford don in his later life), and the narrator of inside political gossip with languid grace was P.N.

Dhar (who was close to Indira Gandhi, and part of what used to be called the 'Kashmiri mafia' around her).

Quite frequently some combinations of these people plus some of the mandarins in different ministries of the government and a scattering of visiting foreign academics would meet in one or the other of the two reigning residential salons of New Delhi in those days, run by two south Indian women married to north Indians. One was presided over by the economic historian Dharma Kumar and her bureaucrat husband, Lovraj Kumar (in his early life he was India's first Rhodes Scholar), and the other run by Devaki Jain, a feminist economist, and her husband, Lakshmi Chand Jain, a Gandhian (in his later life, he was an ambassador to South Africa, but was recalled by the Bhartiya Janta Party [BJP] government in 1998 because it felt that as an ambassador he was not properly enthusiastic in supporting India's nuclear tests). Mrinal was the 'darling boy' in both of these salons. He used to give me a ride in his VW Beetle to these two salons, where I had quite an edifying experience; it gave me a lot of insight into the manners (upscale, whiskey-drenched) and thought processes of the Delhi intellectual and bureaucratic elite.

A different kind of gathering used to take place in Ashis Nandy's small apartment. That crowd was mostly of political scientists and sociologists—like Rajni Kothari, Bashiruddin Ahmed, D.L. Sheth, Veena Das and André Beteille. Mrinal and I were often the only economists there. Kothari was the doyen of Indian political scientists. My leftist friends often did not like him, but in discussions with him I have found his astute understanding of ground-level Indian political processes highly valuable. He and his colleagues had a more society-centric approach, in contrast to the state-centric approach of the leftists. The discussion in the two salons mentioned above was also mainly state-centric.

In a way, this was a reflection of the continuation of the differences among past Indian leaders—Gandhi and his followers emphasized the centrality of village society and community, whereas Nehru and B.R. Ambedkar were suspicious of the oppressive forces of traditional Indian society and sought social justice mainly through the instrumentality of the state. Ambedkar called the Indian village community 'a den of ignorance, narrow-mindedness and communalism'.

Reflecting on these alternative systems of Indian thought, later in the 1980s, I wrote an article on the 'great divide' in Indian social science discourse. I pointed out that the divide in Indian thinking is not 'left' vs 'right', but more in different ideas on state vs society. This sometimes leads to strange bedfellows. State socialists are often in the unwitting company of right-wing nationalists when they both want to strengthen the nation state (against forces of imperialism for the former; against forces of social disunity for the latter), and to follow autarchic economic policies of import-substituting industrialization and large capital-intensive projects. Pitted against them are the motley bunch of anarcho-communitarians, activists involved in preservation of the environment and tribal autonomy, 'subaltern' historians focusing on the lives of the lower social strata, small-is-beautiful enthusiasts, and advocates of decentralization—among great Indian thinkers, both Gandhi and Tagore wanted to promote small self-help communities and to reduce dependence on the state.

Comparatively, votaries of classical liberalism in India have been few and far between. The socialists (in their criticism of 'bourgeois democracy') are almost as suspicious of liberalism as are Hindu nationalists. The experience of the short-lived, ill-fated Swatantra Party, which espoused some classical liberal values, showed that Indian polity in general is not hospitable ground for such values. Even the Gandhians—who emphasize the community—overlook that the traditional community values are highly patriarchal and often illiberal (Gandhi himself was quite authoritarian as a father, husband, and the guru of his ashrams). Today, as a Hindu-supremacist state is trampling upon basic liberties of citizens, many are discovering afresh the old values of liberalism.

From the gatherings at Ashis Nandy's home, and particularly from my numerous discussions with him, I learned to think a bit more carefully about three major social concerns in India.

One was that whenever we economists faced a socio-economic problem that the standard processes of the private market forces did not resolve justly or efficiently, our immediate recourse was the state. We, of course, knew how inept or corrupt the state machinery often was. But the Gandhian in Ashis pointed to many problems which even the best-intentioned or efficient state is inherently incapable of solving. Take the shameful dowry problem in Indian marriage markets. The Indian state tried to solve it by the Dowry Prohibition Act of 1961. But the problem is rampant to this day. One needs social movements and community-level reforms in norms and behaviour—more than state legislation—to make a dent in this enormous socio-economic problem. In such debates, I have, however, argued that while the state is not *sufficient*, isn't it often *necessary* for social change? A law enacted by the state after a process of public deliberation can act as a guiding or catalytic or coordinating force for dispersed social movements. In the US, the civil rights movement acted in unison with some landmark federal laws (Civil Rights Act) in bringing about major (though as yet unfinished) social changes.

Second, I always knew that caste was important in Indian society and polity, but I used to think that in leftist areas like

The Social and Intellectual Milieu in Delhi and Kolkata 127

Bengal, class had significantly overshadowed caste. Talking to the sociologists in the group (including André Beteille, a consummate Bengali with a French father), I realized how limited this perception about Bengal was. Over time, I came to understand that the cultural dominance of upper castes in Bengal is so totally hegemonic that it creates the illusion that caste is less important. In other parts of India, there have been social upheavals partly enabled by democracy, as a result of which middle and sometimes lower castes have at least politically become very important. But in Bengal, even the communist parties are mostly dominated by upper castes—just as in Bengali literature, most of the life stories of the oppressed groups have been, until very recently, narrated by upper-caste writers. Well-intentioned upper-caste leftists try to do something from above about the class oppression of the lower castes, and often overlook the special problems of the latter's lack of dignity and agency that go beyond class oppression. The latter may sometimes side with some leaders who may bring them dignity, even when they do nothing about their economic exploitation. Also, a part of upper-caste hegemony in Bengal lies in making even the upwardly mobile sections of lower castes internalize the cultural norms and mores of the former and get gentrified.

Third, Ashis has eloquently written about the pitfalls of modernity and technocratic development presided over by an aggrandizing nation state. I agree that the nation state often organizes spectacular technological or military extravaganzas and runs mindless gigantic development projects, uprooting communities and disrupting the ecological balance, and that in general the technocratic elite often imposes projects from above—not involving the participation of the local people, instead simply treating them as objects (or targets) of the development process.

But I part company when I see that development itself has become a dirty word with many including some followers of

Ashis (I have already mentioned an article by Steve Marglin on 'Development as Poison'—both Steve and his wife, Frédérique, became devoted disciples of Ashis). Of course, there are alternative types of participatory community-led or decentralized development processes possible, but I do not share the romanticism of many anarcho-communitarians about such development. On balance, I remain a supporter of decentralized development, but there are many complex problems (including those of capture by the local elite or by forces of clientelist politics) even in such types of development which can work against the interests of common people, particularly in situations of socio-economic inequality. In the last two decades and more, I (along with Dilip Mookherjee) have been working on decentralized development to explore some of these problems.

I also part company when I see many anarcho-communitarians and their cultural studies fellow travellers echo postmodernists against expertise, against science, against truth, regarding all objective truth as 'socially constructed' and in the service of ruling powers. As Terry Eagleton, the British literary critic, recently said, '… post-truth politics may have started in the left bank of the Seine, but they ended up in (Trump's) White House'.

Some of Ashis's social-psychological work is indeed impressive. His early work exploring the cultural politics of selfhood and his later psychological analysis of social and political violence of different forms has given us deep insights. Many people do not know that nearly thirty years ago he started a project of psychoanalysis of the Hindu nationalists in India, and, in that connection, he had a long interview with, among others, a then-minor BJP functionary named Narendra Modi. He later described, as reported by *New Yorker* on 9 December 2019, that in that interview he was shocked to find that this man 'exhibited all the traits of an authoritarian personality: puritanical rigidity, a constricted emotional life, fear of his own passions, and an enormous ego that protected a gnawing insecurity.' (Incidentally, the famous 1950 book, *The Authoritarian Personality* by Theodor Adorno and others was the product of research by a Berkeley group of social psychologists.)

In our apartment complex, the Nandys and us often got together, particularly with our small son and their daughter being of similar age. Also, along with Mrinal and Eva, we often went to see late-night movies in New Delhi cinema halls, after our children were asleep—six of us packed in Mrinal's small VW. I remember once as we entered the hall, before the main movie started, there was a sports newsreel where we saw a ferocious wrestler repeatedly headbutting his opponent. At this, Ashis immediately remarked: 'With such beautiful use of the head available, think how we are misusing ours!' (This incidentally reminds me of the memorable headbutt by France's famous player Zinedine Zidane on Italy's Matteo Materazzi in the 2006 football World Cup Final. I was in Italy that day and saw how afterward the bars were agog with creative speculations about what provoked it.)

There was one distinguished economist who did not come to the evening gatherings in our apartment complex, but instead used to wake me up very early in the morning by dropping in after a long walk from his home in the Delhi University campus. It was K.N. Raj, who was the head at DSE, and later vice chancellor of the university. He had then been working on a research project on India's agrarian economy; he showed me some draft chapters of a book on this, which I don't think he ever published. Reading these chapters and interacting with him provided a great deal of inspiration for me in my subsequent work in the area. (Many years later, I tried paying tribute to him by co-editing a collection of essays in his honour.) Among Indian economists, no one else had a larger vision of the structure of the Indian economy, combined with a grasp of the micro features of its diverse aspects.

Raj was a pleasant and unassuming, but excitable man. As vice chancellor he was often facing protests and harassment by the right-wing student groups and the left-wing teachers' union, and he used to narrate his troubles of the previous day to us at that early hour. His young son, Deenu, imitating the protesters, used to lead a march of neighbourhood children shouting slogans like, 'Down, down, Dr Raj', when he arrived home.

7
Exploring Kerala and Surviving Delhi under the Emergency

Soon K.N. Raj gave up his vice chancellorship in Delhi University and moved to his home state, Kerala, and started a new institution, Centre for Development Studies (CDS). He tried to lure me (and Kalpana) to join the faculty there, and even offered to get us land on which he'd persuade his friend Laurie Baker (a resident British-Quaker architect) to build us a low-cost, energy-efficient beautiful house (like his own). At CDS, he not merely provided intellectual leadership, he was the paterfamilias for the group. After a whole day of teaching and seminars, in the evening, he'd visit his colleagues' homes, try to solve their multifarious domestic problems, while his wife, Sarsamma, would minister to their sundry medical needs. Once, driving me to the airport, when I was all praise for the young institution and the community he was in the process of building, he asked me if I had any word of criticism. I told him it was too much of a 'Hindu undivided family' for my taste. Raj corrected me and said it was not 'Hindu'—he did not seem to mind the 'undivided family' part.

While I did not join CDS, though I visited it a few times, Raj did twist my arm to take up the only work I ever did in my life for any government anywhere—he got me to chair a commission of enquiry into Kerala's plantations, appointed by the Communist Party of India (CPI) government of Achutha Menon, a friend of Raj's. Suresh Tendulkar, whom I brought on as a co-member, and I worked hard to write a detailed official report, which insects must have chewed up by now in some ministry dungeon in Thiruvananthapuram, but this gave me an opportunity to travel up and down the countryside, take a closer look at Kerala's remarkable society and economy, and the beautiful lush green landscape.

One early morning, I remember we were driving through a village, and I saw some workers with red flags congregated around a paddy field. I asked the driver to stop and we saw there something remarkable for a remote Indian village: there was a scene of collective bargaining, the leader of the landless workers in the field—a low-caste (Pulya) woman—was doing her hard bargaining with the land owner about the daily wage some distance away, and when they came to an agreement, she waved her red flag to the waiting comrades to signal the agreement and then they all started the day's work.

I also had the occasion to see a different aspect of trade unions in the formal sector in connection with my work on the plantations. I interviewed a large number of trade union leaders, belonging to a whole assortment of political parties. They insistently asked me to recommend to the government nationalization of the plantations (at the time, the large ones producing tea, rubber, etc.,

Exploring Kerala and Surviving Delhi under the Emergency

were mainly owned by British planters). But I asked them that, if after nationalization, the plantations, instead of being run by state bureaucrats, were to be given over to the workers to own and manage, and to share the profits, would they agree. I was struck by the unanimity of all trade union leaders, communist or non-communist, that they were all against worker-managed firms. I partly understood their reluctance because running a firm requires money and facing risks; so I promised also recommending to the government for substantial help in both credit raising and risk bearing—but even then they were all opposed. I felt that trade union leaders had specialized in agitations; they did not want to move over to a new life of responsibility, even if it was for a more constructive role in productive activities and a larger income share for the workers (including the profit share).

As for the plantation owners, we noticed some inconsistencies and gaps in their company balance sheets. The accounts were audited by Kerala's top auditing firm. So we made an appointment with this firm and went with our list of questions; but it was a waste of time as we got nothing but bland, unhelpful answers from the accountants. As we were coming out of their office, we saw in their premises large clay figures of three monkeys, one with hands on its eyes, one on its lips, and the other on its ears—apparently this was their motto. Later in life, I came to realize this was pretty much the motto of even some of the world's top-ranking auditing firms in rich countries.

We also discovered later that what was reported in the plantations' balance sheets was quite different from the confidential accounts they sent to their British owners. Using the legal powers of our commission of enquiry, and guided by our legal advisor (Mohan Kumaramangalam, a veteran leftist lawyer, who told me he was a student at Cambridge in the 1930s), we managed to get hold of those confidential accounts.

During my travels in the hilly plantations, I observed something remarkable around 5 p.m. or so when the siren went off indicating closing time of the plantations or factories. From one hill you could clearly see on the next hill two distinct streams of people coming out of the factory gate—one stream (mostly of women) going in one direction towards their homes, and the other stream (mainly of men) going in a different direction towards the nearby toddy shops. Toddy is the local liquor made from the sap of palm trees.

After the commission's work was over and we were at the point of departing for Delhi, its office arranged for a winding-up party the evening before. The office manager was arranging for bottles of whiskey, beer, etc.; on an impulse, I asked that toddy be served instead. Everyone responded enthusiastically. When the bottles started coming in, wrapped in newspapers, I noticed something scribbled on each bottle in ink. I asked what it was and found out that one bottle was marked as '12.30 p.m.', another as '2 p.m.', etc., and I asked what this meant. They explained to me those were marks of when they were prepared in the day, as toddy did not remain drinkable for long. I had never before encountered alcohol vintage by the hour. (I have to say that all the excitement of my office people was not matched by the taste; I did not particularly like toddy.)

I was once invited by Achutha Menon, the chief minister, to a wedding at his home. I went there with Raj and was immensely impressed by the simplicity of the ceremony and the sparsity in the decorations, jewellery on display and food servings. I asked Raj if this was because it was a communist household or this was the general custom in Kerala. Raj said, it was both; you'd not usually see the north Indian–style extravagance in Kerala weddings.

Later, when I was invited to an ex-royal household by someone who was a descendant of Ravi Varma (a famous Indian painter in the nineteenth century), I was taken to an old palatial building with much less gaudiness than one expected. In the dining hall, lined with large paintings of Varma, I sat down on the red cement floor and my food was served on a banana leaf with several small stainless steel bowls arranged in a semicircle. Before I started eating, my host said that he felt compelled to warn me that the leftmost bowls always contained extremely hot pickles. Apparently, the last Bengali who was a guest in that hall, many decades ago, started on the left and jumped out in distress, and could not finish the meal. That guest was Rabindranath Tagore.

After my many visits to Kerala, I wrote an article, 'On Life and Death Questions in India' for *EPW*, where I highlighted the welfare and demographic achievements of Kerala, the most advanced region in India in terms of many indicators of social democracy. Soon Raj and his colleagues (including my friend T.N. Krishnan) produced a large quantitative report for the United Nations Development Programme, which brought to international attention the so-called Kerala model of development.

Back in Delhi, I was soon after invited to two conferences which were somewhat different from the usual specialized technical conferences I was familiar with. One was a conference organized jointly by the World Bank and the Institute of Development Studies at Sussex on the general theme of how to achieve fair distribution and economic equality without sacrificing economic growth in developing countries. The emphasis was not so much on paper presentation with specialized research, but more on thinking aloud on big issues. The conference was held in the grand surroundings of Villa Serbelloni, the conference centre at Bellagio on a hill facing the beautiful blue Lake Como in Italy (the villa's history goes back a few centuries; it is claimed that Leonardo da Vinci was a guest there).

At this conference, I met a number of important development economists, who became long-term friends; these included Albert Fishlow and Irma Adelman (both of whom were later my colleagues at Berkeley) and Lance Taylor (of MIT, later at the New School of Social Research), apart from Montek Singh Ahluwalia (later a top economic bureaucrat in Delhi) and Clive Bell (later a professor at Heidelberg), who were among the conference organizers and the editors of a subsequent volume titled *Redistribution with Growth* (for which they commissioned me to write a short section).

Montek, Clive and others wrote up a few policy papers drawing upon the conversations at Bellagio, which were then discussed at a follow-up conference at Sussex in September 1973. I particularly remember the date because on 11 September, during a morning session at this conference, the news broke that there had been a military coup in Chile that violently deposed the democratically elected socialist government, criminally aided and abetted by the Nixon–Kissinger administration. The Latin American participants at the conference (which included Alejandro Foxley, who later became a finance minister in Chile after the end of the military rule) became visibly too disturbed to carry on normally for the rest of the conference. (As a side note, 11 September, which happens to be my birthday, is associated with two tragic historical events—once in 1973 in Chile and then in 2001 in the US; recently, looking at my ID and birth date, a shop assistant in the US was expressing unnecessary sympathy for me, but I told her to look at the positive side: This way my loved ones will not easily forget my birthday!)

The Sussex conference also brought me friendship with senior development economists like Gus Ranis (of Yale) and Erik Thorbecke (of Cornell); I also got to know two famed bureaucrat-economists, Mahbub ul Haq (from Pakistan) and Lal Jayawardena (from Sri Lanka).

The other non-specialist conference around that time, where the emphasis again was on brainstorming on big issues, was organized in India jointly by J.P. Naik, the energetic member-secretary of the Indian Council of Social Science Research (ICSSR), and Kalpana (who was then working at ICSSR). It got many of the major thinkers on the Indian political economy together at Lonavala (near Pune), a hill station surrounded by green valleys. During summer, it rains there almost non-stop the whole day, so we were trapped at the residential conference centre, and had no alternative but to keep on talking and thrashing out many issues that usually did not get fully discussed on other occasions. I also got an opportunity to know two stalwart senior Indian economists there, V.M. Dandekar and M.L. Dantwala. Dandekar was a statistician turned economist, a sharp-minded maverick, with leading contributions to measurement of poverty, and designing of crop insurance schemes for farmers and rural employment guarantee programmes for the landless. Dantwala was a foremost agricultural economist, who, in his politics, combined his belief in Gandhian decentralization with ideas forged in his earlier association with the Congress Socialist Party. After dusk in Lonavala, it was quite an experience to listen in to the polemical discussion between these two old friends, one sharp-tongued and the other soft-spoken but spirited, both animated by shots of whiskey.

Around this time, I had got an offer from DSE to fill the chair recently vacated by Amartya Sen. TN was not happy, but after some mulling over, I decided to take it, primarily because I was missing a proper university campus with lots of students around, and also because DSE was near our apartment complex, saving me the long trip to New Delhi every day.

At DSE, even though I continued my large empirical research projects, more of my time went into teaching. I have always been invigorated by teaching students; even apart from teaching, the general presence and company of so many young minds around refresh you. At DSE, my master's students included Bhaskar Dutta (one of the best economic theorists DSE has produced) and Rahul Khullar (one of the ablest administrators DSE has produced). At his graduation, Rahul told me that his own inclination was to do academic research with me, but he had to defer to his parents' strong desire for him to be an administrator. My PhD students included Sudipto Mundle, later a major policy economist. (Towards the end of my stay at DSE, another student, freshly arrived from the UK and seemingly quite radical in his political inclinations at that time, came to see me and expressed his desire to do research with me, but as I was soon to leave, I asked him to look for some other supervisor: this was Prannoy Roy, later a star TV personality and psephologist, and a co-founder of NDTV.)

In the DSE faculty, apart from Mrinal, Dharma Kumar and André Beteille, I was also close to Raj Krishna, a colourful personality and a famed agricultural economist. It is unfortunate that since his untimely death in the 1980s, people seem to remember his describing the first three decades of India's slow growth by the term 'Hindu rate of growth' (a term devoid of its contextual irony becomes rather inane) more than his solid empirical and policy work. There were other distinguished names in the faculty like Sukhamoy Chakravarty (by the time I joined DSE he was mostly busy at the Planning Commission), Prasanta Pattanaik (a soft-spoken social-choice theorist), A.L. Nagar (a guru to many of his students in econometric theory), K.L. Krishna (popular with the students for his indefatigable devotion to teaching and supervision in applied econometrics) and the sociologist Veena Das. (Later Hirofumi Uzawa, who was a professor at the University of Chicago, told me something about K.L. Krishna. Uzawa apparently did not like to teach general classes. So in his first few lectures he'd deal with very tough subjects—thus, by the third or fourth lecture in the term, most students would drop the class, and Uzawa would get relief from teaching it. But one year, he said, there was this Indian student, K.L. Krishna, who'd not drop the class no matter how difficult Uzawa tried to make the subject matter. Here was a case of Japanese toughness matched with Indian tenacity.)

Veena used to mockingly describe economists as mere useful 'handymen' for particular policy jobs, presumably otherwise not very deep or respectable as social thinkers. I was recently reminded of this when I found my friend Esther Duflo (the youngest Nobel laureate ever in economics) describing the economist's role as that of a 'plumber', useful in fixing things. Keynes had also wanted economists to be 'humble, competent people, on a level with dentists', but it is worth noting that he himself went far beyond that level, gave himself the grand role of saving capitalism!

I had missed in DSE two of the towering figures associated with its early days: one was the economist V.K.R.V. Rao, who was a founder of DSE, and the other was the sociologist M.N. Srinivas, who started the sociology department at DSE. By the time I joined DSE, they both had gone back to Karnataka, the state they were originally from, and were associated with the Institute of Social and Economic Change (ISEC) in Bangalore (which was also founded by Rao, the great academic institution-builder). But I did have some brief interaction with both of them later. Once in the 1980s, when I was in a conference in Bangalore, I was summoned by Rao to see him at his home (he told me, 'You cannot come to Bangalore and go away without paying me a visit'), and we had a pleasant conversation. I have met Srinivas briefly in Delhi, but, on a later visit to California, he came to our home in Berkeley. (I remember him pointing to the barren avocado tree in our garden and mentioning that the tree in his home in Bangalore was quite productive.) He told me that he appreciated the fact that unlike most economists, I had muddied my feet by doing field surveys in villages.

Later, I was invited to give the V.K.R.V. Rao Memorial Lecture at ISEC in Bangalore. Before my lecture, Narayana Murthy, a founder of the internationally well-known IT company Infosys, headquartered in Bangalore, whom I had earlier met at a conference in Cornell, invited me to come to what he called the 'campus' of Infosys first, where he showed me around, gave me lunch, and then he and I started in his car for ISEC for my lecture. For the next two and a half hours or so, we were trapped in the very slow-moving Bangalore traffic. This, however, gave me an opportunity to discuss with Murthy, the modest and thoughtful billionaire, extensively on many issues. I had occasion also to know another co-founder of Infosys, Nandan Nilekani, and his philanthropist wife, Rohini. Nandan, the friendly billionaire, is, of course, the father of the world's largest biometric identification programme in India. The first time we met was when I was giving a lecture at Yale, and the whole Nilekani family was in my audience, and after my lecture they came and introduced themselves to me (I think one of their children was a student at Yale at that time). Since then, I have met and interacted with them several times in Delhi and by email.

At DSE, I, of course, very much enjoyed my days there, but some aspects of the university's policy in recruitment and promotion of teachers used to trouble me. Let me just give two examples. One is from DSE itself, but illustrative of a much more general problem in university life. We had a middle-aged colleague who had long wanted to be promoted to Readership (associate professorship), but failed in the usual process, because he had not done any serious research to speak of in many years. He was full of leftist clichés and was popular with some sections of leftist students. He first started complaining that he was being passed over in promotion because his 'right-wing' colleagues (the term used in economics those days was 'neo-classical'—in the same pejorative way the term 'neo-liberal' is used nowadays) were biased in undervaluing his work. This after a time did not work, as even some leftist scholars in the department shared views similar to those of the 'right-wing' colleagues on this matter. Then he tried a different tack.

The university recruitment and promotion process was quite arbitrary. Decisions were taken by a selection committee chosen entirely by the vice chancellor, and, in the committee meeting, the only other people who could take part in the decision were the chairperson of the department and the vice chancellor. Thus, the vice chancellor played a crucial role in the process. So this leftist colleague became noisily active in the campus-wide teachers' union, and soon was influential particularly with the leftists there. On various campus-wide issues, he made it obvious to the vice chancellor that he could make his life difficult. The vice chancellor, a shrewd man, tried to pre-empt him, and knowing fully well his ulterior motive, soon carefully chose a selection committee stacked to select this man. The department chairman, representing the faculty opinion, was in a hopeless minority in this selection process, and the man got what he had wanted all these years.

The second example relates to appointments at a somewhat lower level; this was about the way teachers were selected in the undergraduate colleges affiliated with the university. As a DSE professor, one of my arduous duties was to act as an 'expert' in the numerous interviews of candidates for appointment in some of these colleges. My colleagues had warned me that this duty could be tiresome as the colleges might keep on pressing for their favourite candidates, but they assured me that under the rules, no one could be appointed if I, as the 'expert' from DSE, decided to withhold my signature. The interviews went on for long hours; in some colleges, the selection process was relatively smooth, but in some others it was not.

I remember once in one college the principal had a special candidate in mind, but I found him quite mediocre, and there was a whole slew of other candidates in my judgement much superior, and the best of them, both in interview and in paper qualifications, was a woman, who was quite low in the ranking of this macho man of a principal. After the interviews were over (around 6 p.m.), the war of attrition started, over endless cups of tea and repetitive arguments. The principal kept on pushing his candidate and I kept on saying no. He thought he'd wear me down, but did not succeed. One of his arguments was that the woman candidate would not be able to discipline the classes, which, according to him, contained some rowdy boys. Then around 9 p.m. or so he yielded, but with a threat: 'Okay, Professor,' he said. 'Go ahead, and appoint this female, but if she gets assaulted in class, it's your responsibility.' I said, while finally signing the paper, 'No, it's the college's responsibility to look after the safety of all faculty, male or female.' But this incident left a bad taste in my mouth. (I faced similar problems in a couple of other colleges where they had a preference for candidates from a particular region or community.)

Outside academia, Delhi was a good place for some aspects of pan-Indian culture, say, classical music and dance. It was also a great delight to walk through places where all the major state governments had their emporia, and you could see displayed the fascinating diversity and richness of local arts and crafts from different parts of India. But in my lifelong search for interesting films, Delhi was a bit of a disappointment (even compared to Kolkata or Mumbai). I used to wait for the once-a-year international film festival, which brought not merely some new international non-blockbuster or art films, but also a 'panorama' section for films from different Indian regions. But getting tickets was not easy. Delhi being a bureaucratic city, many of the seats were allocated to bureaucrats (with free passes), and for the rest of the seats sold in movie halls you had to jostle with long lines of people. As with my episode with milk 'tokens' before, I did not want to use my 'connections' to procure free passes, and mostly stood for hours in lines for advance tickets in different movie halls in different corners of this large, spread-out city. In particular, if any film was marked 'A' (for 'mature' audience only), many people took it as a signal for a profusion of steamy scenes in the film, which was an attraction in a sex-repressed society and the crowds in the lines were desperate. Let me relate two incidents in this connection.

Once, I got a ticket for a foreign 'A' film for the matinee show. I had some engagement for which I'd have to rush immediately after the movie was to end. Towards the end, I had already positioned myself near the gate, so that I could beat the crowd at the exit. Suddenly, I was roughly pushed aside by a sturdy fellow, who rushed out of the hall and started shouting to a couple of people outside: 'Give up the tickets, there's nothing in it, only two buttons opened!' I realized these were touts, one of them was in the matinee show to check how steamy the film really was, he was now instructing his fellow ticket scalpers to quickly sell off their hoarded tickets, as their black-market prices were going to collapse as soon as the news about the movie spread to the viewers of the next show.

Another time, I went to see a well-known Argentinian documentary film on neo-colonialism and violence, titled *Hour of the Furnaces*. I think probably by some clerical mistake the film festival people marked it 'A'. As the movie went on, the crowds were disappointed and getting increasingly restless by what they saw—the very few women in it were fully clothed in guerrilla fatigues fighting in the jungles. At one point, sections of the viewers started shouting and demanding their money back. The chaos and mayhem reached a point when the panicked authorities stopped the projector. I'll never forget the screen with the frozen scene—Che Guevara in the Bolivian jungle had just been killed by the CIA-assisted Bolivian forces, and some of them were dancing and spitting on his dead body. And, in front of me, there were these people jumping on their seats, demanding their money back for the lack of sex scenes in the film.

In both ISI and DSE there was one problem I faced in my research that I did not fully anticipate before. Some of the major international journals had a submission fee for research papers which was equivalent to something that would exhaust most of my Indian monthly salary. In the US, authors mostly charged the fee to their research grants, which was not a way out for me. I once wrote from Delhi about this to the executive committee of the American Economic Association (AEA), and suggested that for their journals, they should have a lower rate for authors from low-income countries. I got a reply saying that after careful consideration in their committee meeting they had decided against my suggestion. Their rationale was a typical one for believers in perfect markets: since an article in an AEA journal was likely to significantly raise the expected lifetime earnings of an author, the latter should be able to finance it. (I visualized the dour face of an Indian public bank loan officer trying to comprehend this.)

I also found out that using Indian micro-level data for a research paper in a mainstream American journal in those days was considered so exotic that more often than not the editors, even before reviewing the paper, would immediately suggest sending it instead to an Indian journal or, at best, a field journal.

The other journal-related problem was their limited availability in India. Indian libraries could not afford some of the high-priced technical journals, and for those that they could, by the time they'd arrive in the library shelves, most of the articles had gone rather stale research wise, as researchers abroad, who had seen their working-paper and pre-print versions years before, had already advanced the frontier in that area, before we in India even came to know of the original article. (Today, the internet and social media have largely done away with this research barrier that we had faced.)

Meanwhile, in the political front in India, things were reaching a boiling point. Many of us were dismayed by the arbitrary authoritarian actions of Indira Gandhi. The strike by 1.7 million railway workers—the largest recorded industrial action in the world—was brutally suppressed, with thousands sent to jail. After massive student protests in Gujarat and Bihar, the veteran politician Jayaprakash Narayan (JP)—one of the few surviving leaders then of the freedom struggle, once associated with the Congress Socialist Party, who, after Independence, had declined Nehru's invitation to join his cabinet—called for an all-India resistance movement against the policies of Nehru's daughter. The leftists were divided, some of them looked to Indira Gandhi, supported by the Soviet Union, as the bulwark against 'right-wing reaction', other leftists, along with liberals, protested the encroachments on liberty. I think it was early in 1975 that JP came to Delhi and asked our friend Lakshmi Jain to organize a closed-door evening meeting at his home with some Delhi journalists and academics to discuss some of the burning issues. JP mainly wanted to listen to get ideas for leading his resistance movement. Mrinal and I were invited and went together in Mrinal's car.

In the meeting, the gloom about the future of the country was quite palpable. JP, a sick septuagenarian, seemed despondent, spoke softly and briefly, and then others spoke. After some time, one or two garrulous journalists started dominating the discussion. Mrinal and I decided to go home. As we came out and Mrinal was having a smoke standing in the garden outside, he quietly pointed me to something near his parked car. I saw a man crouching near the front of his car, trying hard in the darkness to write down his licence plate number. This hapless plain-clothes policeman had probably been sent to trace the invitees to this sinister meeting. As Mrinal and I approached the car, the man quickly disappeared into the darkness.

Then late night on 25 June—the day after the Supreme Court upheld a decision of a lower court against Indira Gandhi, and the day on which JP called for the police to disobey orders they regarded as immoral—an Emergency was declared, suspending constitutional rights, and a massive crackdown on most political opposition took place, jailing tens of thousands. There was a blackout on information. Mrinal and I used to get together every day to collate and sift through all the details (much of it rumours) we could garner.

Every evening, a diplomat friend of ours, Sisir Gupta (who was a somewhat mysterious character, it was a bit difficult sometimes to figure out which side he was on), used to come to Mrinal's place and, after imbibing his whiskey, he'd unburden the stories ('from the horse's mouth') and accounts of intrigues that he had collected in the day from different political camps. He used to relate his stories in a conspiratorial whisper; I did not believe all of them, but many of them later checked out right. Some of the stories were about Indira Gandhi's rowdy younger son, Sanjay, and his evil doings, and also how the rest of the ruling party was resenting the overbearing antics of what was called Sanjay's 'Punjabi mafia'—they lacked the social grace of the earlier 'Kashmiri mafia' around the mother.

Most people in the academia I knew were cowering in fear. Mrinal in this context showed a good deal of courage. One day, I was chatting with him in his office when a group of louts with allegiance to Sanjay unceremoniously barged into Mrinal's office and loudly demanded that the major auditorium in DSE be used by them for a forthcoming symposium on Sanjay's 'twenty-point programme' (this was an ad hoc collection of sanctimonious programmes to alleviate poverty, unemployment, etc., just to cover up the odour of their high-handed activities) for which Mrinal's permission as the head of the economics department was needed. Then they also threateningly demanded that all of the department's faculty attend the symposium. Mrinal coolly responded by saying any organization could apply for using that auditorium, and they'd have to go to the office next door for the formal application; and no, he could not attend the symposium as he had already called a faculty meeting at the time they mentioned, but if any faculty member wanted to attend the symposium it was up to them. The louts were not fully happy, but after some grumbling they left the office, chanting slogans like, 'Long live twenty-point programme'.

Humour was one way to help us spend those dark days. Ashis told us a story about a friend who was making a call on his phone, when suddenly someone in the background—who was tapping the phone—said gruffly in Hindi, 'Speak up, we can't hear you.' Mrinal, Ashis and I used to say that Indian authoritarianism would be characteristically inefficient, messy, showy and farcical—more like that of Mussolini's. There was a cartoon around that time by India's best cartoonist, R.K. Laxman, on the order issued to all government officers on a pledge of loyalty to the twenty-point programme: One officer was heartily singing out the pledge, when someone rushed to point out that there was a typo in the official order, he was to 'sign' the pledge, not to 'sing' it!

Most of us were in deep admiration of our DSE colleague Sukhamoy Chakravarty (I used to call him Sukhamoy-da). He was a prodigious scholar, a voracious reader of books (when discussing a book it was not unusual for him to point out to us that the author had slightly changed his position on an issue in question in the third edition in a long footnote), a man of wide intellectual interests, but also a man of charming simplicity and other-worldliness. In my period at DSE, as he was mostly in the Planning Commission, I'd occasionally meet him at his home (or at Mrinal's) in the evenings. I remember one evening I was discussing something with him in his living room, while a whole army of children (his daughter and her neighbourhood friends) were enthusiastically carrying books, shifting them from one room to another corner of the house under the general supervision of his wife, Lalita (his partner and fellow economist since their Presidency College days). At one point, he digressed from what we were discussing, and pointed to the army of load-carrying children, and said, 'You see, this is how the Industrial Revolution came about—on the backs of child labour.'

He had many physical ailments and his life was cut short at age fifty-six. (Later, I gave the Sukhamoy Chakravarty Memorial Lecture at DSE where I saw his daughter again, by then a well-known chemistry professor.) Even though Sukhamoy-da was mainly a theorist, in the last two decades of his life, he was dedicated in search of solutions to India's policy problems. I remember once an Australian economist friend, the renowned trade theorist Murray Kemp, on a visit told me that he had noticed in some of his Indian economist friends (he particularly mentioned Sukhamoy-da and also me) a kind of divided loyalty in their pursuit of economics—even when we were thinking deeply about some theoretical issue at the frontier of economics, half our minds were distracted by the buzzing question: How would all this help India? (He, of course, implied that as a result we would neither scale the theoretical heights we were capable of nor really help India that much!)

What in this context somewhat dismayed me about Sukhamoy-da's dedication to India's policy problems was that he carried this on in serving the government even when it was turning sordidly authoritarian. All through the Emergency days in Delhi, Mrinal and I often privately suggested to him that he was giving respectability to Indira Gandhi's government, but he continued serving until it fell in a discredited heap in 1977. One argument he used to give was that he could change the undesirable policies of the government by working from inside, instead of resigning. This is a common enough illusion many intelligent, well-intentioned people serving a loathsome government have. (I heard that in one meeting with Indira Gandhi, when Sukhamoy-da objected to some policy, she said with an irritated smirk, 'Professor, you must be pulling my leg.') Later I wrote a somewhat satirical piece in *EPW* titled 'An Imaginary Conversation with a Leftist Intellectual in Government', without naming anyone, on the nature of this illusion.

Many people were amused by reading this piece. One of them who discussed it with me in some detail was Amiya Dasgupta, the veteran economic theorist, who was a classmate in Dhaka University of my father and Sachin Chaudhuri. He was then living in Santiniketan after many years in Delhi. I got to know him well when he visited Cambridge in my student days, and then again at his Santiniketan home. I remember one of his stories involving my dissertation supervisor, James Meade. Dasgupta's son, Partha, had married Meade's daughter, Carol. So once Amiya Dasgupta told Meade that the relationship between the two of them could be neatly described by one simple Bengali word, 'beyai', but it was a deficiency of the English language that no simple word could describe it in English. To this, Meade apparently tried constructing a new word: He said, 'Let's see. You are my daughter's father-in-law; my daughter's father is myself—so you are my self-in-law.' This, in turn, reminds me of my Marxist philosopher friend Jerry Cohen (more on him later), who once, in London, introduced to me a highly embarrassed Englishman (who happened to be the partner of Jerry's then-separated wife) by saying: 'Meet my lover-in-law!'

Going back to the dismal Emergency days, I once again realized then how intensely political a person I was. My teaching and research were thriving reasonably; I had, by then, many good friends in Delhi and, in any case, we were busy bringing up our son, Titash, who was not yet five then, growing in the warm and congenial company of other children of his age in our apartment complex. Yet, it seemed that the unaccustomed undemocratic political surroundings had deeply enervated me—as if a human stain had defiled the civic life around to leave an ashen taste in my mouth, as if there was a creeping darkness at noon.

Around this time, one day completely out of the blue, I got a message from the economics department at Berkeley asking me if I'd be interested in visiting Berkeley for a year. The terms were quite attractive: I had to teach part of the year and for the rest of the time I'd be on a Ford Research Professorship. I knew very few people at the department, except for my friends George Akerlof, Albert Fishlow, and to some extent, Steve Goldman (he was a student of Hirofumi Uzawa whom I knew). I did not know much about the Bay Area either. When I was at MIT, one summer, I attended a two-week colloquium at Stanford organized by Ken Arrow and others. At that time, I had a tourist visit to Berkeley for half a day, but I remember liking the surroundings. Of course, I knew about Berkeley's reputation as an epicentre of Vietnam War protests. My friend Avinash Dixit who was teaching at Berkeley at the time of those protests had a rather negative view; he later told me that one of several reasons why he left Berkeley was that tear gas was frequently wafting through the window of his office—for someone from Kolkata that could be part of the excitement of life in Berkeley.

But I was completely unprepared for this invitation. I had quite a few data-intensive projects with a whole research team that were only halfway through, I was not sure if I'd get leave from DSE only a couple of years or so after joining, Kalpana had a job at ICSSR, our son was managing Hindi at the kindergarten school we liked and spoke Bengali at home, with hardly a word of English in his repertoire, and it was going to be a big displacement for him, and so on.

At the same time, I was quite disturbed by the political situation around. I remember one evening asking Sisir Gupta, the diplomat, about his prediction for the next couple of years. He thought the situation was going to get much worse before possibly getting better. After a lot of cogitation, I asked Berkeley if they were prepared to postpone my visit by half a year so that I could wind up a few ongoing things in Delhi. To my surprise, they agreed. So then I had to accept the invitation. In 1976, we were off to Berkeley.

8

A Newcomer to Berkeley

We arrived in Berkeley and found it to be a pleasant place to live. I have a partiality for small university towns that are culturally and politically alive. And yet, Berkeley is not far from a thriving major city (San Francisco: '…The unfettered city/resounds with hedonistic glee,' as Vikram Seth describes it in his verse-novel *The Golden Gate*) on the one hand, and from wide-open spaces, on the other. Nature in Berkeley itself is quite beautiful, nestled as it is on a verdant hillside, facing an ocean and its bay, with gorgeous sunsets over the Golden Gate Bridge (on days when it is not shrouded by the mysterious fog—-which appears almost as a character in San Francisco noir, like in the crime novels of Dashiell Hammett). Once, driving in the dense fog in a winding street in the Berkeley hills, I missed a turn and lost my way; I fondly remembered that famous scene in Fellini's semi-autobiographical film *Amarcord*, where one winter's day in Rimini, his childhood town, the fog shrouds everything, the piazza disappears and the grandpa loses his way home.

I found the people here also somewhat more laid-back than in the intense cities of the east coast. (Once, a friend from New York visiting Berkeley told me that when a shop assistant at the end of the transaction gave him a smile and said 'Have a nice day', his first instinct with his New Yorker neurosis was: 'What? What did she mean?') The cafes, restaurants, bookshops, music stores and cinemas just outside the campus hummed with lively people. Strolling through the Sproul Plaza in the campus you sometimes get an experience associated with the soap-box speakers at Hyde Park in London or the performers in the Latin Quarter in Paris: At one corner, a religious preacher—Bible in hand—is sternly telling us that the wages of sin is death, while a group of non-believers is busy mocking him; at another gathering, some group is loudly bashing Israel for oppressing Palestinians, while some Hillel International students are protesting; at another place, five women are silently standing, each exposing one breast, pointing towards donations for research on breast cancer; at another, some Punjabi men and women are doing a vigorous bhangra dance; at another a group of PETA women for animal rights is protesting the abuse of those rights in university labs; at another, a stand-up comic is entertaining a large crowd; in a quiet corner, you see a man covered with gold dust standing perfectly still like a golden statue and suddenly moving a limb startling everybody ...

In Berkeley streets, I was initially struck by the number of people in wheelchairs and with other forms of physical handicaps. Later, I realized the city being liberal with help for the disabled is a magnet for such people from less-liberal cities. (The same probably goes for the number of homeless people; but, over time, I sensed that the extremely high housing costs in the Bay Area is also a major factor.) There are also many panhandlers—in order to discourage their use of the money collected on drugs or drinks, the city, at one time, introduced a system of vouchers: if you want to give to a panhandler, you hand out a city-designated voucher (which can only be used on food or medicines). Around that time, walking on Telegraph Avenue, I saw a panhandler with a placard saying, 'Keep your goddam voucher, I want beer!'

The left-liberal city government of what was sometimes called the People's Republic of Berkeley in their deliberations sometimes reminded me of the municipal government in Kolkata under the left. A significant part of the day in both used to be spent in passing resolutions deprecating the latest outrage perpetrated by American imperialism or in expressing solidarity with the people of Vietnam/Nicaragua, while small matters like the gaping potholes in the city roads did not get much attention. (In contrast, in some left-run cities of central Italy you'll, of course, see a prominent Piazza Gramsci, but the cities are relatively well-run and maintained.)

In line with the left movements in Berkeley, there have been some historically important cooperative ventures here. For quite some time the supermarket we regularly went to was run by the Consumers' Cooperative of Berkeley, which, at its peak, was the largest cooperative of its kind in North America. One of the first things that struck me as I entered their supermarkets was that there were some goods on their shelves (like cereal brands with too much sugar) which they didn't really want you to buy and they were marked by a distinctive red tape on the shelves, with green tapes indicating the brands they recommended. These coops went out of business by the late 1980s, marred, I understand, by internal disputes about governance and bankruptcy issues. But, to this day, a store next door, the employee-owned The Cheese Board Collective—selling cheese, pizza and baked goods—is doing roaring business; they now have a large network of stores throughout the Bay Area. There is also a popular student housing cooperative in Berkeley which provides affordable housing and meals to more than 1,300 students. You occasionally hear about problems of drug use and cases of irresponsibility of some residents on the use of the commons, but they provide a very useful service in an area of excessive housing costs.

My friend George Akerlof (and his then Chinese wife, Kay) helped us settle down in Berkeley. George sometimes came to take our son, Titash, for a walk in the park. George even now remembers that in one of those walks when he asked Titash how old he was, he got the prompt answer: five years, four months and seventeen days. Titash was then going to a preschool nursery, where I was astounded by how quickly children could learn a new language (English in his case) and unlearn another (his Delhi preschool Hindi).

Titash and I started using the local YMCA swimming pools. But I found the water in the pool for adults too cold for me and tried without success to persuade the authorities to raise the heating in that pool. They advised me to go to the children's pool instead, where my son was. There, the water was comfortably warm, but the level came only up to my knees. The knee-level water reminded me of a story I once read about Groucho Marx. It was a lovely summer day in Long Island and Groucho decided to give his son a special treat by taking him to a local swimming club pool for the first time. But the front desk people at the club told him that Jews were not allowed in the pool. Groucho then reportedly asked them if they'd permit his son, who was half-Jewish, to wade into the pool at least up to his knees.

After I started teaching, I soon realized that several people in the department wanted me to consider staying on in Berkeley, and there was a chair on international trade which they were thinking of filling. When the formal offer was made to me, I was torn. I liked the city of Berkeley (its life, its natural surroundings and relatively temperate climate), the very friendly and good department, and the fact that it was a great university. On the other hand, less than a decade back, I had taken a difficult decision to leave MIT for India on the basis of some deeply felt reasons. (Just before leaving MIT, Roy Radner, who was then the chairman at the economics department at Berkeley had approached me to see if I'd be interested in joining the Berkeley faculty, and I said no, citing some of those reasons. Now Roy was my colleague at Berkeley; he incidentally expressed his interest in my new work on sharecropping.) My research projects analysing NSS data and with Ashok Rudra on village surveys were still ongoing. Of course, the future life of our son was now a predominant consideration as well.

I told myself that the immersion in Indian data was a goal which I had started accomplishing in India in all earnest and it had been an invigorating experience for me—in spite of the various initial aches and pains. It might be possible now to sustain it, though imperfectly, through frequent visits and maintaining the various contacts I had already established. Frequent visits were also the highly imperfect way of keeping up with the cultural and familial connections with India that I valued. We also weighed the largely rote-based, highly competitive, examination-oriented Indian education system for our son's future compared to the more easy-going, laid-back system in California. So I decided to stay on. But even after accepting Berkeley's offer, initial doubts lingered on for a period (so instead of resigning from DSE, I asked for and got an extension of my leave for the next year).

To facilitate my frequent visits to India, I bought an apartment in Kolkata in a building where a couple of friends stayed. Over the years, long-distance maintenance of that apartment has been a challenge, but, with the help of friends, I have so far barely managed it. When I bought the apartment, I had an interesting encounter with the Indian judicial bureaucracy. In the legal process of registering the title to my property in the local land records, I had to go to the local court one day. I had hired a lawyer who said he'd take care of everything; I just had to be in the court to sign some things and pay the requisite fees. After I paid a bunch of fees, the lawyer asked me to sit in the court along with a large number of people there and wait for the judge to come, and formally declare all the documents as valid. At the last minute, the lawyer rushed to me and said I had to pay a bit more. I paid him but asked him why this fee was more than he had originally asked for. He whispered that the judge was asking for more than he expected. For the first time that day, I realized some of those 'fees' I had paid were really bribes for different officials (including the judge) to speed up the process. Just at that moment of my bitter realization, a court functionary loudly asked everyone to rise as the judge entered the courtroom in full regalia and took his throne-like seat. I refused to stand up; the lawyer again rushed to me and said that I could be charged with 'contempt of court' if I did not stand up for the judge. I told him that I had already paid him a 'baksheesh' (tip), and I was not going to stand up for him.

Land title is a tricky matter in India. I once read about a city clerk in Bihar who had not been to his native village for some years where he had owned some land. After many years, he went back to his village and found that, even though he had the ownership documents, his land was now owned and occupied by a complete stranger. He also found that in the local official records he had been declared as 'dead' and his relatives had sold off the land. Soon, he also discovered that in the nearby villages several such people had been deprived of their land in the same way. Once you are declared 'dead' (with a death certificate from a bribed doctor) in the official records, it apparently is extremely difficult to prove that you are alive. But this stubborn man refused to accept it; he got together with all the other such aggrieved parties in the area, formed an organization called 'Dead Peoples' Society', and started marching in a procession to the local offices. I don't know if he finally succeeded.

My project on analysis of NSS-collected data could be carried out in Berkeley. But those days, it was not easy to pry large sets of data loose from a government office—particularly to take the data out of the country. After a lot of effort, and with the help of V.M. Dandekar, who was then the chairman of the NSS Governing Council, I got the permission to bring the data copied in the form of open-reel tapes that were in use at the NSS office in Delhi. The tapes were ancient Honeywell tapes, which I found—much to my distress—that the Berkeley computers were unable to convert. I called the Honeywell company office headquarters in the US and described the problem of tape-conversion I was having. The officer who finally took the call asked me: 'Where are you calling from? The Smithsonian [the museum]?' I felt like saying, 'Yes, the tapes were with the dinosaur exhibits.' After many enquiries and after several days, they told me that the only machine in the whole of the US that could convert such ancient tapes happened to be located not far from Berkeley, in the Alameda naval base. But when I called the naval station on a Thursday, they told me that they were scheduled to junk that machine on Monday—so I better come immediately. I was lucky to save my NSS data in the nick of time.

Since my chair was in international trade, most of my teaching in Berkeley was in that field of economics, both at the graduate and undergraduate levels. The undergraduate classes in Berkeley are large, and mine had sometimes more than 250 students—even though this course was meant mostly for later-year undergraduates.

Large classes bring you in close touch (particularly during office hours) with a refreshing diversity of young people. But they also bring other kinds of experience.

In large, crowded classrooms, the borderlines were always a bit fuzzy—sometimes nearby pedestrians would saunter in just out of curiosity, to hear a funny-looking man speaking in a funny accent; some others were from the aimlessly loitering often mentally disabled street people. One day, as I was teaching, one woman belonging probably to the latter group seated in a back bench suddenly stood up, looked at the ceiling for a minute and then gave out a piercing wail. As I was pondering on how to handle this, fortunately for me, she slowly walked out of the auditorium.

A colleague of mine, Richard Sutch, an economic historian, usually taught a much larger beginning Econ 1 class, which sometimes had about a thousand students. He told me that he regularly took out what was called a 'teachers' insurance'; he said that in a thousand-strong class there were bound to be some crazies who were going to sue you for one thing or another—this insurance was for his legal protection. I said in jest that I had often wondered why in any case we were not more regularly sued for 'malpractice' (like doctors), for instance, for our class teaching not helping them in getting a job.

Once, I had a rather disturbing encounter with an undergraduate student. This was a student (slightly older than usual) in a small seminar class that he took with me. He did reasonably well in that class, if I remember right. A few years after he graduated, one day, he knocked at my office door and greeted me with a lot of warmth, and started narrating stories about the places he had visited in the couple of years he had been out of the country after graduation. He went on and on, and, at one point, I told him that I had another appointment. He stopped, apologized and said that he had come to pick up 'the thing' that he had left with me before leaving the country. 'What thing?' I asked; he said, 'My wife's jewellery box.' I was dumbfounded and said, 'What are you talking about?' He kept on insisting and I tried to explain to him why it did not make any sense for him to leave his wife's jewellery box with a teacher whom he hardly knew, and even if he had tried to, why would that teacher keep it. He started sobbing and said that his relationship with his wife was already on the rocks, and this was going to make it much worse. At that point, I politely but firmly asked him to leave the room. Later, when I narrated the story to Kalpana, she said I was lucky that the student at the end did not bring out a gun and shoot me.

At the beginning, I did not teach much development economics, even though my research was increasingly in that field. The content of an international trade course was more streamlined and thus easier to teach, whereas that of development economics was inherently more amorphous, as it was really all of economics but applied to a bewildering diversity of countries having most of the world's population. I used to tell students that Tolstoy's famous quote from *Anna Karenina* that 'happy families are all alike, but each unhappy family is unhappy in its own way' also applied to the diverse country conditions of economic misery.

My colleague Albert Fishlow used to teach a graduate course on macro development, mainly based on his interest in Latin America. Albert had a large number of Latin American graduate students; his office was near mine and, on days he held office hours, the hallway was agog with Spanish- or Portuguese-speaking students talking among themselves. I knew some of these students as they took my international trade class and also as I often served in their dissertation committees chaired by Fishlow.

Some of these students are now in different official or academic positions in Latin America or in international organizations. One of them, Mauricio Cárdenas, was for a time the finance minister in Colombia. When I was invited by Universidad de los Andes in Bogotá to give a keynote lecture at a conference, they asked Mauricio to introduce me. In this introduction, Mauricio said, among other things, that when after his Berkeley days he was wooing his girlfriend (later wife), an economics student, he tried to lure her by promising his notes from my class in Berkeley. Little did I know that my lecture notes on the dry subject of international trade could serve as an aphrodisiac!

Slowly, I worked out a graduate micro-development course, which I started teaching, and I was soon joined in this by my French colleagues and friends, Elisabeth Sadoulet and Alain de Janvry of the department of agricultural and resource economics. Both of them had done a great deal of research in developing countries in three continents. (For a time, Alain was also the coach of a soccer club for young people that my son, Titash, played in.) Some of my lectures later formed the basic materials for a textbook, *Development Microeconomics* that I published in 1999 (jointly with Christopher Udry, a student and then a colleague of TN—TN was by then teaching at Yale, after leaving ISI, and he had introduced Chris to me).

Even though our textbook has received praise from different quarters, I think its publication was, unfortunately, badly timed. Around this time, the turn of the century, development economics took a major turn towards more refined empirical, rather than theoretical, work (which got increasingly reflected in the subject's course materials at different American universities), whereas our short textbook deliberately dealt almost entirely with theoretical issues, though drawing insights from our own empirical work (in South Asia in my case, sub-Saharan Africa in the case of Chris).

About a year after joining Berkeley, we bought a house on the hill above the campus, facing San Francisco Bay. With hardly any savings in my kitty, I had to take a huge mortgage to buy it. (My father in India, when he heard this, quickly converted the large dollar amount into a gigantic figure in rupees, and gave up all hope that I'd ever be free of the shackles of debt.) So whenever any visitor came to our house and went gaga over our spectacular Bay view, I used to say, 'Yes, we eat the view.' From the house, it is about a two-mile walk down a steep hill to the campus, but walking up is tough.

By then, for the first time in my life, I had acquired a car (I learned driving by attending an evening school run by the city—the various sections of this evening school were indeed quite impressive, teaching all kinds of useful skills from plumbing to auto repair at nominal fees. I wish municipal governments in India could arrange for such schools even on a small scale!). But in the Berkeley campus, parking your car is not easy. The university charges a substantial fee for the parking permit, but I soon discovered that the permit was only a 'hunting licence', it was very difficult to get parking space anywhere near my department if you arrived after 9 a.m. No wonder the main coveted reward the campus gives to its Nobel laureates is a dedicated parking spot; in October, when the prize is announced and if any Berkeley faculty gets it, a mock collective sigh goes up in the campus: 'There goes another parking spot!'

I have heard that when Clark Kerr was the chancellor at Berkeley, he was reported to have said that he had figured out the ways of keeping the three main groups in his charge happy: the faculty by getting them more parking space; the undergraduates by giving them enough opportunity to have sex; and the alumni with football games.

Clark Kerr, originally a student and then faculty at the Berkeley economics department, was particularly famous for his reform, when he became University president, of the California education system into a much-copied three-tier system: the top tier with the main campuses of the University of California, the middle tier with the California state universities for the bulk of undergraduates in the state, and, at the large-base bottom, the community colleges with the vocational and transfer-oriented programmes. This was an attempt to achieve a remarkable balance in the public higher education system, between access to education, the need for vocational education for the majority and for academic excellence for a smaller number of qualified students.

As a centrist liberal, this man got hit from both sides. In 1964–65, Kerr bore the brunt of the student protests in Berkeley. In 1967, he was hounded out of his university presidency by the newly elected governor of California, Ronald Reagan, who considered Kerr as much too liberal and whose election campaign had promised to 'clean up the mess at Berkeley'. At his dismissal, Kerr commented that he was leaving the presidency of the university just as he had entered it: 'Fired with enthusiasm!'

In the Berkeley hills, there is a campus bus, but the nearest bus stop is about a one-mile walk from my home, if you take a shortcut through a meadow, but it gets quite muddy in the rainy season. Still, after some years, I opted for taking the campus bus rather than my car on weekdays. One regular passenger I used to meet in the bus was a distinguished nonagenarian, Charles Townes, who had won the 1964 Physics Nobel Prize for inventing the laser (later, he was also involved in the team that discovered the black hole at the centre of the Milky Way galaxy). In a campus lecture that I once gave on globalization, I was thrilled to see him at the front in the audience. He was active in the campus even in his hundredth year, shortly before his death.

I also came to know that he was a deeply religious man. He claimed that his invention of the laser came to him like a 'flash', akin to religious revelation. When he got the 2005 Templeton

Prize that celebrates scientific and spiritual curiosity, he said that 'Science and Religion are quite parallel ... Science tries to understand what our universe is like and how it works, including us humans. Religion is aimed at understanding the purpose and meaning of our universe, including our own lives.' This reminded me of what Tagore said to Einstein on the relation between Science and Religion when they met at the latter's home in Berlin in 1930: 'Science ... is the impersonal human world of Truths. Religion realizes these Truths and links them up with our deeper needs; our individual consciousness of Truth gains universal significance. Religion applies values to Truth.' Einstein did not fully agree with Tagore, and nor do I, with either Townes or Tagore. Einstein later said, 'Science without religion is lame, religion without science is blind.' In any case, no one can deny that in interpreting facts scientists cannot be independent of values (this is an important issue in some debates in life sciences now), and I also understand a bit about the possible appeal of deep spirituality even for atheists.

It used to be quite an experience for me to see astute Marxist scholars around me in Kolkata deeply moved by some of Tagore's spiritual or devotional songs. Many non-believers share the sense of wonder at the vastness and the as-yet-unresolved mysteries of nature, and are moved by the ability of spirituality sometimes to capture the infinite beauty of the universe, particularly when expressed in the form of art or music. Why does an irreligious person like me sometimes get goosebumps from listening to religiously inspired classical music (both Western and Indian)? Why do non-believers find healing properties in Gregorian chants? I am also reminded of a short unfinished essay that was found in my Marxist philosopher friend Jerry Cohen's table in Oxford after his sudden and untimely death, where Jerry says that one beautiful morning in Oxford he came outside, looked around, and felt deeply thankful and blessed—he then asks, thankful to whom? Blessed by whom?

As with Charles Townes, I came to know, only marginally, another great scholar in Berkeley outside my department; this was Steve Smale, who got the Fields Medal in Mathematics in 1966 for his work in topology in higher dimensions. Smale actually had an honorary appointment in our department, but I hardly ever saw him there. Most of the time, I saw him walking leisurely in different parts of the campus, with a slight inward smirk, as if he was amused by himself. He was an activist in the anti-war and the free speech movements in Berkeley. He co-founded the Vietnam Day Committee, whose most prominent act was a 1965 Oakland demonstration intended to stop troop trains. When, the next year, he received the Fields Medal at the International Congress of Mathematicians in Moscow, he held a controversial press conference there in which he criticized the actions of both the US and Soviet governments. I once went to a campus lecture given by him on a game-theoretic interpretation of international relations. Over the years, he also amassed one of the finest private mineral collections in the world. Many of Smale's mineral specimens can be seen in the book, *The Smale Collection: Beauty in Natural Crystals.*

In other Berkeley departments, the pre-eminent people I became friendly with included the sociologist Peter Evans, Janet Yellen at the business school (currently the US treasury secretary), Pravin Varaiya in the electrical engineering and computer sciences department, Michael Watts in the geography department, Robert Cooter in the Law School, the Sanskrit scholar Robert Goldman, and the Sanskrit and Tamil scholar George Hart. At frequent gatherings at George Hart's home, we met many South Asian scholars. On Tamil religious occasions, George used to perform ritual puja at home, sometimes even wearing a sacred thread for his priestly role—he jocularly claimed that he came from a 'Boston Brahmin' family and was thus entitled to wear the sacred thread!

I also knew Bharati Mukherjee of the Berkeley English literature department. Born and raised in Kolkata, she was an award-winning American writer (she'd insist on her Americanness); her fiction is about the internal culture clashes of the Indian immigrant's experience in the US. Conversation with her over a dinner at her home and later in the campus made me see clearly the differences between our attitudes to our immigrant status. She found it difficult to understand the inherent resistance and ambivalence I have inside me to a complete assimilation into American culture. She used to celebrate what she called her cultural and psychological 'mongrelization'. Later, she wrote a piece in the *New York Times* on this subject, differentiating herself from her sister, Mira, who had also migrated to the US around the same time, in early youth. She wrote:

> Mira and I differ in the ways in which we hope to interact with the country that we have chosen to live in. She is happier to live in America as expatriate Indian than as an immigrant American. I need to put roots down …The price that the immigrant willingly pays, and that the exile avoids, is the trauma of self-transformation.

Maybe I too have been avoiding this trauma.

In the Berkeley business school faculty, for a time in the 1980s, I had a friend whom I had known for many years; this was Sudipto Bhattacharya. He was the son of a Presidency College teacher of mine. Sudipto was an extremely bright finance economist, but since I knew very little of that field, we used to discuss other topics in economics, and on issues of culture and contemporary literature (in which he was remarkably wellread). He was a difficult person, very competitive academically and sometimes bluntly outspoken; he easily offended other people (some of whom had complained to me), but with me and Kalpana he was always very sweet and affectionate. He visited us often when he was in Berkeley, and called us frequently after he left. He lived a rather restless life alone, and sometimes, when he called from London, where he was in his last years, I looked at the watch and saw that it was something like 3 or 4 a.m. in London (though evening in California); he was sometimes worked up about something or someone, and he'd keep on talking, even as I implored him to have some sleep. Then suddenly, I heard about his heart attack and death in London at age sixty. The London School of Economics (LSE) invited me to give the funeral oration, but I did not feel like grieving over him so publicly and ceremoniously.

In my own department, I had many friends in the faculty, but over the years, I found myself developing some kind of a special relationship (born I presume out of an affinity in what the French call 'mentalité', often used in a historical sense) with three Europeans: in the early years, with the senior Italian economic historian Carlo Cipolla and the vibrant Catalonian mathematical-economist Andreu Mas-Colell, and, in more recent years, with the Belgian comparative-systems analyst Gérard Roland.

Even before arriving in Berkeley, I had read some fascinating short books by Carlo Cipolla (on *Guns and Sails* and on *Clocks*), and parts of his edited *The Fontana Economic History of Europe*. (K.N. Raj in Kerala had told me, when he heard that I was going to Berkeley, that he was a fan of Cipolla.) On meeting him, as I expressed my admiration for those books, he presented me with some of them and told me that most of his economist colleagues did not read such books any more. When I pointed out that one commonality in some of his books was that they were centred on early modern Italy, he said that Italy was historically lucky in being geographically situated at the centre of the trade routes between Asia and Western Europe in this period. Later, when he was writing a couple of historical books on the plague in Italy, he told me he was stimulated to write them while thinking about the epidemic of HIV/AIDS that was ravaging several countries around us at that time.

He said that like me he had also come to Berkeley first as a visiting professor, and then decided to stay on. By the time I met him, he was dividing his time: half the year in Berkeley, and the other half in Pavia, Italy, where he was born—until later, after developing Parkinson's disease, he gradually stopped coming to Berkeley. I have been told that in Italy he had an impressive collection of ancient coins, old clocks and Roman surgical instruments. I also came to know that his light-hearted treatise *The Basic Laws of Human Stupidity* was a bestseller in Italy and made into a play in France.

For a period, I was surprised to see him sitting at the back of my international trade class; I soon asked him not to come because the boring theoretical models I was doing in class were worlds apart from the rich historical sense pervading his books. Outside the world of books, Carlo always looked a little lost. Once at his home, his wife, Ora (a Californian woman), described to us how when Carlo in his well-intentioned way tried to help her in gardening, she'd quickly send him back to the house 'as the trees have a way of attacking him'!

Andreu Mas-Colell, a mathematical economist from Catalonia, came to Berkeley before I did. He was a student activist in Barcelona, was expelled from his university for activism (those were the days of General Franco's Spain), and later finished his undergraduate degree in a different university, in north-west Spain. When I met him in Berkeley, he was already a high-powered theorist using differential topology in general-equilibrium analysis, in ways that were far beyond my limited technical range in economic theory. But when we met, it was our shared interest in history, politics and culture that immediately made us good friends, and his warm, cheerful personality was an added attraction for me. (His wife, Esther, a mathematician from Chile, was as decent a person as she was politically alert.)

A few times, it so happened that when I went to see some obscure Latin American film in a special showing at a remote movie hall in Berkeley, at the end when the lights came on, I discovered that Andreu was also in the audience, and then we sat down somewhere to discuss the film animatedly. We used to frequently visit each other's homes. One time, Romila Thapar, the eminent historian of ancient India, came to visit us from Delhi, and we asked Andreu and Esther to join us. Later, he told others about meeting 'this very impressive woman' at our place.

When, after a few years, he left Berkeley—first for Harvard, and then in the 1990s went back to Barcelona—I sorely missed him. At Harvard, Andreu co-authored what is probably the most used graduate textbook in microeconomic theory in the world. In Barcelona, he was a professor at the Pompeu Fabra University. He later joined politics, serving the Catalonian government in different capacities, including as the minister of economy and knowledge in 2010–16. In 2021, he was slapped with a multi-million-euro penalty by the Spanish Court of Auditors for allegedly participating as minister in activities that led to the abortive Catalonian bid for independence; I believe the case is still pending.

Over the years, I have visited him a few times in Barcelona. Let me narrate the rather eventful first time. I was visiting Maison des Sciences de l'Homme in Paris (founded by the famous historian Fernand Braudel) for a month. Kalpana was visiting her parents in India, but I took our early-teen son, Titash, with me. Both of us had Eurail passes, which we used intensively to visit different parts of Western Europe by train almost every week. When Andreu came to know I was in Paris, he called me and demanded that we visit him in Barcelona; he said we could stay in his apartment, as he had to be with his parents in a coastal town not too far away.

So we went to the very crowded Spanish consulate in Paris for a visa on our Indian passports. After spending most of the morning waiting in line, when our turn came, the consular officer took one look at our passports and said there was no way we could get a visa there. He said that as we were residents in California, but citizens in India, according to standard rules, we could get a visa only at a Spanish consulate either in California or in India, not in a third country like France. So we went back to our hotel and called Andreu to tell him that we were not coming to Barcelona after all. Andreu refused to accept that. He asked me to wait near the phone and called back in half an hour and instructed us to go back to the Spanish consulate for a visa. We went there and found our visas waiting for us; I realized how politically well connected Andreu must have been in Spain.

The next day, we took the overnight high-speed TGV train from the Gare de Lyon train station in Paris. We were told that we'd reach Barcelona in the morning. Titash and I fell asleep. When we woke up, we found that the train was stationary at some nondescript stop in the middle of the night, but strangely, there were no other passengers left in the train. It was dark and, for a time, we did not dare get off the train, lest it suddenly started again. But after some more time, we had some doubts, got off the train with our luggage and started walking in the desolate station. Finally, we found somebody who told us that Barcelona passengers had to change to another train (nobody in Paris had told us about this), and if we ran, we could probably still catch it.

We barely made it. In the new, smaller train, an elderly passenger explained to us that most trains from France required a change of train at the Spanish border. The story apparently is that when the Spanish railways were built in the middle of the nineteenth century, the memory of Napoleonic invasions of Spain several decades ago was still fresh, so the gauges in the Spanish train tracks were deliberately made different, to make things difficult for French troops. This was an interesting story, though it may not be the only explanation. (I understand, in recent years, Spanish train tracks were changed to the standard gauge.)

In Barcelona, there was another event for which we were unprepared. Andreu was waiting for us in his apartment. As soon as we arrived, Andreu explained a few things about the apartment and, before leaving and giving me the keys, he said that his father was a locksmith, so the locking system at the front door of the apartment was somewhat fancy and unusual. He gave us a demonstration and left us to see his parents. Titash and I were both sleepy, particularly after the early morning adventure at the Spanish border, and we decided to take a nap before going out for lunch. But, at lunchtime, the intricate locking system, which looked easy enough when Andreu showed us, now baffled us—we could not open the door to go out! In my life, I have been locked out a few times, but this was the first time we were locked in! (I remembered as a child reading the story of Alibaba and the forty thieves, where his brother Cassim forgot the secret code for getting out of the thieves' treasure cave and had to pay with his life for this.) So I had to make an apologetic call to Andreu, who had just reached his parents' home in the coastal town. Poor Andreu had to come all the way back to rescue us. We felt ashamed, but he was his usual cheerful self.

Since that time, I have been to Barcelona quite a few times, mostly in connection with conferences. Almost every time,

Andreu and Esther, for all their busy engagements, took me out for superb dinners. Of course, dinners in Barcelona usually start near about midnight. Over there, even at 3 a.m., the streets are full of noisy crowds—I often wondered when these people slept, if at all, as the offices started in the morning at the usual time.

On my first visit, I went around the museums in Barcelona. I saw the one on Joan Miró, but the Salvador Dalí Museum was outside Barcelona, in the small town where he was born. (The Dalí painting I like more than many of his more famous surrealist paintings is a realist painting of his early youth, the one titled 'Young Woman at a Window', which was not in this museum, but in Madrid). I was pleasantly surprised by the Picasso Museum in Barcelona—its collection was not as large as the Picasso Museum in Paris, but still quite substantial.

Picasso's most powerful anti-war painting *Guernica* I had seen in New York before it moved back to Spain—to Madrid, specifically, where I saw it for the second time on another visit. There is a story that in occupied Paris when looking at a large photo of *Guernica* on the wall of Picasso's studio and the devastation depicted in it, a Nazi officer asked him, 'Did you do it?'; Picasso answered, 'No, you did it.' (There is an alternative story that Picasso actually said this to a Nazi officer with reference to a different painting, *The Charnel House*, which showed a pile of corpses underneath a kitchen table—that was kind of a sequel to *Guernica*.)

After the end of the Second World War, Picasso joined the Communist Party. At that stage, his simple sketches of the 'dove of peace' became an iconic symbol of the international peace movement. Before the first World Peace Congress in Paris in 1949, his friend, the poet Louis Aragon, lobbied hard with the Soviet authorities that Picasso's *Dove* should be officially recognized as the symbol of peace. When he finally succeeded, he rushed to Picasso to give him the news. Picasso reportedly said that he'd not object to his drawing of the dove adopted as a peace symbol, but Aragon did not know that a dove or pigeon was not a peaceful bird at all. If you kept them in a cage, as he himself had personally observed, they could be ferocious with one another. Nevertheless, in 1949, around the time of the Peace Congress when his second daughter was born, she was named 'Paloma' (the Spanish word for 'dove' or 'pigeon').

One of the most memorable sights strewn all around in Barcelona is, of course, the anarchic and fluid geometry of Antoni Gaudi's style in many architectural landmarks. The first time I visited La Casa Mila, Gaudi's iconic work of civic architecture, I walked through and went all the way to the rooftop—there, after a few minutes, suddenly it occurred to me that I had seen this roof somewhere before. I tried hard to remember but could not. Was it in some dream? In the afternoon haze, I sat down there amidst the curving peaked structures for quite some time. Then it slowly dawned on me that it was in this roof that Michelangelo Antonioni filmed a scene of *The Passenger*, a movie of existential ennui; in this roof, the nameless woman in the story (acted by Maria Schneider) decided to help the protagonist (acted by Jack Nicholson) to escape from his previous identity as a journalist. Later, I saw the same rooftop used in Woody Allen's 2008 movie *Vicky Cristina Barcelona*.

Gérard Roland came to Berkeley only around the turn of this century. He grew up in Belgium, was a radical student and, after the student movements of Europe subsided, he supported himself for a time by operating trams in the city. When he was wooing his girlfriend (later wife), Heddy, she used to get a free ride in his trams. (A few years ago, when I visited them one summer in their villa in the Italian countryside near Lucca, Heddy told me in jest that those days she was content with a free tram ride, but now she needed a house in Tuscany to be placated.) Gérard is also a good cook.

As with Andreu, my special link with Gérard was based on our shared interests in history, politics and culture. In addition, his research involves analysing institutional rules in the economic development process and issues of comparative economic systems, which have also been part of my own research themes. He comes to this set of issues from his long-run interest in Russia, in its process of economic transition after the fall of the Berlin Wall, and later in China.

At this point, I might as well give some perspective for my interest in institutional and comparative-systemic issues in the context of the subsequent developments in the discipline of economics. By institutions, economists do not necessarily mean an establishment or organization. They apply the term to imply general rules, practice and custom in economic arrangements. I have earlier talked about my interest in and detailed empirical work on agrarian relations in Indian villages—these relations are often examples of small-scale economic institutions at the microlevel. Thus, sharecropping, that my early work was concerned with, is a prime example of an age-old economic institutional arrangement. Apart from the theory to understand the basic mechanism, my work also went into various empirical features of such arrangements in land, labour and credit markets in peasant economies. I put together much of my empirical work of the previous decade in this field in a book *Land, Labor and Rural Poverty* published in 1984. Then, collecting the theoretical aspects of the work in this area by myself and other fellow researchers, I edited a book, *The Economic Theory of Agrarian Institutions*, in 1989. This book was meant to give the reader some idea of the theoretical frontier of institutional research in developing countries which had been going on, both at theoretical and empirical levels, for the previous two decades. But development economics was considered such a marginal field at that time that I doubt if many people outside the field took notice of this book.

In the 1990s, following Douglass North's work on institutions in Western economic history (and his Nobel Prize on the basis of that work), the literature of institutional economics thrived, mostly using cross-country statistical exercises showing how different performances in different countries in the macro-economic process of growth depends on the importance of the institution of property rights and contract enforcement. It has been widely recognized that this was a major turning point in economics, as orthodox economics concerned with prices and markets, often used to operate in what looked like an institution-free vacuum. (I first met some of these institutional economists in a summer symposium on the subject held in the austere but beautiful Certosa di Pontignano—a monastic complex a few miles north of Siena in Italy, going back to the fourteenth century, but now belonging to the University of Siena.)

For us development economists, however, it was unfortunate that these researchers in post-1990 institutional economics were largely oblivious of the substantial theoretical and empirical work in the previous two decades—the 1970s and 1980s—by a whole array of people on micro-institutions in agrarian relations in poor countries (including issues of property rights and contract enforcement). In most of the later overviews of the literature on institutional economics, there is hardly any trace that this earlier literature even existed. This, as I have mentioned, is an indicator of the exotic/peripheral nature of development economics for the mainstream, at least until the 1990s. Yet, as Joe Stiglitz said in a chapter in my aforementioned edited book of 1989:

A study of less developed countries is to economics what the study of pathology is to medicine; by understanding what happens when things do not work well, we gain insight into how they work when they do function as designed. The difference is that in economics, pathology is the rule: less than a quarter of mankind lives in the developed economies.

In the last couple of decades, this has been somewhat corrected and some of the younger development economists have now been recognized at the frontier of the economics discipline.

Gérard and I had a common friend, Masahiko Aoki, at Stanford University, who came to the subject of institutional economics from yet another angle. Aoki brought in the perspective of the Japanese corporate governance system, where there is a process of reaching an economic arrangement and understanding among the different stakeholders of a firm (business and long-term employees and suppliers) within mainly a bank-centric, rather than stock market–centric, financial system, and aligned with the government as a mediator and coordinator. (Of course, in the last few decades the Japanese system has also changed quite a bit.)

I had briefly known Aoki during my MIT days (he was at that time at Harvard); he and his actress wife once came to have dinner with us. (Soon after I left MIT, his wife died in a freak accident—electrocution in her bathtub at home; Aoki had talked to her from his office only minutes before.)

I came to know him better at Stanford; I have also visited him in Tokyo, where he used to spend a significant part of the year. Once, he took me to a back room of a posh restaurant in Tokyo, where in the whole room there was only the two of us; then, a uniformed chef came, bowed to us and started cooking individual dishes in front of us according to our specifications, served them to us, and then on to the next dish and so on—this was a first-time experience for me.

Aoki wrote his memoir, titled *Transboundary Game of Life*, in Japanese, which recently, after his death in 2015, has been translated into English. Like Andreu Mas-Colell, Aoki also had an activist student past. He was one of the leaders and theoreticians of a radical Marxist student organization in Japan, and was imprisoned in 1960. In the early part of his memoir, he writes about his prison life. The food there was not bad and he adds: '... some dried *hijiki* seaweed (was) sprinkled on top. Even now, when I eat *hijiki*, I am reminded of those days, though not quite to the extent of Proust's madeleine.' But he soon became fed up with the partisan disputes of leftist circles, gave up his activism and went to the University of Minnesota for his PhD. (Andreu also went to Minnesota, but later.) At Minnesota, he was greatly influenced by the distinguished economic theorist Leonid Hurwicz, particularly by his game theoretic approach to understanding social mechanisms.

I have briefly known Hurwicz. He was one of the most charming, as well as polymathic economists I have ever met. He got the much-deserved, but much-delayed Nobel Prize at age ninety, six months before his death. He was of Polish origin but born in Moscow in the year of the Revolution, 1917: '*After* the February Revolution, but *before* the October Revolution,' as he told me. I met him the first year I joined Berkeley, when he came as a visiting professor. He was interested in a whole range of academic disciplines; at different times in his academic life, he had taught mathematics, statistics, electronics, meteorology—apart from economics, a subject in which, by the way, he did not have a degree. He was also a man of infinite intellectual curiosity about most things in life.

Once, when I went to give a lecture at Minnesota, he took me to his office after my talk. We chatted about various things, including my work on sharecropping in which he showed a great deal of theoretical interest. At one point, he took me to one of his large file cabinets stuffed with hundreds of newspaper cuttings on Indian news from newspapers. I was amazed to observe his meticulous interest in Indian political and economic issues, which he had developed ever since he visited India for a year in the mid-1960s.

When he visited Berkeley, one weekend he and his wife came and picked us up, and took us to see elephant seals at the coast south of San Francisco. In the same trip, a professor of statistics in Berkeley, David Blackwell, a friend of Leo's, accompanied us. I had heard about the Rao–Blackwell theorem, one of the most important theorems in mathematical statistics, named after C.R. Rao (whom I have mentioned before as the director at ISI when I was there) and David Blackwell, but had never met him before. When he joined the faculty in 1955, he was the first African-American to be a tenured faculty member at Berkeley. Now, there is a new residential hall for students in Berkeley called Blackwell Hall.

On a cold day, under a grey sky near the ocean, it was quite a heart warming sight to watch these old intellectual stalwarts rapt in childlike curiosity and delight in observing a whole colony of giant elephant seals and their cavorting pups.

9
Exploring China

The interest of both Masahiko Aoki and Gérard Roland in institutional economics easily shaded into comparative analysis of economic systems, including different varieties of capitalism and socialism. Since my student days, I have been acutely interested in comparative systems and their political economy. In this context, like Aoki and Roland, I have closely followed the developments in China. When I was growing up in Kolkata, the leftists around me used to say that the Chinese were better socialists than us; now, in the last three decades, I have heard from all quarters that the Chinese are better capitalists than us. To reconcile the two, I sometimes tell people that if the Chinese are better capitalists now it is partly because they were better socialists then. This is not an entirely frivolous comment. By the end of the Mao regime in the middle 1970s, before Deng

Xiaoping's economic reforms started, Chinese performance indicators in basic health, education and rural electrification showed levels unattained by India even two decades later. This gave China a head start in providing the basis of capitalist industrialization.

The two largest countries of the world with ancient agrarian civilizations, with many centuries of dominance in the world economy in the past (up to about 1800) and with impressive economic growth achievements in recent decades—though with different political and economic systems—draw obvious comparison. But, since 1990, the Chinese economic performance has been far superior, and economically and militarily, the country is now in a different league. My first piece of a comparative study of Chinese and Indian agriculture came out as the lead article in *Journal of Asian Studies* in 1970. Fifty years later, I was still at it, with the my piece on a comparison of the economic governance systems of the two countries coming out in the *China Economic Review* in 2020. Meanwhile, in 2011, I published a book titled *Awakening Giants, Feet of Clay: Assessing the Economic Rise of China and India*. One abiding theme in my recent work has been that China–India comparison is not a simple matter of authoritarianism vs democracy. While there are some undoubtedly positive features of the Chinese governance system, authoritarianism is neither necessary nor sufficient for those features. On the other hand, there are some ugly features of the Chinese system that are inherent in authoritarianism.

My interest in China goes back to my childhood. Very near our house in Santiniketan, there was Cheena Bhavana, the oldest centre of Chinese studies in all of South Asia. It was founded by the Chinese scholar Tan Yun-Shan (we used to call him 'Tan shaheb'), whom Tagore met in Singapore in 1927 and invited to join the teaching faculty in Santiniketan. He was a college classmate of Mao, but thoroughly non-political. I have heard that in 1962, shortly after the Sino-Indian war, when Jawaharlal Nehru, who was his friend, in a convocation address at Santiniketan briefly referred to the war, people found Tan shaheb openly weeping in the meeting.

I remember as a child admiring the calligraphy on the walls of his living quarters. Among his children whom I used to see in the neighbourhood, his young daughter, Tan Chameli (a name given by Tagore), and her brother Tan Arjun were neighbours and playmates of my best cricket buddy of those days, a feisty boy named Suryanarayan (who spoke Tamil at home, but the purest local Birbhum dialect with the rest of us) and his siblings. Tan Chameli is now an accomplished artist in India. Her much older brother, Tan Chung, became a professor in Delhi and the doyen of Chinese cultural studies in India.

The first time I went to China was end of May 1989. Sponsored by the Ford Foundation, I was supposed to give a set of lectures to some graduate students at Beijing and also at Fudan University in Shanghai. This was a tumultuous time of student protests in Beijing. After I, accompanied by Kalpana, arrived there, I was told that my Beijing lectures (like most classes in the universities there) had just been cancelled, though not the lectures at Fudan. Our tickets for going to Shanghai were for 4 June. Meanwhile, my hosts arranged for our visits to the usual tourist spots like the Great Wall or the palace complex of the Forbidden City (by the way, some of the most famous paintings and porcelain of earlier eras originally from the Forbidden City are in the National Palace Museum in Taipei, as I found out a few years later). But I also wanted to go to Tiananmen Square, where the protesters had camped and by then the whole world's attention was riveted. My host professors were not comfortable with this, but, at my insistence, decided that on 2 June some of the students would take us to the square. On the evening of 1 June, Justin Yifu Lin, then a foremost young economist in China—I think TN had introduced him to me, when he was on a postdoctoral fellowship at Yale—came to see us at the Friendship Hotel where we were staying.

Justin already had a somewhat dramatic history. He grew up in Taiwan and, in 1979, when he was on service as an army captain in the Kinmen islands, just off the Chinese mainland, he dived into the sea and swam 2,000 metres to defect to China, leaving behind a pregnant wife and a three-year-old son. On arrival in China, he took on a new name 'Lin Yifu' (in Confucian reference, it apparently means 'persistent man on a long journey'). He later reunited with his wife and children when he went to the US for his doctoral studies. (In 1996, when I visited Taipei to give lectures at Academia Sinica, at a dinner, the well-known Taiwanese economist John Fei told me that if the Taiwanese authorities could get hold of Justin at the time of his defection, he'd have been court-martialled and possibly executed. Even in 2002, when his father died in Taiwan, Justin applied for a visit to the funeral, but he could not go as the Taiwanese army issued a warrant for his arrest.)

When we saw Justin at the Friendship Hotel, he was quite morose. He had been an economic advisor to the reformer Zhao Ziyang, the general secretary of the Communist Party from 1987 to 1989, who lost out in the inner-party struggle with the Party elders, particularly on account of his alleged sympathy with the protesters in Tiananmen Square. Zhao was put under house arrest (where he remained for the next fifteen years until his death). Drinking cup after jittery cup of green tea from the flasks in our hotel room, Justin told me that there was a good chance that he might be arrested too (he said his wife had already arranged a small suitcase for him to carry to jail). Later, when I mentioned this in private to other economists I met in Beijing and elsewhere, they said that Justin being arrested by the Chinese government was extremely unlikely—as a rare defector from Taiwan, he was too valuable an asset for the Party.

On the afternoon of 2 June, accompanied by two students, Kalpana and I went to Tiananmen Square. As we were approaching the Square, looking at the large gathering, the first thought that came to my mind was: in Kolkata, I had seen protest gatherings of such size many times, but what the world was excited about was the fact it was happening at all in communist China. The Square was full of tents where many students were on hunger strike, with colourful placards and banners demanding democratic rights fluttering in the light breeze. I did not see any sign of militancy, but mostly patient persevering protests by mainly high-school and college students. I then talked to some of the student leaders with our student guides acting as interpreters. I remember asking one leader, who was very confident of the success of their movement, that as martial law had already been declared and the army had surrounded Beijing, how could he be sure that the army would not come and crush their protest movement? He led me to the back of the tent and pointed to piles of shirts and other pieces of clothing spontaneously donated by working-class families who came to visit them (out of consideration that it got a bit chilly at night in the Square). He said that the working classes were with them, so the People's Liberation Army (PLA), where the soldiers were from working-class families, would not harm them.

In another part of the Square, I saw a prominent plaster replica of the American Statue of Liberty (donated by an arts school in Beijing), and sure enough, I saw a CNN TV reporter there broadcasting to the world with the statue in the background. I asked a student leader why they had allowed a foreign symbol for their movement, when already critics had described the students as puppets of America? He did not have an immediate answer; he huddled with his associates for a few minutes and came back to me with a defiant answer: 'We deliberately want a foreign symbol to tell people that liberty is something alien in China.'

Looking back, I often wonder if these students I talked to, weakened by their hunger strike, but with innocent animated faces, survived at all when the tanks came rolling the next night (3 June).

I came to know later that the PLA soldiers manning those crushing, pulverizing tanks were brought in from distant provinces—soldiers who did not understand the language of the Beijing students nor did they have much cultural empathy. Large-country governments usually do this. I have heard that in India to crush a rebellion in Nagaland in the north-east, in the past, Punjabi soldiers from more than a thousand miles away were sent; and when a Punjabi rebellion had to be crushed in the 1980s, soldiers from Nagaland were dispatched.

Early in the morning on 4 June, we took a taxi from Friendship Hotel to Beijing airport, oblivious of the dreadful happenings in Tiananmen Square the previous night. I remember the taxi driver, in his almost non-existent English, tried to tell us that 'something' (he was not sure what) had happened in the night in the Square and so traffic was not allowed to go in that direction. By the time we reached Shanghai, our hosts who came to receive us knew. Of course, they could not know it from radio or TV, as there was a news blackout. These were days before the internet, but cross-country fax messages were still active. Beijing to Shanghai messages were blocked, but people in Beijing were sending fax messages to their friends and relatives in Los Angeles, and the latter were sending messages to Shanghai.

We were put up in the faculty guest house of Fudan University. It turned out that our living room in the guest house had the only short wave radio in the whole campus. So for the next few days, endless streams of students and young faculty came to our room to listen to the news on BBC or Voice of America. Even though we had to listen to the same grim news over and over again, this gave me an opportunity to talk to many young people in the campus. Along with discussing the news, I also asked them about their life, their studies, their family backgrounds and so on. In response to my question about what they'd like to do after university, in general, the ones who were more forthcoming or whose English was better would usually say that they'd like to work for a 'joint venture' (joint between a Chinese company and a foreign multinational company). I noticed that these students had often adopted English first names like Max or Susan to introduce themselves, I presume just to make things easier for foreigners—I think the same was probably true for Justin Lin in Beijing. (In recent years, I have noticed a big change in the reverse direction, my friends in China who used to send me emails earlier with their Chinese names in Romanized letters, now almost always use only Chinese characters. So when I receive an email from China, it takes a bit of time for me to know who the email is from; mercifully, the text is in English which helps me understand who it is from.)

Other students talked about their goal to work for the government. To some of the latter, I asked if they trusted the government (after all, they were coming to my room to find out what had happened in their capital city, whereas on Government TV, also in my room, you saw continuous cultural programmes with vigorous song and dance going on, as if nothing had happened, with occasional breaks of martial music). They'd often remain silent on this question. One student who came from a peasant family in a remote province told me that when he was a child, his parents and the government were saying that the

Cultural Revolution was a very good thing; now they'd tell him it was a very bad thing. He said, with a sigh, that now he did not know what or whom to believe. (As they used to say, in other countries the future is uncertain, but in communist countries the past is uncertain.)

At the university, I managed to give only the first lecture. That afternoon, the news came that somewhere near Shanghai students in protest of what had happened in Beijing lay down on train tracks to stop trains; but the first train did not stop in time, and ran over and killed a couple of protesters. The whole city of Shanghai burst out in protest. I saw that bus drivers in sympathy with the protesters parked their long buses diagonally at street crossings, and left, thereby completely paralysing the traffic. My subsequent lectures were, of course, cancelled. But because of the traffic paralysis, we could not go anywhere. For the next week or so, we were trapped. I talked to many more students, some of them took me to see their dorms (which were no less dingy or crowded than some of the shabby college dorms in Kolkata). We walked around every day, but there was not much to see in the campus except for massive statues of Mao here and there.

We were once invited to a gathering of a few faculty members at someone's home. At that gathering, I came to know from one professor that the pay scale of professors at that time was not any better than that of bus drivers. None of them, of course, could afford cars. At one time, the discussion turned to the killings in Tiananmen Square. Some professors spoke out against student protests; they said throughout Chinese history people put a great deal of value on stability, they were put off by signs of chaos and disorder. I told them that I was from India where disorder and protests were part of daily life. I remember then asking why the Chinese government needed tanks to crush these unarmed students, already weak from weeks of hunger strike. I said international TV in the previous weeks had been full of scenes of water cannons used to quell protests going on in East European cities. The room fell silent at my question, until one elderly gentleman said slowly, dragging his words, 'You see, the water pressure around the square is not good enough for water cannons to be used.' (Hence, armoured tanks, he implied.) To this day, I am not sure if he was joking or not.

The university was closed down, and students slowly left the campus (probably on their bikes). The campus became a rather desolate place. One day, some of my host professors came and told us that we had to be moved from the guest house, as the staff there was going to leave soon, and there'd be no one to serve us food. So they had decided to move us to a big hotel at the airport. As roads were blocked for vehicular traffic, they had arranged for a pedalled cycle van which would carry us and our luggage, but it'd obviously take many hours to reach the airport. Flights were still cancelled, but when they'd resume, it'd be easier to book flights from the airport hotel, they reckoned. We then were asked to get ready for our long journey.

But at the appointed hour, instead of a cycle van, a car appeared. Our hosts explained that at the final moment they had found a driver who knew the Shanghai back streets well and he had promised to evade the street blocks by protesters, and somehow take us to the airport. The next hours were quite nerve-racking for us, with a stout daredevil driving recklessly through the lanes and by-lanes of old Shanghai, taking abrupt U-turns whenever he saw people blocking a street, sometimes going fast on reverse through extremely narrow lanes where the walls were scraping the car on both sides. We felt like we were in the midst of a thrilling car chase scene through a slum in a Bombay film. After a couple of hours, we reached the airport hotel—the less said about the condition of the car exterior the better.

I found the big hotel full of Taiwanese businessmen, also waiting like us for the flights to resume. When, after a few days, they did, there was a mad scramble for tickets at the airport. After a lot of hassle, we managed to get a flight to Hong Kong, and from there we went to Kolkata. The communists who ruled the city (and the state) then were in full sympathy with their Beijing counterpart. I remember the first day we arrived in Kolkata, I checked the leading communist party Bengali newspaper *Ganashakti* about what they said on the Tiananmen killings. Not surprisingly, I found the quote from Deng Xiaoping prominent in their headline news: 'If you open the window for fresh air, you have to expect some flies to blow in'; and, of course, you have to swat those flies.

While at the guest house at Fudan University, I had quickly written out two articles on Tiananmen Square, one in English for *EPW* and the other in Bengali for the Kolkata literary magazine *Desh*, for which I occasionally wrote, and had faxed them. Soon after my arrival in Kolkata, both articles came out. One day, a friend of mine, who was a student leader during my college days (though at a different college), and who was now an important member in the central committee of the ruling communist party, came to see me, to discuss Tiananmen. I told him I had nothing to discuss with him, given the asinine position their party had taken. He said my articles had been read and discussed in the party, and that I should not take their party's public statements to indicate that there was no critical internal debate within. I said, 'You guys have long lost the habit of independent thinking. I have no patience with your mumbo-jumbo about "democratic centralism" inside the party, and, in any case, whatever I have to say about Tiananmen, I have said it in those two articles.'

I was also reminded of a conversation I once had with an old college friend of mine, who later, as an academic, had learned Mandarin and visited China during the Cultural Revolution. He was invited to the party headquarters in Kolkata on a weekend to give a talk on the Cultural Revolution to a small group of party higher-ups. At the end of his talk, the big boss asked him, 'Could you give us a real clue about what Mao essentially is trying to achieve through this Cultural Revolution?' My friend, annoyed by the big boss clearly not having paid much attention to what he had said in the previous hour, said, 'Okay, I'd explain it with just one example: It's late in the day, and while we are discussing large issues in this meeting room, I see your janitor is smoking beedi [a cheap, thin local cigarette] after beedi outside, waiting for when the babus [the gentry folk] will be done with their meeting, and then he can close up the rooms and go home. Mao, through his Cultural Revolution, is telling us to wipe out our distance from that janitor, to bring him in and involve him in the discussion, as the issues are about his life too.' Needless to say, after this, the party members never again contacted my friend.

In the last two decades, I have been to China many times—mostly for lectures and conferences primarily in Beijing and Shanghai. Of course, compared to what I saw in my first visit in 1989, China has undergone a dramatic economic transformation. The most dazzling of visible changes are in infrastructure, highways, skyscrapers, bullet trains, airports, etc. There are parts of Shanghai now—say, the eye-catchingly rich Pudong district—where, once while coming out of my hotel, for a moment I was confused if I was really anywhere near the Shanghai city I had seen before. My academic colleagues tell me that the pay scales in top universities are now almost the same as in America, in order to attract top talent back to China. Chinese airports and high-speed trains are certainly more advanced than the ones you see in most American cities. My Chinese students in Berkeley have often told me that in application of digital technology in daily life (particularly in retail trade, local transportation and communication) they are struck by how backward the US is compared to China.

I remember going to a conference in Beijing at the turn of this century, along with several other international economists, which included Thomas Piketty (now of rock star–like fame for his work on inequality). We had arrived at Peking University the day before. In the afternoon, Thomas and his then wife, Nancy, went out for a walk in the streets holding between them the hands of their three little daughters. All the Chinese pedestrians stopped and were gawking at the extremely unusual sight of a family with three children in a country then with the one-child policy. The next morning, our conference was in a room at the China Center for Economic Research in an impressive building that Justin Lin—then head of the centre—said used to be an imperial palace. The first speaker that morning was Piketty and I was to chair the session. When Thomas brought out the plastic 'transparencies' he had for his talk and was looking for a portable overhead projector, there was none. The Chinese, who were using smudgy blackboards in seminar rooms less than a decade ago, had by then leapfrogged to PowerPoint presentations from laptops, skipping the stage of using transparencies. The Chinese hosts were initially nonplussed; then someone said in another part of the campus one might get such an overhead projector in a storeroom, and they rushed to procure it. While we were waiting for it to come, I told Thomas, 'You come from a backward country, France, where you are allowed to have three children and also use transparencies for seminars!'

Chinese advance in technology is not always for general benefit. The technology for surveillance of the citizenry, with Big

Data and facial recognition devices, has become so sophisticated now that it is possible to describe the Chinese state today as approaching 'totalitarianism', in a more accurate sense than any of the earlier loose descriptions of authoritarian countries as totalitarian. More than half of the world's surveillance cameras are now in China, and nine of the ten most-surveillanced cities on a cameras per capita basis are Chinese. The totalitarian state controls and saturates every little bit of social space, and makes possible what the German jurist and Nazi academic Carl Schmitt called 'Totalstaat' in an influential work in 1927. Artificial intelligence is now allowing the Chinese state to reach a degree of control unattained by possibly any other state in history. *The Economist* magazine has called this 'digital totalitarianism' in China.

Even in academia, surveillance cameras are now in most classes. I am told students might *jubao* (report on a professor) on what the latter may have said or done that contradicts a Party policy. There is also a large social engineering project in place in China now (though not yet fully or uniformly implemented), called the social credit system. If you have failed to repay a debt or violated some rules or even played loud music in public, you can get a negative social credit evaluation which is recorded. If you are in the official blacklist, then you may have problems buying train or plane tickets or getting jobs or hotel reservations. In the West, or even in India, this would be considered as unacceptably intrusive, but what is interesting to note is that common people in China are not particularly bothered by this—they often consider it as necessary for boosting public morality. (Some people point out that in the US, the control by tech and credit card companies on your access to services like insurance, accommodation or transportation based on your credit score is not much less objectionable. In some sectors in the US, people have also complained about ubiquity of surveillance.)

As a short-term foreign visitor to China, I have not yet encountered the full might of the totalitarian state. A couple of years before the COVID-19 pandemic, in a conference organized by Justin Lin at Peking University, some of us foreigners openly, though politely, deprecated the recent turn in the country towards heightened repression; our Chinese audience just listened to us in sullen silence.

A few years before that, after my China–India comparative book *Awakening Giants, Feet of Clay* came out, I was invited by Tsinghua University to give a public lecture on that topic. It was quite a large audience and, halfway through my lecture, I thought to myself that I was criticizing India's performance a bit too much relative to that of China. To make some redress, I decided to cite a striking example on the opposite side of the ledger, as it were. I went on to say that both countries had the capital punishment, something that I was opposed to, but there was a striking difference in the way this punishment had actually been carried out according to some Amnesty International data that I had seen, China, at that time, executed every week on average a number that exceeded the total number executed in India over the previous sixty years. When I said this, I heard a soft but distinct whooshing sound rippling across the room. But nobody raised any question about this either then or in the discussion time.

After my lecture, a Harvard professor and China specialist, Dwight Perkins, whom I knew and who happened to be visiting the university and sitting at the front, walked over to me and whispered that if I had said that thing about capital punishment ten or fifteen years ago, the police could have given me some trouble. Later, at the dinner, seated next to me was my friend and ex-colleague from Berkeley, Yingyi Qian, who was the dean of the school of economics; I asked Yingyi if what Dwight said was really true. Yingyi laughed and said, maybe not in so many words but definitely implied, that the Chinese authorities thought that foreigners spoke all kinds of nonsense, but if a Chinese person said the same thing, they could have been in trouble.

I should also mention that when my China–India book was published by Princeton University Press in 2011, the publisher entered an agreement with a Beijing press for bringing out a Chinese edition. When I got a copy of the latter from Beijing, I showed it to one of my Chinese students in Berkeley. He took it and told me the next day that comparing it with the English edition, which he had already read, he found out that most of my statements in the book criticizing the Chinese government or its policy had been cut out. Of course, they did not take my permission, which was in the agreement with Princeton. I wrote to the Beijing publisher in protest, but there was no response.

So, at the beginning of my public lecture at Tsinghua, I told my audience not to read the Chinese edition as it provided a censored and highly unbalanced comparative study of the two countries. The next day, a very shy, nice young woman came to see me. She introduced herself as the translator of my book and kept on profusely apologizing. I did not have the heart to raise the matter of the broken agreement. From my brief conversation with her, I gathered that, as is not uncommon in authoritarian countries, much of the censorship was pre-emptive self-censorship on the part of the publisher, not the government.

I have known Yingyi for many years. Like Masahiko Aoki and Gérard Roland, I have mentioned before, his research was in comparative and institutional economics. He suffered a lot during the Cultural Revolution, but then thrived in the post-reform period and became a major theorist of that reform. He introduced me to a leading Chinese journalist, Xiao Meng. I have met her a few times on my later visits to Beijing. She did not speak much English, but was quite well read in the economics literature. Over the years, she got many of my journal articles translated in to Mandarin.

One time, she took me out to lunch along with some of her junior colleagues. After lunch, she said her home was within walking distance and asked if I'd care to visit. I agreed, and we went to a lovely house with a traditional courtyard and a lot of greenery. In her living room, she showed me a photo of Mao and herself as a teenage girl wearing a red scarf—apparently she was a Red Guard during the Cultural Revolution (later, I heard that her father served as a minister in Mao's government). She knew of my interest in films and so she took me to another room stacked with thousands of DVDs, most of them of foreign films—she said with a large grin that all of those DVDs were, of course, pirated. (I was reminded of Joe Stiglitz telling me that once, while walking in a Chinese city, he saw a big photo of his on the window of a bookstore; he walked in, saw hundreds of copies of his books piled around and soon realized that they were all pirated editions. For a moment, Joe was not sure if he should be sad for loss of his royalty income or glad by this kind of publicity—in the end, he decided to go with the latter, as, in any case, he was not a strong believer in intellectual property rights.)

At the end of my visit to her home, Xiao Meng told me that she was particularly interested in showing me her long-time home because it was soon going to be demolished by the city authorities as part of a big highway construction project. Her associates told me that because she was so well connected, the authorities gave her some time before demolishing the house. I have heard that for common people, quite often when the authorities decide to demolish a house, the residents or homeowners do not get much notice. One morning you wake up and see your outer wall marked with a large Chinese character, meaning 'raze', and that's your notice.

It is difficult to discuss politics openly and intensively with my Chinese friends, but I have some general idea of their political views and how to differentiate their politics. For example, Justin Lin, with a Chicago doctorate, seems to have slowly moved from conservative or mainstream economics to be—in recent decades—an advocate of interventionist industrial policy tinged with Chinese economic nationalism. Yingyi Qian is more of a liberal economist and is wary of Chinese ultra-nationalism, which is rampant now. Another bright liberal economist in the same vein is Chenggang Xu, whom I have known since his LSE days and later in the University of Hong Kong. Discussing with, and reading, Yingyi and Chenggang, I have come to appreciate the unique combination that China has accomplished between political centralization and economic decentralization. Another economist with whom I have profitably discussed the Chinese economic and political system is Yang Yao, who, as I write this book, is serving as the dean of the National School of Development at Peking University. On the basis of these discussions and further thinking on governance issues in China, I gave a lecture at Renmin University in Beijing in 2018. Xiaobo Zhang, the editor of the international journal *China Economic Review* was in the audience; he persuaded me to write it up and he published the article there in 2020.

Some years back, Yingyi had introduced me to the veteran economist Wu Jinglian, one of the major architects of market reforms in China; he presented me with his book *Chinese Economic Reform* and told me (this was around 2010) that he thought the Chinese case was turning into one of crony capitalism. His sharply expressed opinions have often landed him in trouble. During the Cultural Revolution, he was persecuted (including being beaten up, his mother's home ransacked and half of his wife's head shaven by the Red Guards). Again in recent years, hardliners have tried to discredit him as a US spy in the state-controlled public media for his pro-market stand. 'I have two enemies,' he said in a 2009 interview with the *New York Times*. 'The crony capitalists and the Maoists. They will use any means to attack me.'

Some of the more intellectual opponents of the market reformers are with groups like what is called the New Left in China. I came to know two of the leading figures in this group, though they themselves do not like the New Left label (particularly with its Western association): Wang Hui, professor of literature and history, and Cui Zhiyuan, professor of public policy and management, both at Tsinghua University. Their position seems to be against free-market capitalism as well as capitalist democracy, and in favour of more egalitarianism and social justice (understandable in a country that has moved from being one of the most equal to one of the most unequal in the world within just two or three decades).

I met Cui a few times when he was a student at Chicago of my friend Adam Przeworski, the well-known political scientist, and also when he later taught at MIT. Even though Cui was in political science, I found him very well read in economics. For some years, he has been a supporter of capital–labour partnership in the governance of the firm on the lines advocated by my Cambridge dissertation supervisor, James Meade. He has also advocated Meade's idea of social dividend (a form of universal basic income).

I have met Wang Hui in Tsinghua and one time in Delhi. He is one of the foremost scholars of Chinese intellectual history. In a discussion about the state, I found him pointing out that among many large empire states in recent history, China has been rather distinctive in more or less keeping its territorial and bureaucratic integrity even when the empire ended—compare, for example, the aftermath of the dissolution of the Ottoman or the Austro-

Hungarian empire around the time of the First World War with the end of China's last imperial dynasty (the Qing dynasty) shortly before. This continuity in Chinese territorial sovereignty, Wang points out, has some implications for understanding the nature of the rise of China in the current period. This also has implications, I thought, for the continuity of tyranny in Chinese history, including the harsh suppression of the cultural autonomy of Tibetans and Uighurs.

I remember reading the 1992 book by the historian W.J.F. Jenner, *The Tyranny of History*, where he describes one of the basic tenets of Chinese civilization as 'that uniformity is inherently desirable, that there should be only one empire, one culture, one script, one tradition'. This is where I believe lies a basic difference in the historical legacy of the Chinese and the Indian civilizations. India celebrates diversity, in spite of all the messiness, fragmentation and chaos this entails. My Chinese friends, when they go to India, are often shocked by the near-anarchic disorder of everyday civic life. Throughout history, the Chinese have had a dread of disorder (*'wěnluàn'*), which has been used to legitimize repression. The idea of checks and balances, separation of powers or independence of the judiciary is quite alien to Chinese political culture. (A Chinese professor told me that even when liberal scholars in China think about governance reform, independence of the judiciary is almost never uppermost in their minds.)

In 2010, Wang Hui was invited to the same conference in Delhi on social democracy as I was. I have mentioned before about this conference organized by Sonia Gandhi at the Nehru Museum. There, I gave a talk on UBI (Universal Basic Income) for India, where I showed that, unlike in rich countries where this may be too expensive, it is possible for the Indian government to afford a decent basic income supplement for all citizens, if it has the political courage to reallocate some of the existing subsidies that are currently enjoyed by the better-off people. I originally got the idea of UBI from my discussions with my Belgian political philosopher friend, Philippe van Parijs, who had been its major advocate for many decades. He recently told me, after listening to my arguments, that just as Marx expected the socialist revolution to come to advanced countries of Western Europe (Germany, England), instead it came to relatively poor countries (Russia, China), so similarly maybe UBI, which he thought about for rich countries, may first be feasible in poor countries after all.

Sonia Gandhi was seated at the conference round table just next to the person after me. All through the conference, she was taking copious notes, but was mostly silent. Wang seemed to like my talk, but what struck him particularly, as he told me later, was my intervention at a different session. Someone at that session asked me to give my views on decentralization. In view of Sonia's proximity at the table, I decided to take that opportunity to provoke her. I said, somewhat exaggeratedly, that decentralization had very little chance in India—none of the political parties, starting with Sonia Gandhi's own Congress party (then ruling India), seemed to believe in decentralization of power even within their own party, everything was decided by the top brass in Delhi—how could you then expect them to implement genuine decentralization in the country's governance structure? (Sonia did not respond to that in the meeting, but in the next coffee break, when she was rushing somewhere, she stopped near me, silently shook my hand, and went away—presumably indicating that she was not completely disapproving of what I said.)

In the next session, Yogendra Yadav, an important political scientist in India (now also a practitioner), took up the same theme in even stronger language. Wang Hui was startled by such straight talk and criticism in front of a top political leader. I told him that this was nothing extraordinary in India. (That was more than ten years back. I wish I could say that with equal confidence about India today!)

In their search for an alternative non-Western modernity, the so-called New Left in China have sometimes been accused by their liberal critics for complicity with the repressive state. Wang, for example, told me that he was not very keen on the activities of Chinese dissidents (he did not name them, but the most famous dissidents in recent history included the late Liu Xiaobo, who was awarded the Nobel Peace Prize in 2010 and was imprisoned until death, and Ai Weiwei, the artist who was imprisoned in 2011 and is now in exile). He thought the dissidents mainly played up to a Western audience, but were not in tune with what was really going on inside China and the real problems that afflicted the lives of common people.

Some Chinese literature has also reflected opposition to market reform, and the resultant inequality and venality among people, and to the kind of moral wasteland that the frenetic capitalist development has brought about along with a consumerist society run amok. This can be seen, for example, in a best selling novel like *Brothers* by the writer Yu Hua, a close friend of Wang Hui, where the protagonist is a town scoundrel turning into a top national entrepreneur. This kind of theme is, of course, not unfamiliar in India—for a rather strident depiction of this in the literature in English one can cite the Booker Prize–winning novel by Aravind Adiga, *The White Tiger*. But the pace of capitalist development having been much faster in China, one can see why the depiction in Yu Hua's novel comes across as even bleaker, more brutal and grotesque.

In general, my personal preference in literature is usually more for sad novels rather than angry ones. (Recently, I had an occasion to tell Aravind Adiga that I much prefer his earlier, less well-known, piece of fiction, *Between the Assassinations*, where the fury is less strident, instead there is more nuance and aching sympathy, along with an all-enveloping sadness.) In a different and more general context, the well-known Pakistani writer Mohsin Hamid said in a recent interview, 'We live, we die, this infuriates us—but far better that it saddens us, and that we find ways to honour and transcend our sadness.'

10

Reflecting on Comparative Systems and Marx

Since 1990, I have also visited Vietnam a few times. Vietnamese economic reform (called 'doi moi') started in the mid-1980s. On my first visit, I found Hanoi to be more like a small, quiet town in India, with a lot of poverty (and some begging in the streets, but not many visibly malnourished children), while Saigon, or Ho Chi Minh City, was somewhat better off, and more raucous and colourful. One lecture I gave in Vietnam was titled 'The Rocky Road to Reform', where I spelled out the challenges of economic transition from a state-dominated economy; after my lecture, a Vietnamese academic came to me and said, 'Our roads are all full of potholes, so we are used to the "rocky road" of challenges!'

One of the most knowledgeable people in Vietnam on issues of economic reform I met in Hanoi was Le Dang Doanh, who was an advisor to the general secretary of the Communist Party, and later president of the Central Institute of Economic Management—a premier government think tank on economic policy (I actually sought him out at the suggestion of my journalist friend Nayan Chanda, who used to be with the *Far Eastern Economic Review*).

On my subsequent visits, I found out how fast Vietnam was changing. In Hanoi, where I saw mostly bicycles before, it is now practically impossible to cross the road with the unending streams of motorcycles and cars (they'll not stop for you; you just have to take your chance). The Vietnamese economy is now a veritable dynamo of activity in Asia. It started with agricultural exports (like rice and maritime products), but soon followed China, a historical adversary, down the well-worn path of export-oriented, labour-intensive industrialization with foreign investment and learning of foreign technology—combined, of course, with a deplorable state of political repression.

During the Vietnam War days, I used to see the walls in Kolkata streets covered with slogans like 'My *nam* [Bengali word for name], your *nam* is Vietnam'. In one grand gesture of symbolic protest, the street where the American consulate in Kolkata was located was officially renamed Ho Chi Minh Street, so they had to use that street address in their stationery. But real achievements are more difficult than symbolic ones. In recent years, I have told my Bengali leftist friends that Vietnam's population is roughly the size of West Bengal's—it was poorer in 1977 (when the left government started its thirty-four years of continuous rule in the state), but is now far better off, more advanced both in (largely capitalist) industrialization, and in public health and education.

My interest in the political economy of comparative-systemic issues and a generally appreciative, but ever-questioning, approach to Marxian themes, which has persisted ever since my college days, gravitated me to a high-powered but informal Europe–US-based interdisciplinary group of leftist social theorists, which I was invited to join in 1982. This group was started by three prominent left intellectuals: Jerry Cohen, the Canadian-born philosopher in England, Jon Elster, a Norwegian political theorist and philosopher (now at Columbia University) and John Roemer, an American mathematical economist (now at Yale). Their purpose was to study large historical and systemic questions raised by Marx and his followers, but apply rigorous analytical methods to study those questions, and if the age-old Marxist answers were found lacking by this analysis—as they often did—to jettison them for more sustainable answers. The informal name for this group was the study group for 'non-bullshit Marxism' (i.e., Marxism without any dogmatic or obscurantist fog), but the formal name was the September Group, as it met usually in September initially in Europe (Paris, London, Oxford), but, in more recent years, mainly in New York.

Jerry Cohen grew up in a Jewish-communist family of factory workers in Montreal. From 1985 to 2008 (the year before his death), he held the prestigious Chichele Chair in Social and Political Theory at Oxford (Henry Chichele was the founder of All Souls College in the 1430s). Jerry was one of the most colourful personalities I have met in my whole life. His super-sharp intellect as a philosopher was combined with gregarious warmth, compassion, curiosity, and a stand-up comedian's performative skills and irreverent wit. In the evenings of our meetings, and even sometimes during coffee breaks in the meetings, he'd give us memorable performances in skits (sometimes involving great figures of history, like Marx, Thomas Jefferson or Gandhi, or his teacher, Isaiah Berlin), mimicry and songs. I understand his valedictory lecture at Oxford in 2008 included a series of imitations or parodies of many famous philosophers. I read somewhere that the German philosopher Friedrich Nietzsche in one of his letters referred to himself as a satyr, a clown, and said 'the most profound spirit should also be the most frivolous'; Jerry's clownishness sometimes reminded me of that.

He loved spicy Indian food and was chummy with many of the workers and managers of Indian restaurants in Oxford. When he first visited India, he wrote a diary which he gave me to read—every time he had a meal in India, someone would invariably and annoyingly tell him, 'I hope the food was not too spicy'; he thought to himself then that the vindaloo that his friends in the Indian restaurants in Oxford cooked up for him was much spicier. He was fascinated by long south Indian names which he'd come across in his regular reading of Indian magazines; he'd memorize them and the next time he met me, he'd give me tests like where is Thiruvananthapuram?

Jon Elster is the Robert K. Merton Professor of Social Sciences at Columbia University and also honorary professor at Collège de France in Paris. I have found Jon's erudite command over the whole range of social sciences—political science, economics, history, constitutional jurisprudence, philosophy and psychology—really amazing. There was a period in the 1980s and 1990s when he wrote almost one book a year on different weighty issues in the social sciences.

His tome, *Making Sense of Marx*, was a landmark in a meticulous dissection of Marxist ideas, particularly from the point of view of what is called methodological individualism (a term originally coined by Joseph Schumpeter, following the ideas of his teacher Max Weber, to indicate a method giving primacy to explaining social phenomena through individual intentionality and individual action–interaction), so that in understanding class struggle, a collective like a social 'class' may not be taken as acting by itself except through individuals in the class. This keeps us wary of various problems of collective action which Marxists used to glaze over. (Even if you do not believe in methodological individualism, you have to take seriously the relationship between individual choice and the social process in understanding the underlying mechanisms of social dynamics.)

The book also points out that Marxists are often mired in a kind of 'functionalist' fallacy (a crude analogy would be that of a detective trying to solve a murder mystery by just looking for who benefits from the murder, the possible *motive*, without checking into the *means* or how the murder could have actually been carried out). So it is not enough to point out that something happens in a capitalist society because it serves the interests of capitalists. Many ideas in the Marxist tradition did not thus survive Elster's dissection, and some reviewers said that his book should have been more appropriately titled as 'making minced meat of Marx'. Some people called this kind of analysis 'rational-choice Marxism', but intentionality in individual action need not be always rational. In fact, Elster himself had been moving away from the presumption of rationality in individual behaviour. On Marxism, Elster now calls himself 'a faded Marxist'.

The third founder member of the September Group is John Roemer, professor of political science and economics at Yale University. John started as a mathematician, then moved to do his doctorate in economics at Berkeley (interrupted for some years by his Vietnam War protest activities). Using general-equilibrium theory, he reformulated much of the Marxist economic system (giving up things like labour theory of value and keeping his focus on the inequality of ownership of assets under capitalism as the key source of injustice). Later, he provided probably the neatest formulation of the idea of inequality of opportunity, allowing compensation to people with bad luck in the birth lottery, but holding them responsible for their bad choices (like indulging in drugs or in laziness). The World Bank has now adopted his approach in evaluating inequality of opportunity. In more recent years, he has been bravely recasting economic models in terms of cooperative behaviour, based on the moral principle first proposed by the German philosopher Immanuel Kant in 1785—that you should act a certain way only if you're willing to have everyone else act the same way too (thus you should not litter, unless you are willing to let everyone else litter too).

Apart from these three founder members, the September Group, in the first decade or so, included the Marxist sociologist Erik Olin Wright, the historian Robert Brenner, the political scientist Adam Przeworski, the political philosopher Philippe van Parijs, the economist Samuel Bowles, the philosopher Hillel Steiner, the political theorist Robert van der Veen and myself. (Among these people, van Parijs was from Belgium, Cohen and Steiner from England, van der Veen from the Netherlands, Elster and Przeworski regularly commuted between the US and Europe, the others were resident in the US.) In 1986, Roemer edited an anthology titled *Analytical Marxism* where many of us contributed chapters.

In the 1990s, Elster and Przeworski left the group, but others like philosophers Joshua Cohen, Debra Satz and Seana Shiffrin, legal scholar Amy Kapczynski, political philosopher Harry Brighouse, and economists Suresh Naidu (one of my best ex-students in Berkeley) and Roberto Veneziani, and others joined at different times. The untimely death of Jerry Cohen in 2009 and Erik Olin Wright in 2019 dealt big blows to the group as these two were, in some sense, the most dynamic members. Nevertheless, the group has kept on meeting almost regularly for nearly four decades, intensively but congenially discussing one another's recent research, and also making an effort to infuse some new blood in its membership in recent years.

Even though the group has been interested in the important questions raised by Marx, the political views of the individual members have been quite diverse, and also changing over time. While the internal political debates have been energetic, I have never seen any lack of warmth or camaraderie. Once, in a meeting in London, I remember the group seriously discussing if there should be any political-ideological criterion for membership to the group, and, in the end, deciding that coherent constructive dialogue on a set of important issues was more important than adherence to a particular set of political positions.

I have noticed over the years a gradual process of evolution of the views of some of the initially Marx-preoccupied members towards what can only be called a general belief in democratic egalitarianism. Since Marxists take pride in the 'scientific' nature of their analysis, there was a broad feeling that they should abide by what Alfred Whitehead, the British mathematician and philosopher of science, said on the progress of science: 'A science which hesitates to forget its founders is lost.'

Jerry Cohen's grappling with and reflecting on the above-mentioned evolution in an essay in the last decade of his life is quite touching: He quotes from *The Great Gatsby* its last line, 'So we beat on, boats against the current, borne back ceaselessly into the past.' To this he adds, 'I have remained attached to the normative teachings of my childhood, and, in particular, to a belief in equality ... A powerful current bears me back to it ceaselessly, no matter where I otherwise try to row.' He writes: 'Raised as a Marxist my intellectual work has been an attempt to reckon with that inheritance, to throw out what should not be kept and to keep what must not be lost.'

Even though I have attended most of the meetings of the September Group over the last forty years, my own participation in the group has really been more like that of an interested outsider looking in. This is for mainly two reasons. One is that since my research is primarily on developing countries, it had very little overlap with research areas of almost everybody else in the group. I often hesitated presenting my research because I thought the specialized details of my work might bore the rest of the members, even though I knew they'd politely listen to me. So I often participated more actively in the session in each meeting reserved for some topical global issue for general discussion rather than for presentation of original research.

The second reason was a matter of my personal inclination. Even though, over the years, I have been a lucky beneficiary of the high quality of the discussion in a diverse array of disciplines (and wished some of the more narrowly specialized, even tunnel-visioned, economists in my profession were exposed to such richness and diversity of concepts and approaches), I'd sometimes lose patience with the intricacies of ethical-conceptual debates among the high-powered moral philosophers in the group. While they sharpened my understanding of many conceptual issues of social justice in ways which I had not thought about before, I sometimes found that the attention lavished in some of the discussions to ethical purity and depth was out of proportion with the practical political difficulties of even remotely reaching anywhere near the outer, coarser, periphery. As primarily a political economist, I am more interested in the political feasibility of many general ideas of justice and egalitarianism, and the nature of the concrete obstacles, rather than in the ever-finer conceptual refinement of the desirable normative goals. With the possible exceptions of Adam Przeworski and Robert Brenner, most members in the group—at least in the early years—have been more interested in moral-philosophical issues of justice than I have been, after a point.

But, independent of the issues discussed, the sharpness of mind and analytical skills displayed in a warm atmosphere of congeniality has made most sessions a very pleasant learning experience for me for about four decades. Having seen, since my college days, how many Indian leftists keep wallowing in bullshit Marxism, it was indeed a breath of fresh air for me to participate in this group. And, of course, the friendships forged in the meetings have been a great source of joy.

Thinking of my early days with the group, I also remember that once Jon Elster, after a short visit to India, asked me an unexpected question. He said in his visit that the Indians were all very nice to him, but he wanted to know 'in their heart of hearts, what do Indians really think of us, Westerners'. Somewhat flippantly, I said to Jon that people in India thought Westerners were technologically and militarily superior, but definitely inferior in terms of morals and personal hygiene. He said, 'Morals I can imagine, but why personal hygiene?' I then told him a story that I had heard from Sheila Dhar in the Dharma Kumar salon in Delhi that I have described before.

Sheila, wife of P.N. Dhar, whom I have mentioned earlier, was an accomplished singer and writer of books capturing the bygone ambience of the world of north Indian classical musicians that she used to inhabit. She'd narrate her stories with a great deal of raucous humour mixed with empathy (but rendered in a rather bizarre way, as while narrating them she used to keep on crunching ice cubes with her teeth—I was told this was the way she was coping those days with the after-effects of quitting smoking for many years). The story I told Jon was about Siddheshwari Devi, who was a great classical vocal singer from Varanasi. When she was at the peak of her fame, she was once invited to perform at the Royal Albert Hall in London. This was her first trip to a Western country. The day prior to her performance, she arrived at the fancy hotel where she was put up. Going to the bathroom there, she was deeply shocked to realize that Westerners didn't wash their bottom: they wiped it with a piece of paper. The next day, when she sat down to perform on the stage, the thought of singing such heavenly compositions in front of an audience with hundreds of unwashed bottoms so agitated her that she wanted to cancel her performance. After a great deal of persuasion by the organizers she barely managed to sing.

In the early 1990s, shortly after the fall of the Soviet Union, in a meeting of the September Group, I remember Jon Elster telling us that as we were going through a historic transition period, that we should keep in mind that our grandchildren might ask us one day what we were doing in such an epochal time. Looking back, my answer, if my grandchild ever cares to ask me about this, will be somewhat complicated.

The fall of the Soviet Union was a landmark geopolitical event, but people like me from a developing country may look at it somewhat differently from Europeans and Americans. The welcome by the former may have been ambiguous for a transition from a duopoly of superpowers to a monopoly (at least for the next two decades or so). Nor could they think of it as the triumph of democracy over authoritarianism, as the Western support (and worse) over many decades for brutal dictators all over the world (described by 'realist' foreign policy bigwigs in the US as 'our sons of bitches') and their corrupt oppressive regimes has not been particularly edifying.

Leaving aside geopolitics, what about the comparative-economic systemic event? I was never enthusiastic about the Soviet brand of socialism (or for that matter any authoritarian brand of socialism); in many ways, the Soviet Union represented an utterly debased form of Marxist or any humane egalitarian idea. But its fall did represent the demise of the idea of purely state-controlled command-economy socialism. I did spend much of the 1990s thinking of how to reshape an economy that has socialist/egalitarian goals, but makes considerable use of the market mechanism of prices and incentives.

John Roemer and I edited a book on market socialism, and also co-authored an article on the subject for the *Journal of Economic Perspectives*, when Joe Stiglitz was its editor (and I was in the editorial board). There was the old literature on market socialism in the 1930s, in which the Polish economist Oskar Lange and the British-American economist Abba Lerner tried to show the feasibility of socialism with market prices. But they did not quite answer the incisive criticisms of Austrian economists like Friedrich Hayek flowing from the fact that state planners will not have access to private information of individual citizens or to local knowledge. Roemer and I tried, in our imperfect and incomplete way, to update that debate for a world where this informational constraint is important.

We in turn were sharply criticized by the Russian-American economist Andrei Shleifer at Harvard, who was convinced that socialism was neither feasible nor desirable. Around this time, Shleifer was an advisor to Anatoly Chubais, then Russian vice premier and the main architect of privatization in Russia. It is probably unfair to consider Andrei complicit in the oligarchic loot that the Russian privatization spree subsequently amounted to, but, in our academic disputes with him, I could see that he was too quick to dismiss our concerns about privatization and why we thought it was important to consider alternative ways of bringing the market in.

In spite of our sharp differences, personally, Andrei was quite friendly with me. I found him extremely smart and also witty in a sardonic way. Born in Moscow, he migrated to the US in his mid-teens, and claims that he learned English by incessantly watching TV series like *Charlie's Angels*. In economics, he specialized in the field of corporate finance and is one of the most cited economists. I got to know him a little better when he and I were once invited to the same conference on law and economics in Delhi; he hardly knew anybody there, and so we chatted a lot.

To him, the Soviet state was hardly different from a body of organized crime and, after its fall, the sooner one could dismantle the remnants of the public sector behemoths and the elaborate machinery of Party control by whatever means, the better (hence, 'shock therapy'), particularly to forestall any restoration of the rule by those crime bosses. I think it was naïve of him not to think of the real possibility of many of those crime bosses and their cronies mutating into kleptocratic oligarchs, fattened by the spoils of the rigged privatization process. Without the necessarily slow build-up of democratic and locally autonomous political and economic institutions and structures of accountability, you may just replace one kind of mafia rule by another (with the composition of mafias often overlapping).

Today, with Vladimir Putin's murderous mafia state and his revanchist aggressions dominating the headlines, the image of Russia in much of the world is in complete tatters. Thousands of talented people—ranging from scientists to ballet dancers—are trying to leave Russia, ashamed of the country. In this context, going beyond economics and politics, one can say that it is easy to overlook the inner depths of a society which has a long tradition of great literature, music, dance, art and culture, sometimes arising magically from a deep well of pain, outrage and the ravages of history.

I was reminded of this in a trip I took to Moscow for a conference in 2015. During a lunch break, I decided to take a walk in a nearby park. It was early October and already snow flurries were in the air. Near the gate of the almost desolate park, I saw a large statue, which I assumed would be of a military hero or a political leader. But when I looked up, I saw the soft features of a woman in a flowing dress. Because of my ignorance of the Russian language, I could not decipher the name of the person etched at the bottom. But I did notice a bunch of fresh flowers placed there.

Back at the conference, my colleagues informed me that it was the statue of the poet Anna Akhmatova. When I asked about the flowers, I was told that I'd see similar bunches of fresh flowers at the feet of statues of other writers and poets in different parts of the city. Is this arranged by the municipal authorities? I asked. No, I was told, the flowers are regularly put there by the admirers of these writers. I come from a city, Kolkata, where poets are adored and which has probably a larger number of poets per square kilometre than many other cities. But this kind of reverence for poets, writers and high culture among the common people of Russia is impressive by any standard.

Akhmatova happens to be one of my favourite poets. Let me just cite one of her short poems, which to me has a haunting quality:

> I drink to the wreck of our life together,
> And the pain of living alone.
> I drink to the loneliness we shared—
> My dear, I drink to you.
> I drink to the trick of a mouth that betrayed me,
> To the eyes and the look that lied.
> I drink to the terrible world we inhabit
> And to God, who never replied.

In the 1990s, Andrei Shleifer was only one among many in the proselytizing army of reformers who went out to the transition economies, mainly in Central and Eastern Europe, but also in developing countries, to make them ready for capitalism. They were in a hurry to implement reforms of liberalization and privatization according to some general, often one-size-fits-all, formula. The purse strings of emergency financial help by international organizations like the IMF and the World Bank, and US agencies like USAID, were also controlled by stern macroeconomic ideologues of 'structural adjustment'. The reformers were in possession of the canonical gospels which it was their sacred duty to spread among the heathens as quickly as possible, given the golden opportunity after the fall of the godless communists and socialists.

I went to some of the international conferences on the economics of transition in this period, held usually in cities like Budapest or Prague or Riga. Soon I gave up going to such conferences, as I felt I did not know enough about those countries to really say anything that'd make sense to the local audience. But I did go to one organized in Kolkata by the eminent political economist Mancur Olson. (Mancur grew up in a Norwegian-American family in North Dakota. When he came to know that the name Mancur, a traditional name in Scandinavian families, was a variation of the Arabic name Mansoor, he speculated: 'In fanciful moments, I imagine a Viking raid on the Levant.') I had admired his past work on collective action and I thought he deserved a Nobel Prize for that work, which he did not get. When he asked me to contribute to a collection of essays on institutional economics he co-edited, I gladly did.

But on reform-mongering, sometimes he went a bit overboard. I remember he was coming for the conference in Kolkata for the first time immediately after visiting his Mongolian reform project and saw on the road from Kolkata airport to his hotel, many people on the roadside selling small amounts of vegetables and other odd bits. Mancur had a flamboyant dramatic style of talking with a lot of energetic waving of his hands. Next morning in his conference lecture, he said with a flourish: 'India has a great future. A great prospect for market reform here. On my way from the airport, I saw all around me market forces blossoming!' In the coffee break I told him, 'Mancur, those roadside vegetable sellers have been there all over India probably for the last 5,000 years.' I did not tell him that India has markets even in things where markets are missing in advanced capitalist countries: with enough money to bribe you could, for example, buy a driver's licence, even though you did not know how to drive.

Once, in a conference in Berkeley, Mancur gave a lecture in his usual grand style. I also gave a lecture at this conference. My friend Mrinal was visiting from India and attended the conference that morning. He was with his two small sons, whom he got seated for a time at the back of the auditorium. Afterwards, when they were at our house, Mrinal asked his sons whose lecture they liked best. Since I was there, they made some polite noise about my lecture, but the one they liked best, they said, was by 'that lo-and-behold guy', meaning Mancur.

Even though I did not get very much involved in the ongoing international gung-ho reformer frenzy of the economists of transition, I did participate in the mainly political-science project of my friend Adam Przeworski on the transition to democracy. (Adam had by then left the September Group). He was born in Warsaw, Poland; I understand he never saw his father, who was a physician conscripted in the Polish Army just before his birth and killed in the Katyn forest where thousands of Polish officers were killed by Stalin's secret police—I have earlier referred to the famous Polish film director Andrzej Wajda, whose father was also killed in the same massacre. (In 2007, Wajda made a film based on a historical novel on this massacre, what he called an 'unhealed wound' of Polish history.) On 11 September 2001, when Adam saw from the balcony of his office at New York University in Lower Manhattan the burning twin towers collapsing, he was, he told me, immediately and involuntarily transported to his early childhood memories of devastation in wartime Warsaw.

Adam is a distinguished theorist of democracy and comparative politics. In the mid-1990s, he was the leader of the Group on East-South Systems Transformation, which had twenty-one social scientists (including myself) from eleven countries and four academic disciplines. It included some very well-known political scientists like Guillermo O'Donnell, Alfred Stepan and David Laitin. I also got along well with a fellow member Luiz Carlos Bresser-Pereira who was once the finance minister of Brazil, and later served as a minister for some years in the Fernando Cardoso government.

The major question we deliberated on in this group was how to make democracy viable and sustainable in the varied country contexts against considerable economic and political odds. One distinguishing feature of this group was to discard the idea of transplanting the American or West European model of policies and institutions irrespective of local contexts, cultures, political processes and pre-existing institutions. We met at various international venues (including Bellagio in Italy and Antalya, the beautiful ancient Turkish city on the Mediterranean coast). The group ultimately produced a book titled *Sustainable Democracy* published by Cambridge University Press.

Looking back to this period, I can see how my views have evolved over time on the twin transformations that were being attempted—one was on political democratization, and the other on economic liberalization and privatization. Where do I stand on those issues which so preoccupied us in the 1990s? Let me briefly take stock, in a somewhat nerdy way, on a few of the key issues involved.

On democracy, elections have been easily accepted all over (subject to some questions about the nature and conduct of such elections), but liberal values, and primacy of individual autonomy and rights have been much more difficult to take root. As early as 1948, B.R. Ambedkar, while drafting the Indian Constitution, had said: 'Democracy in India is only a top-dressing on an Indian soil, which is essentially undemocratic.' This has been in effect the case in many other countries, particularly where traditional rural societies (and their overflows into urban centres) are important—not just in India, Indonesia, Ethiopia and Turkey, but also in Russia, Poland and some other countries in Southern and Eastern Europe. In such societies, traditional social hierarchies (including patriarchy), and the sense of structured community privileges and loyalties are stronger than liberal values. Even when rights are recognized, the emphasis is more on group rights (for a caste or community) than individual rights.

Adam Przeworski, following Joseph Schumpeter, has a minimalist concept of democracy; he'd certify a polity as democratic if there are competitive elections in which the incumbent has a chance of being voted down. But electoral sanctions are highly imperfect and blunt instruments, and there are many institutional practices that a democracy needs which may disappear in between elections.

Coming from a country of extreme diversity of groups and social oppression of minorities (and dissenters), I insist on safeguards of individual and minority rights as an essential part of democracy. So for me, the institutionalization of those safeguards (through, say, separation of powers, independence of judiciary, free media, etc.) is indispensable. In this respect, as we know, many countries have been recently experiencing a basic erosion of democracy, even though regular and even competitive elections have taken place, and there has been some widening of group rights for some hitherto subordinate groups. Strong despotic leaders have succeeded in turning citizens into fan clubs and have learned ways of turning elections into a referendum on their charisma. Democracy as a peaceful way of processing social conflicts has been on the wane, yielding often to strong-armed majoritarianism (ethnicity or religion based).

On economic reform, I have been a general supporter of liberalizing market reforms, but only with sufficient guarantees of social insurance for those who will inevitably lose out in those reforms, and with sufficient opportunities for the latter to retool and retrain themselves to adapt to the harsh market changes. The alternative of state control often encourages monopoly power of some state bureaucrats and their favourite business cronies, leading to corruption, inefficiency and inequality of a different kind from that generated by markets. If market reform encourages socially undesirable consumerism, as some complain, there are ways of handling this, say through stiff taxation (apart from social reform movements). I am not, however, a supporter of financial liberalization—particularly if it is not substantially regulated.

On the related subject of globalization, the importance of supply chains and crucial imports of essential goods and components for all countries are now widely recognized. I also cannot help but note that many opinion polls show stronger support for globalization among low-income countries today than among many rich countries (which used to preach the virtues of free trade before)—more support among poor female garment workers in Bangladesh or Vietnam than among the industrial working class of France or the US. But I am against unregulated international capital flows.

On privatization, I have found it more difficult to make up my mind, so I'd go by the evidence that may vary from context to context. For every well-run public firm (say, in France or Singapore or South Korea) I can, of course, cite many more instances of taxpayer-funded, bureaucratically run white elephants and disasters from all over the world. A part of the reason why the disasters persist is that they are sometimes monopolies, so they have no urge to shape up or that the bureaucrats in charge presume that in case of losses, they'll be bailed out by the government. For many countries, the government cannot credibly commit to not interfering in the commercial operations of a public enterprise, for all the autonomy promised on their memoranda of understanding. Patronage distribution through public firms and corrupt income through public procurement are much too tempting for politicians.

But the question that arises in my mind in this context is: After privatization, what is the nature of the government commitment to the firm? Most large private firms have to be under the general supervision of a government-appointed regulatory body. Instead, quite often, one hears stories of regulatory bodies being captured by the firm to be regulated. I suppose much depends on the particular politician–business–bureaucrat nexus in different countries. This nexus also influences the price at which a public enterprise is sold; there are many stories of collusive deals of under pricing and defrauding the taxpayer in the privatization process (not to speak of the oligarchic loot in Russia we have mentioned before).

The evidence on privatization of public utilities (like water, electricity and railways) in different countries is quite mixed. Privatization often implies turning a public monopoly into a private monopoly, and thus may not make a firm more efficient. For goods that are tradable, in an open economy, the pressure of cheap imports or of competitiveness in export markets can act as a disciplining factor on the inefficiency of a domestic monopoly—

whether public or private. Also, comparative efficiency should not be judged in terms of profits alone, because a public enterprise often has socially ordained goals beyond moneymaking (like serving remote areas or poor people, which private firms may not do). Even Andrei Shleifer, an ardent votary of privatization in Russia, has co-authored an important article where he shows that privatizing the prison system (which is common in the US) may not be a good idea because there are social objectives (like the humane treatment of prisoners) which cannot be fully spelled out or enforced in a contract with private prisons. In general, I have often felt that in comparing the performance of particularly large firms that are necessarily bureaucratic in organization, private or public, much depends on the managerial incentive structure and corporate culture than on who owns the firm per se.

One area where the performance of public firms may be dubious is in the matter of encouraging productivity-enhancing technological innovations. I have seen leftists often overlooking this aspect. There is new evidence, however, from China that in some tech firms that are under mixed (public–private) ownership or in private firms where the state actively provides a large part of the finance and underwrites some of the risks, considerable technological advance has taken place, particularly in areas like artificial intelligence and biotechnology. Depending on some minimum bureaucratic-professional capacity, the state can sometimes play a catalytic role in the innovation process through coordination and directional guidance, shaping market expectations and making strategic initial investments. There are many examples of all of this cited in Mariana Mazzucato's 2011 book *The Entrepreneurial State*. As she illustratively points out, every bit of technology that makes the iPhone made by a private company (Apple) so 'smart' was government funded/

innovated: the internet, GPS, its touchscreen display, and the voice-activated virtual assistant Siri.

Sometimes the *pattern* of innovation is at least as important as the *rate* of innovation. Much of innovation by private firms is labour-replacing, destroying jobs. But with public firms, or private firms where workers can exert a significant voice in their management, the research may be directed towards more job-creating and labour-empowering innovations and innovations oriented to more social (environmental or public health related) goals.

In all this, I have been mainly contrasting private and public enterprises. There is a whole different area where the enterprises may be run by workers and other civil-society organizations, on which there is some limited amount of experience, which we need to study and draw upon. My late friend Erik Olin Wright of the September Group, had a whole project of what he called Real Utopias (utopian ideals grounded in the real potential for social change—projects that are viable, though may not be immediately achievable) on exploring institutional alternatives to capitalism (some examples already exist, ranging from Wikipedia to the Mondragon Corporation of worker cooperatives in Spain) and on developing forms of associative democracy. In one of the volumes in this project, Joshua Cohen (of the September Group) and Joel Rogers suggest ways of strengthening secondary associations mediating between individual citizens and the state, and thus enhancing democracy—organizations like unions, works councils, neighbourhood associations, parent–teacher groups and women's societies.

My views supporting many institutions of liberal democracy (instead of dismissing it as 'bourgeois democracy'), several of the market reforms and an ambiguous position on privatization confuse, if not alienate, some of my leftist friends. Some years back, after a public lecture I gave in India, a young man stood up and said, 'I do not disagree with most of what you said, but I am wondering, which side are you on?' I said in reply, 'Please find flaws in my arguments, not waste time on searching for my ID card.'

11
Wearing Multiple Hats

In the early 1980s, apart from joining the September Group, there were two other outside organizations I was invited to join which expanded my intellectual horizons. The first was the South Asia Committee of the Social Science Research Council (SSRC) in New York. This committee planned some research projects on different topics of social science in South Asia, and also gave out research fellowships and postdoctoral research grants. It gave me the opportunity to interact with some of the top scholars working in the US on South Asia, including Myron Weiner, the distinguished political scientist, Bernard Cohn, the historical anthropologist, Wendy Doniger, the Sanskrit scholar, Ralph Nicholas, cultural anthropologist of Bengal, Richard Eaton, cultural historian of medieval India, and Ronald Herring, political scientist on agrarian development in India.

Of these, the most colourful person was Wendy, who used to entertain us with her charming stories, often drawing upon the erotic aspects of ancient Hindu texts. Myron, when he was the chair of the committee, always began the meeting with his collection of jokes. He was downright serious, though, in his work where he was insistent in bringing to the attention of Indian policymakers the crucial importance of universal child education and reform of the prevailing, widely connived, practice of using child labour. Ralph used to share with me his stories of his experience of ethnographic work in Bengal villages (he was fluent in Bengali and during his field visits he'd often be chatted up by curious villagers who'd tell him that as he was from America interested in their lives, he must be a CIA agent, and were utterly disappointed when they heard his emphatic denial).

Three of my fellow committee members have become controversial in India in recent years. Wendy Doniger, who was originally attracted to the study of Hinduism as a religion that is more joyful and less puritan than some Western religions, was, of course, attacked by Hindu fanatics for her zestful depiction of the erotic anecdotes on Hindu gods (her publisher, Penguin Random House India, had to withdraw her book *The Hindus: An Alternative History* from circulation). Richard Eaton, a foremost scholar of Islam in India, is of the view that the Hindu–Muslim binary in the understanding of medieval Indian history is a complete caricature—this has also drawn ignorant criticism by the Hindu right wing in India. Ronald Herring, however, has faced the fury of the opposite end of the political spectrum for his view that the militant opposition to transgenic crops (or 'GMO' in agriculture) was not consistent with the scientific field evidence in India that he had looked into.

I was also involved in the organization of three conferences sponsored by the committee. One of them I have already mentioned earlier that took the form of conversations between economists and anthropologists, specifically on their contrasting ways of identifying and measuring economic change in rural India. The second conference was another interdisciplinary one on local community-level response to water management in South Asian irrigation, how, for example, farmers resolve (or fail to resolve) local water conflicts. Both of these conferences took place in Bangalore. The third conference, held at MIT, was mainly around the draft of my 1984 book, *The Political Economy of Development in India*, based on a set of endowed lectures that I gave in 1983 at All Souls College, Oxford.

I was in the South Asia Committee for five years, and during this period the SSRC staff person associated with the committee was David Szanton, an anthropologist, who became a good friend. I remember once David took some of us on a flâneur-like strolling in parts of New York City that tourists do not usually go to (I was reminded of similar strolling I have had in Paris and, of course, in Kolkata). Later, David moved to Berkeley and was the executive director of international and area studies. One of his passions for many years has been to promote ethnic art, from the Madhubani district of Bihar in the Mithila region of India near the border with Nepal, where, for several centuries, women have been painting mythical gods and goddesses using natural dyes and pigments. David and his colleagues regularly arrange to get these beautiful paintings, mostly on religious and social themes, but now also occasionally on political themes, sold in the US and distribute the profits back to these women artists.

The second major intellectual enterprise outside my immediate research I got involved in the early 1980s was the *Journal of Development Economics* (*JDE*), the premier international journal in the field. I was asked to be the chief editor, and initially, I was a bit reluctant as I knew this was going to be a rather arduous job (particularly the administrative part was tedious and time-consuming—keep in mind this was still the pre-internet age). I have been in the editorial board of quite a few international journals (*American Economic Review, Journal of Economic Perspectives, International Economic Review, Review of Social Economy, World Bank Economic Review, Asian Development Review*, etc.), but the load was relatively light, whereas for *JDE* the whole responsibility of running it was mine, and the only administrative assistance I got was from a half-time editorial assistant (I used to employ one of my students for this job).

The person who finally succeeded in persuading me to take the editorship was a Cuban-American friend of mine, Carlos Díaz Alejandro, who used to be a co-editor of the journal. Carlos was born in Havana, was stranded in the US by the rupture in the US–Cuba relation in early 1960s when he was doing his doctorate at MIT (the rest of his life he kept on trying whatever little he could do to improve US–Cuba relation—once, he was part of a group of Cuban exiles that successfully lobbied Fidel Castro to release some political prisoners).

He was a professor at Yale for about fifteen years. He primarily worked on Latin American economic history (concentrating on Argentina and Colombia), macroeconomic crises, and international finance, none of which was in my area of specialization. But along with his sharp intellect and very warm personality, his interest in history, politics and culture made the two of us good friends almost as soon as we first met. He was in general very popular among development economists, and large numbers of young economists in Latin America adored him. In any discussion group, his pleasant manners, collection of historical anecdotes and his considerable erudition borne very lightly made him easily the centre of the group.

Once on my visit to New York, he called me and invited me to a Sunday brunch at the prestigious Yale Club in midtown Manhattan. With twenty-two floors it is, I am told, the largest college clubhouse in the world—very posh and with a great deal of restrictions in membership (which for a long time was confined to 'pale, male and Yale' people) and dress code. I did not know all this, and I arrived at the appointed hour at the gate in a very casual dress. They'd not allow me to enter without at least a tie. Carlos had not yet come, so I was loitering nearby waiting for him. Soon, I saw coming from a distance not Carlos, but a common friend, Ronald Findlay, and a fellow invitee to the brunch; from that distance, Findlay was dangling a tie for me. When he came near, he said, 'I knew the Berkeley hippie would not have a tie on him, so I brought an extra.'

I had known Ron Findlay, a warm and amiable distinguished professor at Columbia University, for many years. Even though our common research in the area of international trade and development originally brought us together, later I found out about his deep scholarship in economic history, as reflected in his panoramic perspective of the global economy in the co-authored book titled *Power and Plenty: Trade, War, and the World Economy in the Second Millennium*. In fact, I have known very few economists who were as well read in diverse areas of social sciences and history as Ron. I have been to his New York apartment a few times and seen the massive piles of books on all kinds of subjects in his study.

He was born in Burma, but, at age seven, the Second World War and the invading Japanese army forced him and his family to flee, and trek hundreds of miles of hazardous forested territory to reach India. After his MIT doctorate, he went back to teach at Rangoon, but soon the military coup and the rise of xenophobic and autarchic rulers made him leave the country. I have heard that while he was still in Rangoon, Joan Robinson, my Cambridge teacher, once, on her regular visit to India, made a special trip to Rangoon to meet Ron. Taking him on an energetic walk around a lake, she tried to convince him why he was wrong on a formalization he had attempted of her ideas in a journal article.

When Carlos finally arrived and met us at the gate of the Yale Club, I asked him to complain about the gatemen blocking the entry of the guest of a big-name Yale professor like him. He laughed and said, 'If I complain to them, you know what they're going to do? They are going to push me off to the kitchen in the basement where half the kitchen workers are Cuban.' With Findlay's tie, I gained entry into the building and in one of the first staircases came upon a wall full of photographs of several generations of the Bush family (all Yale men going back to, I believe, 1844)—a family I did not much care for. The club atmosphere was as glittering as it was suffocating, but the food was good.

The last time I saw Carlos was also in New York, where, at a dinner party, much of the time we discussed literature. I told him that even in my limited reading of the great literature of Latin America, I was getting a bit jaded by magic realism, but, at the beginning, how I was obsessed with *One Hundred Years of Solitude* by Gabriel García Márquez. The first time I read that book in my youth, it was a case of 'love at first sentence':

> Many years later, as he faced the firing squad, Colonel Aureliano Buendía was to remember that distant afternoon when his father took him to discover ice.

I had also noted that the concept of historical time in that novel was cyclical, not linear, in a way that was akin to the cycles of time in some ancient classics in India. (I had discussed this with the historian of ancient India, Romila Thapar, who referred me to her article on 'Cyclic and Linear Time in Early India' in a 2002 Cambridge University Press volume on time.) Carlos, in turn, said that he had read very little of Indian literature, and, of course, whatever he had read was by Indian writers in English. He was keen to read some of the vernacular literature that was translated. When we parted, I think in a subway station in Manhattan, I promised to send him some time a list of a few such translated novels of different Indian languages.

I came back to Berkeley and shortly afterward, one morning in July 1985, I was shocked to read in the *New York Times* about his death from pneumonia at age forty-eight. I rushed to the office of my colleague Albert Fishlow, who knew him well, and Albert told me that Carlos died from AIDS-related pneumonia. I also did not know that he was gay.

Looking back, at the last dinner party in New York sometime the conversation had turned to E.M. Forster's novel *A Passage to India* (maybe apropos the recently released movie based on that novel, directed by David Lean), and someone in the party speculated that the character of Dr Aziz in the novel might have been based on a homosexual affair that Forster had had with an Indian on his first visit there. I remember Carlos corrected him and said that Forster's first full-fledged homosexual affair took place much later with a man in Egypt. I remembered being impressed by how well informed he was on Forster's life. (Much later, I read somewhere that Forster did fall in love with a young Indian man named Syed Ross Masood, but Masood did not reciprocate, and Forster left India in some despair; I also came to know that literary critics now think that the Dr Aziz character is partly based on Masood.)

Albert Fishlow and I went on to organize a symposium of articles in memory of Carlos in a special issue of the JDE. Later, it came out as a book.

Some years after Carlos died, another friend and another noted development economist, Hans Binswanger, was diagnosed as HIV-positive. He initially took that as a death sentence and gave away much of the material things he had. But, by then, the new antiretroviral drugs were in use, and possibly because of them, he lived an active life for another quarter-century, until he died in Pretoria, South Africa, in 2017 at age seventy-four. In 2002, shortly before he left his World Bank job, he founded and endowed an NGO in Zimbabwe, that supported about 100 mostly HIV-positive children and their families by providing education, supplemental healthcare and counselling. In South Africa, he married his boyfriend, Victor, in a traditional multi-day Zulu celebration. Since then, he has always identified his last name as Binswanger-Mkhize.

Hans was born in Switzerland to a prominent Swiss family. He was a major agricultural economist with pioneering work on peasants' behaviour in the face of risk. This work was based on experiments carried out in India. I think I met him first in Hyderabad at ICRISAT, the International Crop Research Institute for Semi-Arid Tropics, where he was the principal economist for five years, before joining the World Bank.

In 1977, he invited me and Kalpana to present papers at a conference in Hyderabad on the subject of rural labour markets (later, he co-edited a book where these papers were published). I remember the lavish party he threw for all the conference participants at his home, which was a stunning converted fortress in Hyderabad. The intensive ICRISAT village studies that started under his leadership in India made possible data-intensive work by many agriculture researchers all over the world, and generated, over the years, hundreds of PhDs. Since then, I have interacted with him many times, particularly when he was doing some policy work for the World Bank on land reform in South Africa.

He came to Berkeley and addressed my graduate seminar on economic development. I last saw him at a meeting in Delhi, just a couple of years or so before his death.

In 1984, after some strong persuasion by Carlos, when I finally accepted the editorship of *JDE*, I insisted with the Dutch publisher that the rather stiff submission fee for articles in the journal had to be waived for authors resident in developing countries. The publisher reluctantly agreed, but later quietly raised the submission fee for authors of developed countries. When I saw that, I insisted that the submission fee would be largely spent on paying a token honorarium to the referees who had been reviewing papers pro bono earlier. The publisher agreed, and I made the honorarium payable only to referees who did their reviews within two months, and even the latter were given the option to donate the honorarium to a general fund in Berkeley. With the money in the latter, I started an annual *JDE* award for the best development economics graduate student in Berkeley.

One immediate effect of the waiver of submission fee for authors resident in developing countries was that it led to a hefty increase in submissions from the latter countries, particularly from the two large ones, China and India. Unfortunately, most of these articles were really not of publishable quality. But I thought *JDE* could do a valuable service to these authors by giving them some careful comments on their articles, which they often did not get in the limited academic circumstances of their workplace. The downside of this for me was that some referees were getting annoyed that we were sending them articles that were clearly unpublishable. At the cost of increasing my workload, I stepped up my preliminary screening of these articles, to weed out those that were particularly weak. (Talking of service to developing countries, once an article from China was a reasonably good one in terms of the mathematics in it, but the English was barely comprehensible. So I asked the author to get the English vetted by someone knowledgeable in the language. The author in sending the revised version said he had done so, but still much of the text remained incomprehensible. So my editorial assistant and I sat down together and corrected the English line by line, and we finally published it.)

In the academic world of economics, publishing articles in a major journal is more important in promotions than even publishing books. This inevitably leads to tensions with and pressures on the journal editor who willy-nilly becomes a gatekeeper for the profession (one rejected author even screamed at me over the phone and said that I was acting as a 'censor'). Around that time, *JDE* was getting I think about eight hundred articles a year, of which, on average, less than 10 per cent were accepted (usually after significant revisions). The publisher allowed me only two co-editors, to whom I channelled some of the articles for decision-taking; even so, I was handling nearly six hundred articles a year myself.

This was a big burden, and the main chore was to find appropriate good-quality reviewers. With the proliferation of journals, there is 'overfishing' in a small common pool of good reviewers. It was not uncommon to find referees for a paper only after a frantic search for many weeks and only at our fifth or sixth attempt—in the pre-internet age all this was done by regular mail. Once two such referees per paper agreed to do the job, then the thankless task was to pursue laggard referees, and I did this with some unpleasant persistence just for the sake of fairness to the authors. I was used to hearing from impatient authors about the delay in review, but when in the UK research-funding agencies started giving some weight to a whole department's research productivity, I started getting appeals from UK department chairpersons for expediting the review of an article by a department member because their promotion decision or departmental evaluation was nearing a deadline. I tried my best to help, but it was not entirely in my hands.

One intellectually exciting windfall for the editor of a premier field journal is to be able to directly watch how the research frontier of the subject keeps moving. One also gets an opportunity to marginally shape the direction of research in the field. For example, I felt that not enough work was being done in theoretical aspects of development economics, so I organized some special issues of the journal to give some prominence to work on those aspects. (Paul Krugman, a frequent referee and occasional writer for the journal those days, was among those who helped me in this.) Similarly, on empirical work, I felt that not enough attention was being paid to data quality, so I invited T.N. Srinivasan to guest-edit a symposium in the journal on serious data quality issues in developing countries.

An editor can, of course, be misled by preoccupation with conventional wisdom and guided by the tunnel vision of many standard referees on a given topic, and not have the open mind of visualizing completely new directions. My friend George Akerlof told me that the paper that finally got him the Nobel Prize was initially rejected by some journal editors. Paul Krugman has also written that the paper that got him the Nobel Prize was rejected by some mainline journals. Outside economics, I remember the case of the brilliant physicist Satyen Bose of Kolkata, whom I have mentioned before, who had sent his path-breaking paper in 1924 to a prominent science journal in London where it was rejected. He then mailed a copy to Einstein, who immediately recognized it as one of the most important findings in quantum theory. Bose never got the Nobel Prize, but most of the particles in the universe got named after him (bosons); later, several Nobel Prizes have been awarded on work related to the boson.

I edited *JDE* for eighteen years and, in the first dozen years or so, I used to be inundated with empirical papers doing statistical exercises on cross-country data easily available from the publications of international organizations. I have never been a fan of such cross-country statistical exercises, as they hide a lot of inter-country variations that are due to reasons (economic, political, cultural) that are not immediately observable in the data, even apart from the large data comparability issues across countries. Also, in such inter-country data sets, a continental country like China or India (where even some of the provinces are larger than most countries in the world in population size) provides one data point just as much as a speck of an island in the Pacific Ocean gets—this is like the United Nations General Assembly rule of 'one country, one vote'. Like the proverbial little Dutch boy, I, as the editor, had my finger in the dike as it were, and tried what little I could to stem the flood of such papers sent for publication in the journal in this period.

I also have some experience of observing how data used to be 'manufactured' for some countries. When I was a student in Cambridge, I had a fellow student who was writing a thesis on the Jordanian economy. Once, I asked him if he had data from Jordan on some of the complex issues of industrial structure he was dealing with. He said, of course not; so he had got from the library some data reports from India and Nigeria, and whenever he found data from Jordan missing, he interpolated the numbers from those in India and Nigeria. Half in jest, I asked him why India and Nigeria—was it because geographically Jordan was located about halfway between the two countries?

I once attended a UN conference where the main participants were officials in charge of data collection in different international organizations. I remember one official candidly saying that he had some quota for producing international statistical tables, and, as the deadline for the annual submission of those tables approached, many data cells were still blank because for some countries the data were simply not available; what he usually did then was to look at the data of adjoining countries and, if they existed, he'd simply interpolate and fill the blanks. I appealed to some of these international data generators to colour-code the data in the published tables—the data that were okay to use should be in green, those that should be used with caution in yellow, and the data that were risky to use in red. In response, they pointed to the footnotes in small print below the tables where such words of caution were mentioned, but I knew most users of data did not bother to read them and merrily went on to crunch them indiscriminately into their statistical analysis.

The situation is, of course, much worse in some countries when data are manipulated to please the political bosses. I have heard quite a few stories about Chinese official data, particularly at the provincial level and below. This is understandable in a country where promotion of local officials depends partly on the data of how well the local economy is reported to be performing. Independent sample survey data become particularly important in this context. As I have mentioned before, under the leadership of Mahalanobis, for a time, India was at the frontier of good-quality survey data collection. (As I have mentioned, when the Chinese Premier Zhou Enlai came to India in the 1950s he spent quite a bit of time with Mahalanobis to find out about the source of India's achievement in such data collection.)

Unfortunately, those days are gone. Survey data collection has been in some disarray in India in recent decades. But, as noted before, under the current political regime, some data which turn out to be unflattering for the rulers are suppressed. For example, in a country with large numbers of poor people, official poverty estimates have not been available for the last ten years. An elaborate survey was carried out by the National Statistical Office for the year 2017–18 and after the data were tabulated, some of the key results came out in the media. It soon turned out that those results implied an increase in poverty since the last estimate taken six years earlier. The administrators immediately blocked the official release of the report and said that something must be wrong with the data. After all, how can poverty increase under the glorious rule of the current supreme leader?

I have heard of a story from the ancient Indian fables collection called *Panchatantra*, where, with great fanfare, the king once banished poverty from the land. One day, a man from the margins of his kingdom came to his court and said with folded hands, 'Your majesty, you've banished poverty, but that wretched fellow has taken shelter in my home and refuses to go.'

I left the editorship of the journal in 2003. Shortly afterwards, two development economists, Tim Besley of LSE and Mark Rosenzweig of Yale University, honoured me by bringing out a special issue of the journal for me, on the basis of some papers presented at a conference for this purpose held at Harvard. They even invited me to submit a paper at that conference (which I did in collaboration with Dilip Mookherjee). The papers for the journal were all peer-reviewed in the usual way. I joked with Mark that in order to showcase how strict and upright the review process of the journal was, they should consider rejecting our paper for that special issue.

In the mid-1990s, along with journal editing, I did another job in Berkeley which was even more arduous, but also in some ways quite exciting and instructive. I was invited by the campus academic senate to serve for three years in a high-powered committee that decided on all appointments, promotions, salaries and merit payment increases for all Berkeley faculty (then roughly about 2,000 in size). This committee is called the Budget

Committee in Berkeley; technically it advises the chancellor, but the latter took our advice in 99 per cent of cases—in the less than 1 per cent cases when the chancellor did not follow our advice, the rule was that they were obliged to meet us in a special session of the committee and explain why they would not follow our advice (most often this involved some legal issues) and we had a chance to rebut their arguments.

Working in this committee gave me valuable insights into the process of how a top public university like Berkeley, even though substantially more constrained in terms of resources compared to the rich, heavily endowed private universities in the US like Harvard, Princeton, MIT, Stanford, Yale, Chicago, etc., could maintain its high ranking in terms of academic excellence in most disciplines. I thought the insights I got from my experience would be of some use in the reform of the public universities in India. I wrote a couple of op-ed pieces in Indian newspapers and gave some public lectures in the country with suggestions for reform on the basis of my Berkeley experience, but very few people paid much attention to it—probably because people thought my ideas were utopian in the Indian context.

The Indian public universities have for long been severely hamstrung by heavy-handed political and bureaucratic interventions, overregulation and mismanagement by different governments. (At one time, Jean-Jacques Laffont, a leading French economist whom I got to know reasonably well, gave me a qualitatively similar account of problems afflicting French public universities.) It Is widely believed that the current right-wing government in India has a distinct political-ideological agenda of washing away the remnants of left-liberal ideas from universities, mangling the curriculum of history and culture in universities (and schools), and of installing a narrow and essentially anti-science, Hindu-supremacist ultra-nationalist viewpoint.

One way Berkeley maintains its record of excellence is by zealously guarding faculty autonomy in appointments, promotions and salaries, and by a continuous process of merit reviews. The Budget Committee, answerable only to the academic senate representing the faculty, guards the latter's interest in keeping high academic standards. Every department carries out frequent and, at some intervals, particularly intensive reviews of faculty merit (on three usual criteria of research quality, teaching performance—where student evaluations of the teacher taken every semester play an important role—and university service), and at every important step gets confidential reports of evaluation from academics in other universities. The department faculty votes on its decision, and the department chair explains that decision and passes the whole file on to the dean, who adds their own evaluation and passes on the whole file to the Budget Committee.

The committee has nine members, and each of these members is assigned several disciplines; in my case, for example, I had to handle files from economics, political science, business management, public policy, mathematics, statistics and a few other departments. After studying each of these files, and depending on the stage of promotion, forming an independent subcommittee of evaluation (with a member from the department, but mostly from other campus departments, and sometimes from outside the campus) and getting their report, I'd prepare my report on a candidate on the basis of all those multi-stage evaluations and mine.

Every Thursday morning, the whole committee had a meeting where each of us would have to present our report and defend it for each case in our charge. (One regular item where I had to put up a stout defence was on why a relatively junior economist had to be paid a salary which sometimes exceeded that of even a distinguished veteran in the physics department. I had to resort to what Paul Samuelson in his elementary undergraduate economics textbook called the 'water-diamond paradox'—everybody knows water is much more valuable for life than a diamond, and yet the latter fetches in the market an incredibly high price.) Then the whole committee would take a decision on the file and pass it on to the chancellor, who would take the formal final decision.

The politicians, particularly the governor of California, get involved in the process of selecting the super-administrators called the regents of the University of California, and the latter are involved in the selection of the chancellor (apart from long-range planning and university policy, particularly with respect to undergraduate student admission numbers and tuition fees). But as the chancellor used to accept almost all our decisions on appointments and promotions, the faculty autonomy from politicians remained largely protected. In my three years in the Budget Committee, with hundreds of cases, there was only one case where the chancellor decided to override our decision on what he called legal grounds of affirmative action. In the special session of our committee, where he had to come and explain his decision and face our questions, he came with the university lawyer in tow, who explained to us that even though he understood the academic grounds of our decision (to deny a tenure in a particular case), if the candidate went to court, the university might have to go through an expensive legal process where the ultimate outcome would be quite uncertain. This lawyer had to face sharp questions from us, particularly from the faculty member in our committee who was from our law school.

One major way California politicians affected the university was in terms of the total education budget (particularly the part assigned to the University of California system), which determined, for example, the general cost of living adjustment to our annual salary, apart from student admission numbers and fees, repair and construction of buildings and other facilities. Of course, over the years funds from the California budget have been a diminishing part of our total campus budget, and the campus independently raises funds from donors—in this, of course, Berkeley is less successful than private universities with wealthy alumni. As a result, tuition fees for students have been steadily going up, and even though they are much lower than in most private universities, this hurts the access for large numbers of students and diminishes the general public nature of the university.

In years of tight budgets, the university may cut down on new hires, but tries its best to guard the part of the budget that is earmarked for merit increases on the basis of the intensive merit review process I have described above. One of the toughest battles the committee usually had to fight was in cases when a rich private university tried to lure away a 'star' professor from us by offering much higher salary, research money, laboratory resources, etc. Even there, Berkeley often tried to match some of those offers by deftly juggling the salary scale. One of the first words I learned when I joined the committee was 'decoupling': this was the name for tortuous departures from Berkeley's standard salary scales mostly to withstand the salary offers from other universities. Of course, the authorities would often remind people of the non-monetary advantages of remaining in California, with its climate and other benefits (obviously of not much use for offers from the nearby rich private university, Stanford). I remember once the governor of California, while cutting the university budget, told people how much of what he called 'psychic income' California residents enjoyed—to which many protested and said that at the next election they'd contribute to his campaign fund with 'psychic dollars'.

One possible downside to the principle of faculty autonomy is that with full autonomy some universities could degenerate into cosy, nepotistic clubs of rampant mediocrity. Sociologist

Diego Gambetta has described (he wrote about it in general terms in *Politics, Philosophy and Economics Journal* in their April 2012 issue) such a system of collusive mediocrity in some Italian universities—a culture of mediocrity where mediocre people get other mediocre people around them and thrive in a cocoon of comfortable cronyism, a culture that is quite familiar in India as well. Autonomy vs cronyism is the inexorable dilemma of a higher education system.

In the US, this problem has been mostly averted by a culture of constant competition among the better universities—they raid one another for the best faculty and try to generate a critical mass of good faculty and students. Students also gravitate to where the best faculty are. When professors move from one university to another, they move with the whole paraphernalia of funded research projects, labs and affiliated students. So it'll be costly for a university to lose its good faculty members, if it fails to provide a stimulating environment.

It is, of course, not easy to reproduce this culture of competition and mobility everywhere, but one can try, with some external monitoring mechanisms in place. Periodic reviews of a whole department by outside professional peer groups of academics, particularly if the review report is taken seriously by the external financial authorities in the allocation of faculty slots to the department, can be a significant deterrent to indulgence in mediocrity. In many fields, competitive research grants from external funding agencies are an important source of finance for a US university (in the form of overhead costs charged to the grant), and mediocre people failing to get such grants can become financially costly for a university.

Apart from mediocre faculty, the other related problem of autonomy may be in encouraging low-quality degree giving. The solution to this is not state or regulatory interference. The ultimate solution will have to be the market test. Job-givers will not value such degrees given by universities that abuse their autonomy, and students will soon find this out. This kind of cutting-edge competition, both in recruiting faculty and in quality education for students at least in the better universities, has been slow to come even in advanced countries like Japan or in Europe—it has been at the root of the relative attractiveness of the US academia in the last at least sixty years.

Another interesting aspect of American academia is the role of young faculty in the decision-making process. When a new appointment is made, either at the junior or at the senior level, all of the departmental faculty including the junior most members take part in the faculty meeting. This makes for more informed, diverse and vigorous discussion, and inhibits cliquish appointments. The chairperson of the department in their report summarizes the thrust of the whole discussion, apart from the final vote count.

In general, compared with much of the rest of the world, younger members of the faculty here play a more active part in most departmental matters. In fact, when I first joined Berkeley faculty, I noticed that the departmental deliberations were dominated by thirty–forty-year-olds, and the veterans, including even Nobel Prize winners, did not have the major voice, or at least a voice proportionate to their eminence. This kind of culture with the premium on youth ultimately acts as a major source of dynamism in American academia. Of course, there is also a downside: younger members sometimes, not always, display a tendency to follow certain fads or fetishes, a passing craze or fascination with some dazzling methods or techniques, which may not stand the test of time or are not sustainable from the larger viewpoint of the whole discipline. But, on the whole, I have to say that I have been invigorated by the quality of faculty discussion and the collegiality with which it is conducted in my department.

Berkeley is widely regarded as the best public university in the world. This, of course, depends on the definition of a public university. The high-ranking Cambridge and Oxford universities in the UK are public in the sense of large subsidization by the government, but the private endowments and assets of these two old universities far exceed those of Berkeley. In fact, when I went on a visiting fellowship (at the invitation of my friend Jim Mirrlees, whom I have talked about earlier) at Trinity College, Cambridge, twice in the period 2002–04, I came to know that not merely Trinity was the richest college in the UK, its landholdings alone in vast tracts of the surrounding countryside, largely bequeathed by King Henry VIII, exceeded $1 billion in value.

I remember asking Amartya Sen, then the master of the college, how much of his time as the head of the college was spent on raising funds. (This was uppermost in my mind, as shortly before then I was asked in Berkeley if I'd like to take over the job of a dean, and I immediately said no; not merely that I did not have much administrative skills, but also that I heard one main task of a Berkeley dean was to raise funds from donors, a skill in which I was singularly deficient.) Amartya-da told me that Trinity was so rich that he not only did not have to raise funds, he had to preside over some meetings where—following a Cambridge tradition—he had to take decisions on sharing some of the riches of the college with the less well-off colleges. How I wish the US had a similar tradition!

The Master's Lodge, where he lived, had nineteen bedrooms, one of which was permanently reserved for the possible occasional visit by a member of the royal family. In some small ways, I partook in Trinity's riches: most afternoons, if it did not rain, Kalpana and I enjoyed walking in the large, beautiful, lush green Faculty Gardens, and the food at the High Table for the faculty was good, unusually so for an old British establishment. (For an

Indian philosopher friend, Arindam Chakrabarti, who was also visiting at that time, and who was not just a strict vegetarian, he'd not even touch onions and garlic, the kitchen staff would serve specially cooked meals just for him at the Table.) I was told that the kitchen at Trinity was the inventor of an English, less sweet than the French version, crème brûlée, known as 'Trinity burnt cream', first introduced at the Trinity High Table in 1879.

My first night at dinner at the High Table, I heard Amartyada saying grace in Latin; I later told him that I almost saw him slipping into the shoes of his grandfather, who used to preside over ceremonies in Santiniketan, chanting in Sanskrit.

12
Life in English Academia

After my student days in Cambridge, in my professional life, I have been to Britain many times, occasionally for lectures and conferences, but sometimes, more formally, on visiting assignments. The latter—except for the two terms at Trinity College, Cambridge, as a Visiting Fellow—have been more to Oxford and LSE. This may be partly because, for some time, there was a relative decline in the quality of the Cambridge economics department after the internal troubles and the exit of some big names that I have alluded to before. In Oxford, I have been on formal visits to All Souls College, St Catherine's College and Nuffield College.

The first time in Oxford, I was a Visiting Fellow at All Souls College in 1983. The occasion was an invitation to give a set of endowed lectures at the college, named after S. Radhakrishnan, who used to be a philosophy professor and Fellow at the college, and later President of India. Amartya-da was then a Fellow at that College. I remember I arrived one afternoon straight from California and Amartya-da said he'd take me to dinner at the college and explain the various quaint customs practised in this college founded in 1438.

The college had no undergraduates and hardly any graduate students, only Fellows. I already knew that it had the reputation of being a Tory citadel, and rather stodgy and rigid in its customs. After a great deal of contentious debate, it admitted women only in 1979. I had also heard the story of the famous historian and Shakespeare scholar A.L. Rowse, who, at age twenty-two, sat for the Prize Fellowship Examination at All Souls and did well in the written exam. But then there was another hurdle to cross: he was invited to the dinner to check his table manners. At the end of the dinner, the pudding was served, and on top there was a cherry. Rowse did not know the correct manner of disposing the cherry stone that was in his mouth. He pondered about alternative ways, but could not make up his mind, so he swallowed it. He did get the fellowship, but even when he was past ninety years in age, he told a journalist that he still had not figured out what was the proper way of tackling that stone at the All Souls dinner table in 1925.

At the dinner table, most of the time Amartya-da and I talked to each other. At one point, I whispered to him that all around us there seemed to be many distinguished-looking people, but he had not introduced me to any of them. He looked around and said to me into Bengali: 'The people tonight at this table can be classified in two groups—one obnoxious, and the other highly obnoxious.' That sounded like a good enough explanation. After dinner, when we were parting company, I told him that he had explained to me about the customs at lunch and dinner times, but what about breakfast? He said he never had breakfast at the college, but it should be simple, as it was self-service and he pointed me to the breakfast room.

The next morning, I went to that room and saw a scattering of a few elderly dons, each seemingly absorbed in his *Daily Telegraph* newspaper, and grunting a perfunctory 'Morning!' at me. I then served myself some cereal and took from the table a copy of *The Guardian*, and sat down in a quiet corner. Then I realized that I had not brought a napkin; so I went back to the table and saw some neatly folded cloth napkins and some paper napkins. I started taking a cloth napkin for myself, but immediately a distinct shudder rippled through the room. For a moment I was confused and didn't know what had happened. All these fuddy-duddies were obviously watching me from behind their newspapers. One of them then kindly came over and explained to me that cloth napkins were for permanent fellows, and as a Visiting Fellow I was entitled only to paper napkins!

Jon Elster, who I think was a Visiting Fellow one year earlier, had warned me about a particular Fellow of the college. This elderly gentleman would apparently ask me about the area of my research, and finding it out, he'd then mention a few books, which Jon assured me I would have never heard of. Then he'd try a few other books, which also I was unlikely to have heard of. Then he'd gently exclaim, 'Oh! I thought these were pretty central to your area of research!' and move away. I did meet this gentleman; in fact, he invited me to tea in his large office in one of the college towers. He did not tell me about the books central to my area of research. It is possible he did not consider me worthy of playing his little one-upmanship game.

At the first day of my Radhakrishnan lectures at All Souls, there was a minor fracas about my attire. Amartya-da thought I had to wear a gown while lecturing, so he procured one and gave it to me the day before. But when I went to the lecture hall, Amartya-da rushed to me and relieved me of the gown; if I remember right, he said he had just found out the protocol was that the lecturer in the college could wear a gown only if he was at any time an Oxford student or faculty, which I was not. (Talking of gowns, I remember a story I heard when I was a student in Cambridge. In those days, undergraduates were supposed to wear a gown whenever they went out in the evening. A senior don, called a proctor, and two university officials, known as bulldogs, would punish any gown-less student they caught and would fine them. It used to be quite a sight in Cambridge streets in the evening to see these three chasing some students with their own gowns flying in the wind. The story I heard is about Roger Bannister famous for running the first sub-four-minute mile in 1954. As a student from Oxford, he once went to Cambridge and, in the evening, was confronted by the proctor. 'Excuse me, sir,' said the proctor, 'are you a member of this university?' Bannister made a run for it, with the bulldogs in pursuit. After about a quarter of a mile, Bannister waited for his pursuers to catch up. 'No,' finally said Bannister, leaving the panting bulldogs in some confusion.)

On the last day of my lecture at All Souls, a man from the audience came up to me and introduced himself as Peter Dougherty, an editor (and part-owner) of what used to be called Basil Blackwell Publishers (I met him again much later when he was with Princeton University Press). He said if I wrote up my lectures as a book, he'd like to publish it. The book was published the next year, 1984. Recently, I was approached by an Oxford group of young faculty saying that they'd like to hold a conference at All Souls to celebrate my original Radhakrishnan lectures. I gave an inaugural lecture at this conference, reflecting on the theme of change and continuity in Indian political economy since 1983, and the others made presentations on themes related to my original lectures. A book finally came out of this conference, titled

Class and Conflict: Revisiting Pranab Bardhan's Political Economy of India, edited by Elizabeth Chatterjee and Matthew McCartney and published by Oxford University Press.

On a visit to All Souls College in the late 1990s, one day I chanced upon some scenes of a movie being filmed in the lane next to the college, where the whole lane, with medieval-looking architecture, was taken over to recreate the time of Paris shortly after the French Revolution. The movie was *Quills*, which is about the last years of Marquis de Sade's incarceration in a lunatic asylum. Standing on the roadside, I saw the guillotine going up and down, and there was a basket where the severed heads from a distance looked quite real. Later, I did watch the movie when it came out in 2000 (Kate Winslet, an English actress I like, was in it).

During my first visit at All Souls I came to know a distinguished Bengali philosopher and Sanskrit scholar, Bimal Matilal, who was a Fellow at the college; he also held the same Spalding Professorship at the university that was held by Radhakrishnan several decades back. He firmly believed that it was unfortunate that Indian philosophy 'has remained identified with mysticism and mistakenly thought to be inseparable from religion' (to quote from the preface he wrote for his book, *Epistemology, Logic and Grammar in Indian Philosophical Analysis*). Through his many writings, he tried his best to convince Western philosophers about looking at Indian philosophy as a rigorous, theoretical, logical and analytical enterprise, incorporating in its own way most issues addressed in Western philosophy.

I had much to learn from him and I asked him to join me for dinner at the college. He said he did not go to college dinners any more. As an explanation he said in Bengali to me, 'There are "scorpions" out there at the dinner table. Amartya-da with his urbane sophistication can deftly handle them. But I am a country bumpkin from Joynagar [his birthplace in rural south Bengal], I cannot handle these people.'

One day, he said that after dinner he'd come and pick me up from college, and we'd go see a movie (*Heat and Dust*, an Ivory-Merchant production based on a novel by Ruth Prawer Jhabvala). But he said it was difficult to even double-park near the college gate, so I should wait outside the gate exactly at 8.50 p.m. when he'd come with his car. That evening, I had my dinner at the High Table, and it ended around 7.45 p.m. The young English mathematician I was talking to at the Table urged me to join him in the adjacent room for dessert and Madeira wine. I thought it was more than one hour before my appointed time at 8.50, so I agreed. Already a line formed for moving to the dessert room; unknown to me the line had quickly arranged itself in terms of seniority of the Fellows, with whoever happened to be the seniormost that night at the head of the line. The line then marched on to the next room where we seated ourselves with the senior most Fellow at the head of the table.

I talked mostly to the same young man, and at around 8.30 I was going to take leave of him and start my leisurely saunter to the college gate. The young man hushed me and forced me to sit down. Apparently, the custom was that you could not leave the room until the head of the table did, and, by that time, he was fast asleep after his glasses of Madeira. This continued for some time and Mr Head of the Table was still asleep. I explained my urgent need to my companion. Around 8.42 p.m., he joined me in making tingling noises with spoons and wine glasses. Fortunately, that worked to wake up the old man, and I could get my release and ran fast to the gate, where I saw Bimal's car approaching.

In my several subsequent visits to Oxford (and once in Berkeley when he was visiting), I always made it a point to meet

Bimal. But soon he was diagnosed with terminal cancer, and the last time I saw him, a few months before his death at age fifty-six, he was at his office, where he was lying on a bed and still tutoring a few students, though his voice was feeble. When I quickly said good bye, I'll never forget the soulful eyes with which he looked at me from his bed. The official name of All Souls College is 'College of the Souls of All the Faithful Departed'; this college is associated with the memory of two of my dear departed friends who were both philosopher Fellows at the college: Jerry Cohen and Bimal Matilal.

In the early 1990s, I was a visiting fellow at St Catherine's College and an academic visitor at Nuffield College in Oxford. At Nuffield College at that time, two friends from my Cambridge student days were Fellows, Jim Mirrlees and Christopher Bliss. (I think Jim was mostly away during my visit, and graciously asked me to use his large office at Nuffield.) The other person I used to see there off and on was Tony Atkinson who became the Warden of Nuffield shortly afterward. I knew Tony since our student days in Cambridge. Like me, he also moved from one Cambridge to the other—to MIT—roughly around the same time. Both of us were heavily influenced by our teacher, James Meade, though Tony never did a PhD (as used to be the old British tradition—neither James Meade nor Joan Robinson had a PhD), Tony did not follow Meade in the latter's work on international trade as I did, but in some other respects, he broadly followed the footsteps of Meade, apart from sharing his personal characteristics of modesty, decency and a positive vision of the future. Tony was certainly among the best economists of my generation, with pioneering work on inequality, poverty, public policies, redistributive taxation and welfare. He was also an advocate of UBI. I had co-authored a chapter for the *Handbook of Income Distribution* that he co-edited with François Bourguignon, a French development economist friend of mine.

Among Meade's international trade students, one of the most famous was Max Corden (who grew up in Australia after fleeing Nazi Germany), also a very decent, cordial man, who was a Fellow at Nuffield College, but had left for the US some years before my visit. I had known Max since his earlier Oxford days. Whenever we met, we shared our experience and memories of our common teacher, James Meade. Max was of the opinion that whatever people later discovered to be important in international trade theory was somewhere in the dense prose of Meade's two big volumes on international trade, published in the early 1950s.

In 2003, I was invited to give the first Max Corden Lecture at University of Melbourne, where Max had just resettled after years in the US. My topic was 'Globalization and the World's Poor'. In his preliminary remarks, he said, sweetly, 'I am glad Pranab is here, but why is there a lecture in my name? I am not dead yet!' In my audience, I was pleasantly surprised to see my friend Jim Mirrlees, who was visiting Melbourne. Max is actually still going strong at ninety-five, and the last Corden lecture given just before the pandemic was by Paul Krugman, also on the topic of globalization.

By then Jim Mirrlees, having retired from Cambridge, was living in Hong Kong, first as a professor in the Chinese University of Hong Kong and later the master of a college there. The last time I saw him was when he came to a lecture I gave at the Hong Kong University of Science and Technology in 2012. He fell severely ill a few years after with a terminal illness, was flown from Hong Kong in a stretcher to his home in Cambridge, where he died. He loved playing the piano, and Patricia, his wife, wrote to us that on the day of his death a special concert with a viola player and pianist from the London Symphony Orchestra was arranged, which gave him some happy moments.

At St Catherine's College, Oxford, I was mainly invited by my friend Sudhir Anand, who is a major economist on inequality, development and health. (I think Sudhir was among the childhood playmates of Salman Rushdie when they grew up together in Bombay.) Both Nuffield and St Catherine's were among the more recently established colleges in Oxford and were less encumbered by the quaint customs of the older colleges. Our son, Titash, who was then a physics undergraduate at Berkeley, spent his education abroad programme at St Catherine's, and my visiting fellowship time partly coincided with his time there. His physics tutor at St Catherine's, Neville Robinson, introduced us in a tea party at his home to his son, Andrew Robinson, a writer and a biographer of both Rabindranath Tagore and Satyajit Ray.

At St Catherine's, I also remember meeting John Bayley, a Fellow there and a professor of English literature at the university. I had read quite a few of his essays on literary criticism in the *New York Review of Books*. He was the husband of the writer and philosopher Iris Murdoch. Iris once described him as 'perhaps the greatest [literary] critic since Coleridge'. We attended a talk by both of them, where it was quite a touching sight to see how much care he was taking of Iris. Later, of course, when Iris lost her extraordinary mind to Alzheimer's disease, he was her meticulous caretaker, accounts of which are reported in his book *Iris: A Memoir of Iris Murdoch*, which was made into the 2001 film *Iris* by Richard Eyre. I recently read about Iris Murdoch in her youth being part of an Oxford quartet of women philosopher friends (the others were Elizabeth Anscombe, Philippa Foot and Mary Midgley) who tried to 'do philosophy in a more engaged, creative and open way' than the male Oxford philosophers of their time.

When John Bayley came to know that I was coming from Berkeley, he said he'd share a guilty secret with me. When he and Iris were visiting Berkeley, and staying at the campus Faculty Club, once on their walk they saw and were tempted by fresh California asparagus being sold at a bargain price. On an impulse, they bought some without thinking what they were going to do with it. In their Faculty Club room, cooking was strictly prohibited. The two of them finally decided to ignore this, and quietly and surreptitiously boiled the asparagus in their room and went on to enjoy it. I saw in his face the memory of that guilty pleasure, as Bayley chuckled to himself.

In Oxbridge colleges, I have met so many amiable, decent people, yet there is something to Amartya-da's reference to the 'obnoxious' and 'highly obnoxious', and Bimal Matilal's reference to the 'scorpions'. I don't think they were referring to people who were necessarily racists or to conservatives still suffering from lingering imperialist delusions. Of course, there are snobs and curmudgeons all over the world, but I have found some Oxbridge dons taking a special pleasure out of what can only be called refined malice and suave verbal expressions of sheer bile. For a mild version of this, let me recount a possibly apocryphal but highly credible story. I have heard of two elderly dons busy talking in the college lounge, when they were interrupted by a hapless young American visitor who wanted to know where the nearest 'restroom' was. One of the dons told him, 'You go down the hall, turn right, and you'll find a door saying "Gentlemen", don't let that deter you, you go right in.'

The absurdity is not confined to dons; it can also be among some students, particularly those described as 'toffs'. In a recent book titled *Chums: How a Tiny Caste of Oxford Tories Took Over the UK*, the journalist Simon Kuper writes about how a section of smug, snobbish, entitled group of his Oxford classmates in the mid- to late 1980s blustered their way up the English totem pole. One of them, the ex-prime minister Boris Johnson, even wrote (published in *Have I Got Views for You*) in a tongue-in-cheek way about his Oxford group: 'what a sharp-elbowed, thrusting and basically repellent lot we were'. (Self-deprecation of this kind is part of the arrogant style of 'toffs').

My son, Titash, used to be a cellist at the Berkeley Youth Symphony Orchestra. For some years, I used to take him to a cello teacher, Megan, who'd give him private lessons at her home for about an hour; I used to wait outside in my car and take him and his large instrument back home when he was done. Once, Megan's husband, a distinguished British cellist (and at one time, Megan's own music teacher), saw me waiting and invited me inside. We talked for a while, and as I was enquiring when he had moved from Britain, he started talking somewhat nostalgically about the 'green and pleasant land' of the English countryside, and then abruptly said, 'It's such a beautiful country, but if only the people were nice!' I was surprised and said that the proportion of nice people was probably about the same in all countries, but he did not agree. I did not explore his particular experience with not-nice people, but it kept me wondering.

(Let me take this opportunity to also mention a somewhat peculiar experience I once had while waiting in my car for Titash to finish his music lesson. One day, a gentleman in that somewhat classy, quiet neighbourhood approached me and said that he had often found me in a car there, though I clearly did not live there. So he wanted to know what I was doing. I thought of telling him that I was casing the neighbourhood to plan my next burglary.)

I have sometimes flippantly told others that in England, in public spaces, sometimes I have felt as if English mothers have instilled in their children two strict lessons: one, never talk to a stranger unless you really have to, and two, don't express your emotions in public. When I first went to England, travelling in a train was a strangely eerie experience for someone used to the noisy, messy, nosy extended family–like experience of being a passenger in an ordinary Indian train. If you are lucky to get a seat in such a train in India, very soon someone will ask for your 'good' name (once my half-French sociologist friend André Beteille, who looks like other Bengalis, told me that other passengers in a train were confused by his name and asked what caste he belonged to, as many Indian surnames are indicators of caste). Then they'd ask about your family; if you look young, whether you are married; if married, how many children, etc. And if they like you, they'll insist on sharing their food. If you are reading a newspaper, other passengers will take away some pages you are not currently reading for them to study. In trains in England, people hide themselves with newspapers in front of them and, once, a friend told me that when he was trying to see the headline of his neighbouring passenger's newspaper, this man moved aside in his seat and held the newspaper at such an angle that the headlines were no longer visible.

In Oxford, I used to visit the historian Tapan Raychaudhuri (whom I knew from his DSE days), a distinguished historian of Indian social, economic and intellectual history, a fellow of St Antony's College; but I visited him mostly at home, since he was at his best in that surrounding as a raconteur of juicy stories and his wife Hashi-di prepared delectable dishes for us to savour. (By the way, Hashi-di's sister, Sonali Dasgupta, caused quite a stir in 1957 when she left her husband and child in Kolkata and ran off with the great Italian film director Roberto Rossellini, and lived with him for a time in Rome, as he was breaking up with his famous actress wife, Ingrid Bergman.)

Once at their home, Tapan-da took me to the back of their house where the river Cherwell flowed. There was a wooden bench by the river where we sat down and chatted. I asked Tapan-da if that lovely area was part of his property. He said no, it was part of a common property for all the neighbours. But then, he said, for all practical purposes it had become his private property, since when he'd sit there, none of his English neighbours would come out, lest they'd have to engage in casual conversation with him, even though these were reasonably nice people and he had good relations with them. The social anthropologist Kate Fox in her popular book *Watching the English: The Hidden Rules of English Behaviour* writes, 'Social dis-ease is the central core of Englishness.'

On expressing emotions in public, the British stereotype of reticence and the stiff upper lip is, of course, wellknown. In the film version of *A Passage to India*, there is a scene where you see the characters Ronny and Adela watching a horse race from the racecourse gallery. Then it goes roughly like this: After some silence, they break up their long-standing engagement to be married in just a few clipped sentences, with no raising of voices, and then keep on watching the race as if nothing has happened; after some time, one of them says, 'We are being rather English about it, aren't we?', to which the other replies, 'We are English after all.'

On 31 August 1997, the day Princess Diana died in a car crash, I happened to be in England, and I saw on TV thousands of English people openly and uncontrollably weeping in the street. On this day of tragedy, I thought I was witnessing a major rupture in English character. Virginia Woolf famously wrote in her essay 'Mr Bennett and Mrs Brown' in 1924, 'On or about December 1910 human character changed.' I don't quite know about that, but on or about 31 August 1997, maybe the English character changed.

In recent years, the institution in England I have visited most frequently is LSE—in 1998 as a STICERD Distinguished

Visitor, and in 2010–11 as a BP Centennial Professor (this was shortly after the disastrous BP oil spill in the Gulf of Mexico, so I hesitated telling people about my designation), and numerous times as visitor just for a few days. Most of my interactions were with the development economists Tim Besley and Maitreesh Ghatak in the economics department, and with the political-economy scholar Robert Wade, economist Jean-Paul Faguet and some years earlier, John Harriss (the political sociologist specializing in India) in the International Development Department. Apart from departmental seminars, I also gave three somewhat public lectures in a large London School of Economics (LSE) auditorium, once on China and India, once on a new agenda for global labour, and the third time on my recent book on democratic disenchantment.

In earlier decades, on my way to or from India, I'd often stop in London, and go to LSE and spend some time with my friends, including Nick Stern and Meghnad Desai (since then, both of them hold the title of Lords). Meghnad once invited me to visit the House of Lords, showed me around and took me to lunch there. Meghnad, with his distinct Afro hairdo and all, has always been a flamboyant character. He used to claim to be a Marxist economist. Rumour had it that he and his first wife (Gail, who I think was related to the wealthy Guinness family) had a summer villa in the south of France, where reportedly the only book on the shelf was *Das Kapital*. During the Vietnam War days, he was active at the LSE protests against the war. I was told that my teacher Frank Hahn, who had moved from Cambridge to LSE by then, once suggested to Meghnad, in a characteristic Frank Hahn way, to publicly immolate himself in front of the LSE building in a spectacular anti-war protest gesture (around that time, some Vietnamese monks immolating themselves in protest in Saigon had hit the headlines). Later, Meghnad became one of the Margaret Thatcher–admiring (or –internalizing) Labor Party members. Now I hear in India he is a Narendra Modi admirer. He is also the chairman of the Meghnad Desai Academy of Economics he has founded in Mumbai.

In my transit stops in London, I used to stay with my historian friend from college days, Premen Addy, and also occasionally with Sudipta Kaviraj, an erudite scholar of Indian politics and intellectual history (then teaching at the School of Oriental and African Studies, now a professor at Columbia University) and his musician wife, Nilanjana. Over the years, I have seen London visibly changing. Now it is a vigorous, youthful, dynamic, cosmopolitan city—of course, largely unaffordable except for the financially better off. Even some of my French friends say that London now has some of the top-rated French restaurants. Good restaurants in London are expensive even on my American salary. Some of London's wealth is derived from the thriving financial district ('the city'), and from the investments by kleptocratic oligarchs of the whole world. Once the capital of a plundering empire, London has now become the preferred laundromat for the world's corrupt money.

This, of course, has never blinded me to the fact that some of the world's best writers, journalists, theatre actors, etc., are in London or thereabouts. In economic journalism, for example, *The Economist* and *The Financial Times* have remained among the very best in the world—I regularly read them for their usually coherent, well-informed arguments expressed in crisp witty prose, even though I may not always agree with them (I give myself a useful exercise: if I disagree, I should be clear in my mind exactly why; I often consider them as intelligent opposition, which I am afraid I cannot say about the *Wall Street Journal*).

I have always been a fan of the BBC, probably Britain's most important public cultural institution, but successive attempts by

Conservatives to dismantle it have made it much weaker than before, with its budget cut almost to the bone. Even apart from the culture, to an institutional economist like me, the BBC in principle is a reasonably successful example of a public institution—funded by and accountable to the public, but retaining a great deal of autonomy and independence in its day-to-day functions (the severity with which it still criticizes the government or bites the hand that feeds it is a shining example for other countries). For all the propaganda against it, the BBC has retained its popularity with the general public. In 2015, the government asked the British public for their views on the BBC and received 192,000 responses, of which 97 per cent were favourable. Its fans in the rest of the world are even more numerous.

I was thrilled when about a decade ago, after my China–India book came out and I was visiting LSE, I was invited to appear in the BBC for an interview on the theme of the book; I just had to walk across the road from LSE to the building where the BBC used to be. (In the middle of the interview, they took a short break, but I was told that immediately after the break and before the interview resumed, following a practice in their programme, they'd surprise me with an unrelated question. It turned out to be about what kind of a practical invention I'd like to see in the world at large. I said I'd like an invention where I could carry something like a mobile phone in my pocket which would constantly monitor certain vital parameters of my health, so I could get a sufficiently early signal to get medical help if necessary. This was long before any of the current wearable health devices on the market now was anywhere in the horizon. So I now feel prescient.)

I have already mentioned before about British supremacy in the world of theatre and detective fiction. When visiting LSE, I have often walked across the Waterloo Bridge over the river to watch a play at the National Theatre on the South Bank. Recently, some

Berkeley cinemas have had programmes of showing full videos of plays under the 'National Theater Live' programme. This is a good way of showcasing the quality of British theatre to the wider world. (During the pandemic, you could see some of their plays free online.)

Every year, I look at the list in *The Guardian* for the year's best British detective novels and read some of them. Recently, I wrote an article on my reflections on feminist crime novels. In that connection, I read quite a bit of Scandinavian noir and some good recent American writers (like Laura Lippman, Lisa Unger and Megan Abbott) but also quite a few British ones (for example, Erin Kelly's taut psychological novel *He Said/She Said*). More than dramatic murders and mayhem with beautiful female corpses or exploits of femme fatales (often creatures born of male anxiety) in male crime novels, some of the feminist crime novels (mostly by women, but some by male writers) prominently feature meditations on rape, suicide and child victimization. Both vulnerability and agency of women with impaired and world-weary female protagonists are upfront in the feminist crime novels. The exploration of the inner lives of women, slow development of characters rather than fast-paced action ('less gunplay, more foreplay'), emotional damage in domestic settings and relationships—these are often in the main focus. In any case, we've come a long way since the days of Miss Jane Marple with her knitting needles.

I don't usually read many spy stories which thrived during the period of the Cold War in my youth, but I'll be amiss if I don't mention about my fascination bordering on reverential awe for the spy stories of John le Carré. His real name was David Cornwell. An English patriot, disgusted by Brexit, he wanted to remain European, and shortly before his death in December 2020, he gave up his British citizenship, and took an Irish one.

He was helped by the Irish writer John Banville to trace the Irish roots of his grandmother. By the way, John Banville used to write crime fiction under the pen name Benjamin Black. I have read most of the latter's crime novels, as I have read almost all the espionage stories of le Carré, including his posthumously published *Silverview*.

The plots in le Carré's books are nuanced and complex—the real-life double agent Kim Philby, one of the infamous 'Cambridge Five' spies, said in a letter to Graham Greene in 1982 that he found le Carré's plots 'more complicated than anything within my own experience' though 'they were good reads after all that James Bond nonsense'. The plots involve the morally compromised spies of both the West and the East, their sordid hypocrisies and games, the office drudgery and the bureaucratic turf wars, all narrated in a taut and witty style. But the all-pervasive theme is one of betrayal both in personal and public lives.

The writer Ian McEwan said that le Carré had gone far beyond 'being a genre writer and will be remembered as perhaps the most significant novelist of the second half of the 20th century in Britain'. Philip Roth called le Carré's semi-autobiographical novel *A Perfect Spy* (a perfect spy is the one who betrays everybody), when it came out in 1986, 'the best English novel since the war'. It is a kind of meta-fiction, with stories within stories, largely based on the author's tortuous relation with his own father, Ronnie Cornwell, a charming swindler in real life.

I personally prefer his Smiley–Karla trilogy, three novels where the central focus is on the intricate and treacherous cat-and-mouse games between George Smiley, a world-weary, clear-headed, donnish, badly dressed (his clothes 'hung about his squat frame like a skin on a shrunken toad'), cuckolded old spymaster, called back from retirement, and his fiendishly clever Soviet rival,

Karla (the only time they ever met was briefly in Delhi airport). Of the trilogy, I like *Tinker, Tailor, Soldier, Spy* the best. I saw the superb seven-part BBC TV serial on this in 1979–80, where the masterly Alec Guinness acted as George Smiley—his acting in that series is so indelibly etched in my mind, I just cannot think of anybody else in that role (in the 2011 movie based on the same novel, Gary Oldman acted well in that role, but I still could not accept him).

It is worth noting that even le Carré's traitors are at heart English patriots; the 'mole' in *Tinker, Tailor, Soldier, Spy* when outed, says that he lost his allegiance to the West when, after the Suez crisis in 1956, he realized the waning influence of the British on the world stage and their abject subordinate status to the Yankees he so disliked. There is also an Oxbridge connection in recruitment of young, educated spies, apart from the long shadow of the betrayal by the Cambridge spies in the Smiley novels. In an early novel, George Smiley is nostalgic about his days with the spymaster in Oxford, when 'you took your orders over a glass of port in his rooms at Magdalen College'.

Le Carré introduced some new terms in the espionage literature, which have now become commonplace, like mole, joes, honey trap, scalp hunters, babysitters, lamplighters, etc., which actual spies apparently use now. He told an interviewer that KGB training schools allegedly used his books as essential reading. More interestingly, when Yevgeny Primakov, a former KGB head and later Russian premier, came to London in the mid-1990s, he sought out le Carré and told him about reading his books. During their meeting, someone asked Primakov which character in the books he identified with. 'George Smiley, of course!' Primakov replied.

I have enjoyed, but was less enamoured, with his 'angry' polemical novels in the post-Cold War days—*The Night*

Manager (about international arms dealers), *The Constant Gardener* (scandal involving global pharmaceutical companies), *Our Kind of Traitor* and *Single and Single* (about international money laundering), *A Most Wanted Man* (about international terror, torture and migration), etc. As I have said before, I prefer sad novels to angry novels.

13
Policy Economics and the Indian Elite

Among other things, LSE is associated in my mind with bringing me in touch with one of the most remarkable persons I have ever met in my life, and someone who has been a dear friend over nearly four decades since then. This is Jean Drèze.

I think it was in the mid-1980s that Nick Stern at LSE introduced me to Jean. I have known Nick since he was a student of Jim Mirrlees at Oxford. Once when I was teaching in Delhi, Nick and my Cambridge classmate Christopher Bliss (both of them teaching at Oxford at that time) asked me to suggest an Indian village they might pick which they then wanted to study intensively. I remember telling them to choose a village that had been surveyed before so that they had some benchmark information, and directed them to the Agro-

Economic Research Centre of the DSE, which over many decades carried out village surveys in different parts of northern India. They finally chose a village, Palanpur, in western Uttar Pradesh, about 200 kilometres from Delhi, which had been surveyed by the centre. Over the last fifty years, the team has studied this village intensively and repeatedly, which is quite a unique achievement in the interface of development economics and economic anthropology.

Jean, after finishing his PhD at the ISI, went and lived in this village in 1983–84 as part of that research team. Apart from doing research, Jean kept notes on his life in general in that village, and, on the basis of those notes, his friend Luc Leruth recently wrote up a fictionalized version in a novel titled *Rumble in a Village*, which, of course, went far beyond the economic and social data collected, into the cultural and emotional lives of villagers—their jealousies, intrigues, corruption and violence, as much as their love, compassion and friendships. In this context, let me quote from Jean's comments on love in Palanpur village in his preface to the novel, which, I'd say, applied in large measure to even many of the urban areas I was familiar with in my early youth:

> At one level, love is a bit of an obsession among Indian youngsters. Popular songs, for one, have few other themes. If a future historian tries to understand today's India through the prism of popular films and songs, she will probably think that romantic love bloomed all around. The reality, however, is almost diametrically opposite, at least in Palanpur. Even as young boys and girls listen to love songs and dream of a sweetheart, the actual prospect of reciprocated love is virtually nil. In the conservative environment of Palanpur, where everyone is watching everyone else, a love adventure can be very risky, and should it be discovered, retribution

is likely to be swift and brutal (especially if the love birds belong to different castes). Matrimonial arrangements, for their part, are business-like affairs that often turn sour on the very day of the marriage ceremony.

I may add that, even in Indian lower-middle-class urban or semi-urban life, the elderly relatives who will fondly tell you mythological stories of divine love, including erotic love (say, between Krishna and Radha, which has been given expression in the lyrical poetry of many Indian languages, including Bengali), will glower at you if you express your tenderness for the girl or the boy next door. This, I believe, is ultimately part of the economic and status insecurity of their lives; they are always afraid that youthful indiscretion and audacity by youngsters may take them out of their control, which ultimately may imperil the family's economic security (in terms of old age support) or 'honour' in society (largely involving female sexuality). Even 'honour' killings by the family arising out of some love affair among its younger members have not been absent even in cases where the family had migrated to the UK or US.

Jean was born in Belgium in a distinguished family; his father, Jacques Drèze, was an eminent mathematical economist (his mother ran a home for battered women). We were fortunate to get an article from Drèze senior in the book on market socialism that John Roemer and I edited in the 1990s. The day I first met Jean at LSE, he wanted to sit down with me and discuss a few things; I told him I was busy in the day in a meeting, and then I had a few appointments, but I'd find him in the evening if he gave me his address and telephone number. Jean flashed a large grin and said he had neither an address nor a phone (these were the days before mobile phones). For a moment I was taken aback, then slowly realized he actually lived with the homeless in a nearby park (in a wet, cold London). In the mornings, he'd come to LSE, take a shower, and then start his teaching and research. I became immediately attracted to this character. The next few years when he was teaching at LSE, I'd make it a point to spend some time with him whenever I passed through.

One time, he told me he wanted to see the inside of a jail and find out the conditions of British prison life. How could he make sure he got arrested, though—after all, he was a pacifist, so could not commit any violence. So once, in front of a policeman, he started painting a pacifist graffiti on the wall, and was duly arrested. But his court case, being on a trivial matter, kept on being adjourned by the busy judge. One time, when the judge was at the point of adjourning it once again, Jean stood up and told the judge that he was definitely guilty and would be grateful if he was immediately sent to jail, as the summer vacation at LSE was ending and he was supposed to start teaching soon. (I was reminded of the report of a trial of Gandhi in the 1920s in British India. After the prosecutor brought a charge against him in court, Gandhi apparently stood up and told the British judge that his law infringements were much more serious and numerous than what the prosecutor had pointed out. He then made a long list of those himself in front of an astonished judge and pleaded guilty to all of them. Gandhi, of course, used this as political theatre of colonial law-breaking.)

Another time, when I saw Jean at LSE, he invited me to a dinner he'd be cooking that evening at a large, abandoned hospital building that he and the other homeless in the area had occupied. This was in a desolate and rundown part of London, somewhere near the Oval cricket ground. I found the place after quite a bit of search; it was dark inside as the building had no electricity, and there were a few candles burning. As soon as Jean saw me, he told me he had just finished cooking chicken curry (he himself is a vegetarian) and asked me to take a plate and a seat. There were about thirty other people in tattered grubby clothes and wraps and blankets, seated already, so I seated myself next to one of them at the end of a long table. Jean at the centre of the table was serving everyone from a pan; in the flickering candlelight and dark shadows, from a distance, the whole scene looked a bit like Da Vinci's *The Last Supper* with the Christ figure in the middle. (Being a film buff, my memory also flicked for a moment to a sinister caricature of *The Last Supper* in Luis Buñuel's 1961 Spanish film *Viridiana*, where the people at the table were homeless beggars, with the Christ-like figure in the middle being that of a blind beggar—this film won the Palme d'Or award at the Cannes Film Festival, was banned in Spain and denounced by the Vatican.)

While eating, I started talking to the man next to me, who was obviously enjoying his chicken curry, with gravy dripping from his copious facial hair. I asked him how he came to know Jean. He said he did not know him. That morning, he had been released after twenty-four years in jail (in Britain, that length of jail term is for really horrendous crimes; I didn't dare ask him what he had been punished for); after all these years, he had no friends or relatives, he did not know where to go; someone pointed him to this place, where he might get some food and a place to lie down. He then said that he presumed I too must be looking for shelter there. For a moment I did not know what to say. Later, one line from a plaintive Paul Robeson song (an African-American spiritual from the Civil War era) kept ringing in my ear: 'Sometimes I feel like a motherless child/A long way from home …'

A couple of months later in Berkeley, I got a letter from Jean, saying that they had established a commune in that abandoned building; it ran reasonably well for some time, but then, as usually happens with such communes, it broke up on account of various internal tensions and conflicts. The police were now set to evict them, but meanwhile, the commune had incurred a lot of debt. Jean asked me if I could send some financial help, which I immediately did. When Jean thanked me for this, he enclosed a published diary on the basis of his experience of this commune, *No. 1 Clapham Road: The Diary of a Squat*. This was an activist's account of the inner dynamics and tensions of building cooperatives and communes—a subject in which, as an institutional economist, I have had a long-standing academic interest. (One of Amartya Sen's relatively neglected articles has been on the conflictual problems of labour allocation in a cooperative enterprise, published in the *Review of Economic Studies* many decades ago.)

Jean's commune of homeless people also reminds me of the system of mutual aid that I once saw in a village of beggars a few miles away from Santiniketan. Ashok Rudra and I once decided to go and visit this small village (rather a hamlet) and observe first-hand how these destitute people managed to live. We arrived at the boundary of the hamlet in a hired cycle rickshaw and then started walking somewhat aimlessly. Soon we were followed by an intensely curious, bright-eyed Muslim teenage girl with a baby in her arms (by the way, India is the country with the largest number of child brides and teenage pregnancies in the world). We started talking to her, and she was highly amused by the unfathomable craziness of city people who wanted to know about their living conditions. She immediately appointed herself as our guide in visiting the beggar households, including her own (where she served us tea in clay pots). She said twice a week, they'd go in a group to the Bolpur open marketplace (haat) where they begged from the shoppers. Some of the households also had very tiny plots of cultivable land where they grew some paddy and vegetables. What was remarkable was the network of mutual help among the beggar women. In one dilapidated hut we visited, there was an elderly woman who could not go to the marketplace to beg the previous day as she had come down with a fever. We saw other village women bringing their cooked food to feed this ailing woman. A young girl in the neighbourhood started oiling and combing the hair of the elderly woman to make her presentable to the city visitors. I still remember this touching scene and the general spirit of incredibly upbeat camaraderie, conversation and banter among these poorest of women.

The last time I saw Jean at LSE was I think early in 1991 when the Gulf War was about to begin. Jean was in a hurry: he was organizing an international group of pacifists determined to go and place themselves in between the two armies in the battlefield—the Iraqi and the American—in their desperate attempt to stop the war. Jean asked me if I'd like to join him in his trip to the Iraq–Kuwait border. I have to say I chickened out.

After LSE, I have seen Jean Drèze mostly in India, usually in conferences in Delhi and Kolkata, and at Amartya Sen's home in Santiniketan (where he used to stay whenever the two of them were writing books together). The Kolkata conferences were the annual ones that Amartya-da used to organize for some years, held usually at the Taj Bengal five-star hotel, which Jean would refuse to stay in. While others would take the two-hour flight from Delhi to Kolkata, Jean would take the twenty-four-hour train in the crowded second-class compartment. Then he'd call me and often stay with me in my Kolkata apartment. If Kalpana was around and it was winter, she'd warm the bath water for him and arrange a comfortable raised bed for him; but Jean would refuse even those minor luxuries and insist on taking cold showers and sleeping on the floor.

During his days at the DSE faculty, he'd stay in a nearby 'jhuggi' or slum (with his newly married activist wife, Bela Bhatia). Soon he became an Indian citizen and started devoting more of his time to social activism and less on teaching. He left Delhi and was first in Allahabad, and now for some years has stayed in Ranchi. But much of the time he'd be on the road, walking, biking, and occasionally in crowded trains and buses. Once, I remember getting a long email from him describing his walking trip ('padayatra') to one of the poorest villages in Kalahandi, Odisha. He had heard of near-starvation conditions there. As he was walking, he saw a man carrying a load of vegetables on his head, going to the marketplace several miles away. He started walking along and talking to him (probably in Hindi, which Jean speaks much better than I do), and found out that the man had not eaten anything since the previous day or so, and was hoping to eat after he sold his vegetables in the market. At one point, Jean offered to carry the load at least part of the way to the market. The man emphatically refused, but Jean kept on nagging him. After some time, the man yielded, but when Jean tried to take the load on his head, it felt so heavy, Jean wrote to me, that he almost fell on the ground—just to think that this wiry little man was carrying it for miles on an empty stomach!

It was amazing to see how quickly Jean could switch between his academic and activist roles. From his intensive research in issues of poverty and welfare policies—in the writing of his books with Amartya-da, the latter has often claimed, of course, with charming modesty: 'I have a nice arrangement with Jean; he does most of the work and I get most of the credit!'—to his public speaking (Jean is a very cogent, forceful and persuasive speaker), to his writing of frequent newspaper columns on various topical policy problems, he'd move seamlessly to his life as an indefatigable

Policy Economics and the Indian Elite 273

social activist. I used to introduce him to other academics as 'Jesus Christ with a laptop'; now in Indian academic and activist circles everybody knows him.

For a time, he served in the National Advisory Council for Sonia Gandhi; in that capacity he is widely regarded as the architect of two of India's central welfare policies for the poor in the last two decades. One involving a substantial expansion in the public food distribution system, the world's largest, and the other involving the world's largest rural public works programme (in the latter policy, the co-architect was another social activist member of that council, Aruna Roy). It is probably correct to say that of all the academic economists in India, no one has been as effective as Jean in terms of such singular policy achievements helping hundreds of millions of poor people.

I know how much he had to fight for these policies, particularly for the rural public works programme. Once, in the early years of this century, I got a frantic email from him saying that many of the important policy economists of Delhi were mildly or strongly opposed to the rural works programme (they mostly considered it a waste of money). He knew that I was a strong supporter, so he pleaded with me to immediately write an op-ed defending the programme in a leading newspaper to generate some support among the opinion-makers of Delhi. I remember then immediately talking to Abhijit Banerjee at MIT, and the two of us quickly drafted a supportive joint op-ed and published it in Delhi. Jean was pleased and claimed that it helped him at an important stage of the debate in the policy circles. Nowadays many more economists in India, probably a majority, support the programme. Even Modi, who when he came to power in Delhi in 2014 called this programme a 'dole' and a 'monument of failure' of the earlier government, has depended on it repeatedly for his subsequent need for the votes of the poor. Even now, Jean keeps on fighting for those two welfare programmes, as various lapses and distortions take place in their implementation at the ground level.

Over time, I have noted in Jean a certain impatience when fellow economists raise objections to his policy ideas. He seems to occasionally consider them as obstacles in his mission to help the poor or a distraction from his single-minded pursuit of that objective. He and I have talked about this, and I have a feeling that sometimes the social activist in him gets the upper hand, and he is too quick to dismiss the academics' points as minutiae, if not positively hindering his good cause. This is, of course, understandable, as it is tough to always keep the delicate balance in oneself between an activist and an academic.

This brings me to the subject of my own attitude to policy economics. From time to time, I have made policy prescriptions (most recently for ways of inducing job opportunities for the underemployed, for wealth and inheritance taxes, and for UBI as providing some minimum economic security in India), but I have to admit that I am not always fully comfortable with making pat policy prescriptions, unlike many of my fellow economists for whom the main mission is to come up with appropriate policy solutions to economic problems. I guess I am too much of a political economist and obsessed with understanding the political constraints in the local context of the real world, which often make the possibility of an effective implementation of many policies that look immaculate on paper rather remote or they have unintended consequences. The discipline of political economy is as yet in its infancy in understanding the forces and motivations behind formations of political coalitions and different kinds of group bargains that work in different historical contexts to ensure a particular policy to be feasible and successful. (A leftist friend of mine and a star in the Berkeley electrical engineering faculty, the late Pravin Varaiya, used to tell me that until he got to know me, he, like most engineers, used to think that many socio-economic problems could be easily 'fixed', but by talking to me, he claimed, he became more aware of the complexities around most such problems.)

In India, I have personally known some of the best economist-administrators like I.G. Patel, V.K. Ramaswami, Manmohan Singh, Vijay Kelkar and Montek Ahluwalia in the government, and heads of the central bank like C. Rangarajan, Bimal Jalan, Y.V. Reddy and Raghuram Rajan, apart from Patel and Singh who had also served in the latter capacity. And Manmohan Singh was, of course, the reform-ushering finance minister, and later the Prime Minister—honestly, I could have never imagined this nicest and gentlest of persons I have known could ever be the Prime Minister for ten years in the rough and tumble of Indian politics. When he was the Prime Minister, I often avoided his company—for one thing, the elaborate network of security around him put me off: I remember once invited to his home for dinner I wanted to take a recent book of mine to present to him, but the security establishment, following their rulebook, disallowed it as a possible terrorist weapon.

Many of these economist-administrators have been advocates of economic reform, which I am generally in favour of. But sometimes their enthusiasm for market reform, based on the idea of ensuring more market competition, has not been matched by enough concern for preventing corporate concentration and the thriving of oligarchy, which threaten the Indian economy and polity. Besides, to me, economic reform also should include land reform and taxation of the wealthy, administrative reform, regulatory reform preventing the capture of regulatory bodies by politicians and administrators serving vested interests, reform of governance in the corporate firm giving more voice to the workers and other stakeholders, and electoral reform mitigating the influence of big money on politics. Many of the reform-mongers are less vocal about these other kinds of reforms.

I have also wondered about how deftly my economist-administrator friends managed to combine their steadfast belief in some policy ideas with the need to navigate the muddy currents and crosscurrents of the prevailing political deals. This is too complicated and treacherous a world for me to even contemplate ever playing an active role. I have also seen some economists having an exaggerated notion of their influence on politicians. More often than not, economists get used for the politicians' purpose, rather than the other way round. So throughout my professional life, whenever someone asked me about participating in the government, I have generally evaded the issue by telling them how painfully aware I was of the severe limitations of my capacity outside the academic cocoon. Among the names mentioned above, Ramaswami (we all fondly called him 'Ramu'), while in the government, kept on contributing to academic research and publishing in journals, until a freak tragic accident at his home cut short his life at age forty-one; this happened the first year I arrived in Delhi. In 1997, I gave the Ramaswami Memorial Lecture at DSE.

On two different occasions I was asked by people at the World Bank if I'd like to take the job of the chief economist (and senior vice president). I almost immediately said 'no', mainly because of my above-mentioned ambivalence on policy prescriptions (amplified when applied to many different countries I knew little about). Of course, the politics of US administrations with which the World Bank top leadership was inextricably linked played some role in my mind—even though this job was not directly connected with US policy, I was not comfortable with the possible image of complicity. I was also not sure of my administrative skills, though this job was more on policy persuasion in the international arena and on research administration inside the World Bank, rather than on the chores and functions of a standard bureaucracy. One advantage the holder of this job had was to be involved in potentially shaping the research direction in development economics, as they had probably the largest development economics research department in the world both in terms of resources and personnel. I took part in this in a small way as I served for some years in the research advisory body for the chief economist at the World Bank.

I also knew that some of my illustrious friends have worked on this particular job (like Stan Fischer, Michael Bruno, Joe Stiglitz, Nick Stern, François Bourguignon, and later Justin Lin, Kaushik Basu and others). On policy issues in some sense, Joe Stiglitz's time on the job was the most interesting and intriguing. In international fora, Joe as chief economist and senior vice president often openly criticized the World Bank (and particularly, IMF) policy thrusts, much to the dismay of the US Treasury. I remember I once went to a conference in Rio de Janeiro with Joe, and in the morning at the breakfast table, Joe with a bemused look and a smirk showed me the big headline in the local morning newspaper with his photograph. I told him that I did not read Portuguese. He said someone told him that the headline said something like: 'World Bank Chief Economist blasts World Bank economic policy!' Of course, this situation did not last long, and Joe had to leave the job soon.

In the world of development policy economics, in recent years experimental methods have become prominent. They have shown in a statistically 'clean' way how some policies, mainly in the areas of health and education, work effectively in particular micro contexts (application of these methods has been rewarded by Nobel Prizes to three of my brilliant friends, Esther Duflo, Abhijit Banerjee and Michael Kremer). But the jury is still out on how generalizable and reliable the micro results are; and also controlled experiments are difficult or sometimes even impossible to apply to many cases of large, one-off, real-world decisions that a policymaker has to take. There is also some risk that the current glamour of experimental methods may be diverting attention from some of the big questions of development economics that remain unresolved. It is also the case that in its search for theoretical and empirical rigour, the profession undervalues the need for in-depth country or regional studies of political and economic processes, which sometimes provide deeper insights into the origin and persistence of poverty than those gleaned from either cross-country standardized data or the micro experiments. But there is no doubt that new doors have been opened in policy economics, and vigorous attempts are being made in improving those experimental methods, particularly in the areas of 'scaling up' and extending the domain of interest to more politically sensitive areas (like governance).

One of the first experiments in the political economy of governance, my area of special interest, was carried out by Leonard Wantchekon. I have known Leonard for many years. He grew up in a small village in the West African country of Benin. He was a leftist student activist fighting for democracy in his country and was expelled from the University of Benin and later jailed for many months. He told me how he finally escaped from prison in 1986, fled to Nigeria, then to Canada, before doing his doctorate at Northwestern University in the US. Now a professor at Princeton, he had contacts with some of the past student activists in Benin who were by now important politicians, and with their help, he carried out actual experiments in political campaigns to see how voters in Benin reacted to different political-economic messages. Unless you are lucky to have such political connections or know some NGO which will

Policy Economics and the Indian Elite 279

follow your (expensive to carry out) suggestions, it is difficult for others to do many of the experiments.

Not involved in the application of such experimental methods, and as a political economist, I have all along felt more comfortable in trying to understand what has happened than in prescribing what should be done. Following the title of a debut collection of short stories by the writer Jhumpa Lahiri, I am more like 'an interpreter of maladies' than a medicine-prescribing 'doctor'. (Lahiri got the idea of her book title when she heard from an acquaintance in Boston that he worked as an interpreter for a doctor who had a number of Russian patients who had difficulty in explaining their ailments in English.) Much of my professional life, I have been trying to get an understanding of the incidence of economic maladies all around me (poverty, unemployment, inequality and insecurity) more than that of finding quick fixes. I am less helpful in response to Lenin's famous question in his 1902 pamphlet 'What is to be done?' One year later, in 1903, Bernard Shaw, incidentally an admirer of Lenin, wrote his play *Man and Superman* where he says, 'Those who can, do; those who can't, teach.' That probably describes me.

In 1998, when Amartya Sen got the Nobel Prize it was a big event for us development economists. Even though the prize was announced primarily for his contributions to social choice theory (in particular, his exploration of the conditions that permit aggregation of individual preferences into collective decisions in a way that is consistent with individual rights), the prize committee also referred to his work on famines and the welfare of the poorest people in developing countries. Even this fractional recognition of his work on economic development came after a long neglect of the field in the mainstream of economics. The only other development economist recipients of the prize had been Arthur Lewis and Ted Schultz simultaneously decades back.

As development economists, we all grew up on the classic 1954 article by Arthur Lewis, which, as a combination of economic theory and a sense of rich panoramic history, still remains exemplary in the whole of economics. As someone born in the island of St Lucia in the Caribbean, he was the first economist from a developing country to get the Nobel Prize. I met him at Princeton shortly after he got it. John Lewis, another professor at Princeton who was a specialist on development aid and on India, whom I had known for some years, took me to have lunch with Arthur Lewis, whom I found to be a simple and charming man. (I still remember him, with his suit and tie, lying down flat on the floor of the faculty lounge to show John a particular exercise that he was advising John to do to cope with his back problem.) Shortly afterwards, I was invited, I think by Carlos Díaz Alejandro and Gus Ranis at Yale, to contribute a chapter in a book they were editing in honour of Arthur Lewis. In this chapter, I formalized and expanded on an idea on some historical aspects of tropical trade that he had exposited in a set of lectures in 1969 in Sweden.

From Lewis and Schultz there was some continuity to Amartya-da in their development thinking. Amartya-da's early work followed the structural role of labour in the development process that Lewis envisaged; and his later work on education and health followed on Schultz's emphasis on human capital. But in the intervening period, both social choice theory and development economics, in which Amartya-da specialized, had been marginalized, so much so that I remember on the day of the announcement of his prize in 1998, I met a young well-known American macro-economist, who asked me, with genuine puzzlement in his voice, 'I understand he is an Indian, what kind of economics did he do?' This also indicated to me how absurdly narrow the specialization in different fields in economics had become.

Amartya Sen is, of course, much more well known among philosophers. When he was at Oxford, the philosophy seminar where Ronald Dworkin, Derek Parfit, Amartya Sen and Jerry Cohen taught, argued and sparred with one another used to be described by students as 'Star Wars'. (Before he went to Harvard, Berkeley economics and philosophy departments made him a joint offer; before the offer could be made, I was appointed the chair of the committee that was in charge of writing a report on his work. The usual procedure in such committees was to do a detailed evaluation of the candidate's major pieces of research. I noticed that the philosophers in the committee were too impatient about this procedure, considered such an evaluation of Amartya-da's research redundant, and wanted to get out the offer immediately.) Beyond economics and philosophy, Amartya Sen has, of course, been one of the most celebrated public intellectuals in the world.

A Nobel Prize gives the winner, among other things, a megaphone; some use it in the international public-intellectual fora to draw attention to their favourite causes, others do not exercise that option. Among economists I know well, I have seen Joe Stiglitz, Paul Krugman and Amartya Sen making good use of this megaphone, but others, like George Akerlof, have been more diffident in using it.

As a public intellectual, Amartya-da is widely known as an untiring champion for the cause of mass education, healthcare, and women's autonomy, and for promoting democracy and public reasoning, values that he has explicitly linked in much of his later work, notably in his book *Development as Freedom*. In 2006, in a public conversation in San Francisco between him and me that was organized by the *California* magazine, I pointed to him a possible contradiction in his public causes, and his prompt answer was an indicator of his clear thinking on such important issues; it also happened to bring out one strand of commonality between his and my research. So I am taking here the liberty of quoting an excerpt from that conversation, which was published in that magazine.

> PB: Democracy obviously has been a favorite cause of yours. Another favorite cause has been that of mass education, basic health, and women's rights. When you combine these two sets of causes, one cannot help but notice that there could be a disjuncture, not in the realm of your ideas but in the real world of politics. The conditions of basic health and sanitation and primary and secondary education are simply appalling in India. Yet, the electorate does not penalize politicians when they fail to deliver these services. And the conditions continue to be appalling, election after election.
>
> AS: A very interesting question, Pranab. Let me say three things. First, democracy is basically a permissive system. Some of the issues of deprivation are very easy to seize in terms of media and political opposition. Like famines. Hard to win elections after a famine. It's hard to prevent newspapers writing editorials, unless you censor them, criticizing the government if famines occur. So these things get immediately politicized. The rest require a lot of effort. In India, the gender issue—when I first started working on it, you were one of the first to be involved in that. You wrote this great paper 'Life and Death Questions in India'. I think you have had the same experience as I had, the people treating it as your and my amiable eccentricity that we are concerned with the gender issue. But nobody thinks

like that today. If the Indian Parliament is debating today as to how to ensure that a third of the parliamentarians are women, something has changed—and changed as a result of politics, particularly the women's movement ... So my second point is that the democratic critique is still, even in India, making a difference.

My third point is that democracy is primarily, as I see it, not just voting, but public reasoning, government by discussion. To initiate the discussion is a contribution to democracy. You might not have thought that your 'Life and Death Questions' was a contribution to Indian democratic practice, but that's what it was because a lot of people read it and were inspired by it and moved by it.

I have known Amartya-da well since my student days in Cambridge and spent many hours chatting with him on various economic, political, cultural and, of course, personal issues (he has been a mentor for me for many decades), at different international venues, often at his homes in Santiniketan, Delhi, Oxford, London, and the two Cambridges. He is a connoisseur of good food and wine. Once, I remember he invited me to his home near Harvard, and when I arrived, he said he had made a reservation for the two of us (his wife, Emma, was away to England) at a nearby Chinese restaurant (both of us like Chinese food). While walking to the restaurant, I was puzzled seeing him carrying a paper bag with a bottle of the choicest wine from his cellar. As soon as we entered the restaurant, the manager did, without any exchange of words, what seemed to me like a familiar routine: He relieved Amartya-da of his paper bag and disappeared into the kitchen. Apparently, the restaurant did not yet have the licence to serve alcohol. So a kettle came to our table, from which the waiter kept on filling our little tea cups with superb French wine instead of green tea. I was more than a willing accomplice in this delicious illegality.

After his Nobel Prize, it became more difficult to have leisurely chats with him, as the demands on his time from others multiplied manifold. When his prize was announced, I got an urgent message from Krishna Raj then editor of the *Economic and Political Weekly* that they were bringing out a special issue on Amartya-da that week for which he needed an article from me by the next day, which I had to fax. This brief article was mostly on his research, but I could not help taking the opportunity to comment on the hoopla in India that I had already started hearing about. Maybe I had been jaded by knowing and watching a number of Nobel laureates around me in the US, and the agitation in a prize-starved country of billion-plus was probably understandable. But I thought it was a bit too much when I heard that numerous boys born that week in Kolkata hospitals were named 'Amartya' by excited parents. So in that article I quoted a couple of famous lines from Bertolt Brecht's play *Life of Galileo*: When a dispirited pupil Andrea on the occasion of Galileo's fall says, 'Unhappy is the land that has no hero', Galileo replies, 'No, Andrea, unhappy is the land that needs a hero.'

This quote had a fallout. When, in a couple of weeks after my article came out, Amartya-da went to India on a triumphal arrival, he was almost immediately interviewed by Doordarshan (then the main public TV station). Within a few minutes of the interview, the breathlessly effusive interviewer asked for his reaction to Pranab Bardhan's criticizing him in the pages of *EPW*. Amartya-da wanted to know what I had said, and he was told about the quote from Galileo. His answer was, Amartya-da later told me, 'Pranab was criticizing not me, but you.'

Later, once in Santiniketan, when both of us were on a short visit, he asked me over tea at his home when I'd be taking the train back to Kolkata. When I told him that I was going back by the afternoon Santiniketan Express the next day, he immediately said he too was taking the same train and proposed that we travelled together so that we could chat on the way. I immediately said, 'No way, I am not going to travel in the same compartment as you; you are like a film star, I'd be stampeded by the adoring, autograph- and photo-hunting crowds around you.' (In my mind flashed the scene in Satyajit Ray's 1966 movie *The Hero*, where the matinee idol was travelling in a train and at every station where the train stopped the crowds were desperate to have a glimpse of him.)

The next afternoon, I took my seat in a different compartment in the train, and prepared to get cosy, as I usually did on such journeys, with a Bengali novel or magazine. At one point before the train started, I heard some commotion and saw from my window large numbers of people on the platform rushing to a compartment a few doors away. But unfortunately, in the journey that afternoon, I could hardly avoid the Amartya Sen-phenomenon. My fellow passengers had seen him board the train; soon, my whole compartment was agog with loud multilateral conversations about his various public achievements, speculations about his salary, about his personal life, his mother, his first wife (who was an accomplished Bengali writer) and the circumstances of their divorce, his children (one of these children was a film actress, whom did she resemble, the father or the mother), his various wives and other women in his life, and so on. A large part of it was the usual half-truths and imaginary gossip that hover around a celebrity, but it spoiled my reading plans as I could not plug my ears off the very public discussion around somebody whom and whose family members I happened to know reasonably well. Thus, I avoided being stampeded, but not being bombarded with unnecessary and gratuitous babble.

The Western admirers of Amartya Sen as a public intellectual may not be aware that he is actually in a long line of globally engaged cultural elite that Bengal has produced. (This is true to some extent of the elite elsewhere in India as well, particularly around Chennai and Mumbai.) One aspect of this phenomenon is worth reflecting on. These members of the cultural elite were well versed in the manifold offerings of the West, but they came to them with a solid grounding in the cultural wealth of India. Take Ram Mohan Roy (1772–1833). He was, as Nehru describes him in his *Discovery of India*, 'deeply versed in Indian thought and philosophy, a scholar of Sanskrit, Persian and Arabic ... a product of the mixed Hindu–Muslim culture ... the world's first scholar of the science of Comparative Religion'. He contributed to the development of Bengali prose. He was a social reformer in Hindu society, actively engaged in serious religious debates with Christian missionaries in India, and a champion of women's rights and the freedom of the press (standing up against colonial censorship). Yet, when he went to England, he caused some stir as the urbane face of a reforming Indian society, was active in campaigning for the 1832 Reform Act as a step to British democracy. The philosopher Jeremy Bentham reportedly even began a campaign to elect him to the British Parliament (but Roy caught meningitis and died in Bristol soon after).

The line of cosmopolitan Bengali public intellectuals later, of course, included Rabindranath Tagore, the statistician Mahalanobis, the scientists Satyen Bose and Jagadish Chandra Bose, Satyajit Ray and Amartya Sen—all of whom were deeply immersed in indigenous culture and vernacular literature. I have already mentioned that Mahalanobis was a whizz-kid in the Bengali cultural world and that he was deeply involved with Tagore. I have also already mentioned about Satyen Bose's enthusiasm for science writing in Bengali. Jagadish Chandra

Bose was not just an international pioneer in the investigation of radio and microwave optics and of plant physiology, he was the father of science fiction writing in Bengali, and his 1922 Bengali collection of essays *Abyakta* is a landmark in Bengali literature. Many people do not know that Satyajit Ray's main source of income was not his internationally famous films, but writing books in Bengali mainly for children and adolescents—many Bengali youths knew him more as the creator of a famous detective character 'Feluda' and the editor of a popular children's magazine, *Sandesh*, founded by his grandfather. (When our son, Titash, was growing up, the task of reading bedtime stories to him was on me, and I read many of the 'Feluda' stories to him in Bengali.) When I went to college, one of the first things I read of Amartya Sen was an article by him on unemployment in a popular magazine in lucid Bengali prose. I also remember in the early 1990s, one day at Ashok Rudra's home in Santiniketan, the two of us and Amartya-da spent a whole evening on honing good Bengali synonyms for technical terms that the latter was going to use for a Bengali book of his on economics.

This grounding in the vernacular for these and other Bengalis (including myself) creates an asymmetry in our encounter with Western intellectuals. Quite often, it has struck me that we know much more of their literature, culture, history and philosophy than they do of ours. This gives Bengalis (and other like-minded Indians) a certain confidence in dealing with Western influence—we bask in its illumination and absorb it to the fullest, without getting unanchored from the rich Indian indigenous roots.

Recently when the *New York Times* books section interviewed Amartya-da and asked him what moves him most in a work of literature, he said: 'I don't think there is a shared object that moves me in every case. Rather, it is how a book develops and makes room for interesting ideas. In one way or another, we should be able to accommodate "Hamlet" and the sonnets, Goethe's "Faust" and the fifth-century Sanskrit poet and playwright Kalidasa's "Meghaduta"(The Cloud-Messenger).' When they asked him which books were currently on his nightstand, his reply counted in the same breath the recently published biography of Mary Wollstonecraft by Sylvana Tomaselli as well as some well-known selections from Bengali poems by Tagore and Nazrul Islam, and the third-century Indian writer Shudraka's revolutionary play 'Mricchakatika' (The Little Clay Cart).

When I discussed with my friend Sudipta Kaviraj at Columbia University about this particular asymmetry in our encounters with the West, he, in his typical erudite way, referred me to the discussion in Georg Wilhelm Friedrich Hegel of the 'master-slave dialectic': Hegel says that the 'slave'—that is, all people who have less power and live under someone else's dominance—have to be cleverer in their understanding and negotiation of the world, because they have only intelligence as their weapon. Cognitively, they thus have a fuller view of what the world is really like than the 'masters'. Sudipta calls this 'cosmopolitanism from below' in the colonizer–colonized intellectual interaction.

Of course, there was a time when the colonizer simply dismissed the cultural wealth of the colonized. Lord Macaulay's well-known *Minute on Indian Education* (1835) contended that 'a single shelf of a good European library was worth the whole native literature of India and Arabia'. The arrogant parading of such colossal ignorance on the part of the colonizer persisted for more than a century after. What to me is more interesting is the reaction of the colonized elite to this, even lingering in the post-colonial era. Some part of this elite remained imitative in fawning admiration of the West—'mimic men' to use the title of a V.S. Naipaul novel. Another part, probably larger in number today, resorted to resentful rejection and hostility to the West.

These latter in their politics belong both to the left and the right. The left will give the usual anti-imperialist rationale for their rejection of the West, even though in their rejection of the Western cultural legacy of the liberal order they will, ironically, quote in justification either Marx–Engels or, more recently, Foucault–Derrida, as if the latter are some Eastern sages.

The right in India will show disdain for Western culture, harking back to the glorious past of the Hindu civilization where everything that is worth knowing is in the ancient Vedas (or in Islamic culture, to the glorious earlier part of the previous millennium). I have often noted a streak of deep inferiority complex underlying both these strands of intellectual discourse of 'protesting too much'—on the left, a licking of the wounds left by the imperialists and blaming all present failures to them (as if we don't have the capacity to mess up on our own), and on the right, empty bragging to cover up their intellectual hollowness, or what Joseph Conrad once termed the 'exasperated vanity of ignorance' (and, of course, lapping it up if by any chance praise from some Western institutions comes their way). In contrast with these strands, the leading type of Bengali (and as I said some other Indian) cultural discourse has been somewhat exceptional in confidently assimilating whatever is good in Western culture and yet not losing one's footing in their indigenous legacy of language, literature and culture.

Unlike those with this kind of confident assimilation, there are others for whom militant antipathy is often the default reaction. Let me give an example from the mundane experience of adversarial social interaction with Westerners. I was once travelling in a car driven by a fellow Indian on a California freeway. At one point, I saw a car in the adjoining lane when the driver lowered his window and shouted at us, 'Go back to fucking Mexico!' My companion became very angry, but I tried to calm him down, and said that unless some direct harm was caused, he should only feel pity for such ignorant racists (just as when I first read Lord Macaulay's remark quoted above about the literature of India and Arabia, I did not feel anger, only pity for his ignorance). My Indian companion then grumbled, 'In any case, why should I go to Mexico?' I told him that the confusion was understandable as Mexico shares some latitudes with parts of India (Mumbai and Mexico City are roughly on the same latitude) and the skin colour of people, and that the stereotypical immigrant in California was more likely to be from Mexico than from India. I also thought to myself about the advice that the Duke gives to Desdemona's father in *Othello*: 'The robb'd that smiles steals something from the thief/He robs himself that spends a bootless grief.'

The confusion about Mexicans and Indians also reminds me of an incident I faced in San Francisco one night as I was returning to Berkeley after watching a late-night movie at the San Francisco International Film Festival. It was about midnight, and I had to rush to catch the last underground (BART) train to Berkeley. Being the last train, it was jampacked, I could barely stand, clutching a handle inside the train. Very soon, I found out that next to me and pressed against me was a drunken Mexican. Even he mistook me for a fellow Mexican and started speaking to me loudly in Spanish (as if I was a long-lost amigo). I tried to tell him that I did not speak Spanish; when it finally dawned on him, he then switched to English and, much to my distress, soon started to vent his anger in that language against 'gringos'. In the pressing crowd, it was difficult for me to move away, as he went on '... You see these gringos have stolen our land ... California belongs to us ... but take it from me, we're going to take this land back ... You see all these gringos, they may look nice, but let me tell you, they're all full of shit.' I was thinking if a fist fight was to start then, in that crammed space, I was sure to get some blows and my jaw broken. Fortunately, the surrounding 'gringos' remained resolutely impassive.

In parts of Western academia, there were some other ramifications of the colonizer–colonized cultural interaction that came to my attention when I settled in Berkeley in the late 1970s. I saw in the left circles in Berkeley and elsewhere in coastal US an environment of encouraging the tolerance for a certain facile form of 'third-worldism'. Among radical or even liberal Western intellectuals it gave rise to a lot of chest-beating for the harm their governments and businesses had done elsewhere. Without denying the ugly reality of this harm, and the genuine distress about this among many of my leftist friends, I should also mention that I have sometimes sensed in others a whiff of pious condescension in the sympathy or a kind of showy competitive radical chic. I remember once reading a satirical verse on this:

> I am sorry for what my people did to your people,
> It was a nasty job.
> Please note the change of attitude
> On the bumper of my Saab.

(At the same time, I think V.S. Naipaul in his typical dyspeptic way goes a bit too far on this when he pours scorn on some Western radicals, 'the people who substitute doctrine for knowledge and irritation for concern, the revolutionaries who visit centres of revolution with return air tickets ... all those people who in the end do no more than celebrate their own security'.)

And taking advantage of the guilt trip of the Western liberals, a whole section of 'third world' intellectuals had covered their mediocrity with anti-imperialist or post modern rhetoric and also sometimes touching on holier-than-thou race-gender sensitivity buttons, all with the purpose of smoothening their climb up the academic ladder, which otherwise would have been difficult for them to reach. For a time, I became rather allergic to such rhetoric, the fashionable atoning/appeasing kind on one side and the self-serving kind on the other, proliferating in seminars and campus debates. These games are, of course, more easily played in the softer disciplines in academia, but I also remember once sharing a cab in New York going to JFK Airport with a Latin American mathematical economist who tried hard to evoke third world camaraderie in me and went about telling me that 'the gringos even steal our theorems'.

14
Academic Life in Berkeley

Being in Berkeley for more than four decades, I have met and encountered many leftists and several of them are/were radical in their politics—though in recent years the radical fervour has been somewhat on the decline even in Berkeley. I remember reading some time back one east-coast journalist describing Berkeley, with a dollop of exaggeration, as moving from being the left capital of the US to being its gourmet capital. This transition is, of course, most well known in the case of Alice Waters who, a Berkeley activist in the 1960s, started her iconic restaurant Chez Panisse in the next decade, though she herself considers the novel approach to food embodied in that restaurant—insistence on fresh ingredients and cooperative relations with local farmers—as growing out of the same counter-culture movement. (Her transition was, of course, much more agreeable than some of the militant Black Panther leaders of 1960s Oakland turning to Christian evangelism.)

In campus politics, the decline in radical fervour became plain to see in the first decade of this century during the Iraq War. There were protests in the campus, but nowhere with the same intensity that was observed during the Vietnam War. I think this was partly because the military draft had been lifted meanwhile so young men from middle and upper classes, which are in large numbers even in a public university like Berkeley, were no longer conscripted—wars in America now (as has been the case always in India) are largely fought by poor people. So the Iraq War was not an immediate threat or interruption of life for the young in the campus.

Also, wars are now less dependent on soldiers on the battle field, and more on computers and precision-guided weapons. Targets in West Asia are hit by missiles directed from a situation room thousands of miles away. A large part of conducting a war is now almost like an amplified version of a video game played by young military operators. I have often told my American friends that without improvements in American school education, particularly in geography and history, the rest of the world is in great peril. You can almost imagine a military operator with poor education exclaiming from his air-conditioned office in a military base somewhere in the Arizona desert: 'Oops, I just wiped out the wrong town/village in whatever is the name of that shithole country where we are fighting!'

And, of course, with poor knowledge of world history, American politicians and military planners heedlessly bumble into alien places like giant zombies, causing mindless destruction and mayhem. (When Titash was in school, I saw how little of history of other countries American kids learn. As an attempt at partial compensation, part of my bedtime stories for him for a time involved books on world history. The most useful book for this purpose was Jawaharlal Nehru's *Glimpses of World History*, which he wrote in the early 1930s from British prisons in the form of 196 letters to his young daughter, Indira, in lucid English prose. These were letters, written from his heart, introducing his daughter to the story of human civilization as it unfolded in different parts of the world. I thought Titash would be bored after a point, but he remained an enthusiastic listener till the end, largely because of Nehru's style of storytelling meant for a young loved one. When the book came out the *New York Times* described it as 'one of the most remarkable books ever written'.)

Another contrast with the Vietnam War time was that many otherwise liberal Jewish members of the faculty and students (wrongly) thought that the Iraq War would enhance Israel's security. I remember around the beginning of the war, Andrei Shleifer came from Harvard to give a seminar at Berkeley, and we took him to the Faculty Club for lunch. It so happened that morning the *New York Times* had carried a full-page petition signed by many Nobel laureates to stop the war. My friend George Akerlof was one of the signatories. At the lunch table, Andrei, who was an ardent supporter of the war, started taunting George about his signature in the petition (the subtext was as if he was betraying the Zionist cause). George became uncomfortable and started scratching his head in some confusion. I could not take it any more. I turned to him and said, 'George, you did absolutely the right thing. Andrei is not realizing the big mistake he's making.'

In more recent years, I found the leftists among students and young faculty much more preoccupied with identity issues (race, gender, sexual orientation, etc.) than on class issues. Over the years, the gulf between them and socially conservative but class-conscious blue-collar workers has widened on such issues. I used to associate identity issues more with the right wing earlier, but this has been a major change lately. This is a big problem now for social democrats in their efforts to mobilize the support of working classes.

On economic–systemic issues, the radicals I came across in Berkeley and elsewhere, mainly among non-economists, were often utopian socialists. They were moved by the primacy of social justice in their value system and did not have the patience to think through the various trade-offs that one has to keep in mind in a real-world economy or polity, even in pursuit of worthwhile social justice goals. For example, for effective redistribution and vigorous social welfare over the long haul, one needs to ensure a viable system of continuous innovations in place to keep the economy prospering and the state coffers filled, and this may require some encouragement of capitalist enterprise and profit-minded creative thinking. In social–democratic Scandinavian countries, by and large, they have worked out a system in which workers have an assured, well-functioning welfare safety net, but they have also made sure that the incentives for private business innovations remain strong—in the global index of innovations, the Scandinavian countries remain among the highest in the world ranking, in spite of high tax rates.

Economists are more adept at thinking of the various trade-offs involved in the pursuit of social justice, but many of them are conditioned to think that there is an inevitable equity–efficiency trade-off—so that if you want more social justice and equality, you have to give up on efficiency, and waste a great deal of resources that could have been used in enlarging the social pie for everybody; in such cases, redistributive transfers have been compared to carrying water in 'leaky buckets'. I think recent advances in economic theory and actual experience have shown that equity and efficiency can actually be complementary even in an otherwise broadly capitalist framework. For example, a properly designed and implemented land reform even in a private enterprise agricultural context may improve both productivity and equality. Leftists need to further explore the various possibilities of this kind (I'll come back to this).

Leftists are in general correct in viewing many economists' approach as much too narrow in being individual self-interest-centric, that they often overlook the importance of community-level cooperation, where egalitarian efforts may build trust and solidarity. An unequal and divided society makes social cooperation difficult, and may, in the end, harm all. As the Anglo-Irish writer Oliver Goldsmith famously said in his 1770 poem 'The Deserted Village', which I read in school: 'Ill fares the land, to hastening ills a prey/Where wealth accumulates, and men decay.'

Of course, as I have discussed before in the context of anarchists and communitarians, there are forces of both conflicts and cooperation at the community level, and one has to be wary of the romantic illusions some nurture about the local community. If one takes the three social coordination mechanisms that are important in most societies—of the state, the market and the community—all three have both many advantages and pitfalls, and a sane social thinker has to take a balanced approach. Such balance is often missing in both the left and the right.

In economics, the analytical framework to study both conflicts and cooperation in interactive human decision-making is provided by game theory. I was first exposed to elementary game theory when the professors in my undergraduate days in Presidency College, Kolkata, told us about the ideas in the landmark 1944 book *Theory of Games and Economic Behaviour* by the mathematician John von Neumann and the economist Oskar Morgenstern. Then, for me, there was a long gap. In my studies and research in the two Cambridges, I was too busy with the theory of economic growth, and, on my return to India, I was preoccupied with village studies and analysis of rural institutions in India. So when I went to Berkeley I found out that people did not do much of growth theory any more and the new fad was about game theory—transformed in the intervening period by the application of the ideas of John Nash, the Princeton mathematician, and also by those of the Berkeley economist John Harsanyi and Reinhard Selten of Bonn (the three of them got the Nobel Prize in 1994 for their contributions). I decided to attend a couple of courses in Berkeley in game theory (including one by my then colleague Drew Fudenberg, now at MIT) to make myself familiar with the basic concepts and their applications, but I could not say I really mastered it.

John von Neumann was the Hungarian polymath who had revolutionized several subfields of mathematics and physics, but also made path-breaking contributions to economics and in the invention of the atomic bomb, nuclear energy and digital computing. Some people think he was probably the most intelligent person who ever lived (possibly using a special definition of intelligence). I once met his daughter, Marina Whitman, an economist, and simple-mindedly asked her how it felt to grow up as the daughter of such a genius. I still remember her cryptic answer: 'Better than being the son of a genius.' I see that in a recent biography of von Neumann by Ananyo Bhattacharya, Marina went a bit further about her father: 'He tended to be oblivious to the emotional needs of those around him.' Marina was two when her parents divorced; her father agreed to let her live with him only after she turned twelve, when he could be sure that she was 'approaching the age of reason'.

I have heard many stories about him. When at work at the Institute of Advanced Study at Princeton, he'd often play very loud German martial music on the gramophone in his office, which used to annoy people in the neighbouring offices, including Albert Einstein. Despite being a bad driver, he loved driving, often while reading books, leading to various accidents and arrests. In the one-hour train journey from Princeton to Penn station in New York, he'd challenge anyone to give him the toughest mathematical problem which he'd then solve before the train reached Penn station.

He died of cancer at age fifty-three. After his terminal diagnosis, for the first time in his life, he faced something he could not take control of, and I read somewhere that for a time the neighbours used to hear at night the howls coming from his home. But on his deathbed, he reportedly entertained his brother by reciting the first few lines of each page from Goethe's *Faust*, word for word, by heart.

John Nash's life was written up by the journalist Sylvia Naser (I remember discussing it with her when we met once) in her book *A Beautiful Mind*, later made into an Oscar-winning movie. The book covers Nash's years at Princeton and MIT, and also his years of struggle with paranoid schizophrenia and slow recovery (and the strength and large-heartedness of his El Salvadoran wife, Alicia, throughout—Alicia did physics at MIT and was a student of Nash). The Nobel Committee had considered Nash's name for quite some time, but was unsure about his mental condition, lest something embarrassing happen at the ceremony. Jörgen Weibull, a Swedish economist, was discreetly sent to Princeton to check up on him, and Weibull came back with renewed confidence as an advocate for awarding the prize to him. (John Nash and Alicia died in 2015 when their taxi crashed on their way home from the airport)

The Nobel Committee's anxiety about avoiding embarrassment at the ceremony reminds me of a story I have heard about the Physics Nobel laureate—and the great prankster—Richard Feynman. When the prize was announced in October 1965, Feynman was, of course, enormously pleased, but then one of his Caltech colleagues told him that at the ceremony he had to be very careful. After getting the prize from the king of Sweden, he'd have to retreat with his face towards the king, he should not show his back to him as that'd be disrespectful; and, mind you, there were some steps he'd have to negotiate while retreating, and it'd be embarrassing if he were to tumble there. So then Feynman started practising walking backwards in the staircases of Caltech. Soon he became so good at it, he started leaping two steps backwards at a time. Caltech students apparently used to gather and observe this strange sight of the big-name professor walking backwards on the staircase, jumping two steps at a time. I don't know if he performed this feat in front of the king the following December.

As with game theory, I also attended some courses in Berkeley in another relatively new subject for me, psychology and economics (later called behavioural economics). In particular, I liked the course jointly taught by George Akerlof and Daniel Kahneman (then at Berkeley psychology department, later at Princeton). I remember during that time I was once talking to George, when my friend and colleague the econometrician Tom Rothenberg came over and asked me to describe in one sentence what I had learned so far from the Akerlof–Kahneman course. I said, somewhat flippantly: 'Kahneman is telling us that people are dumber than we economists think, and George is telling us that people are nicer than we economists think.' George liked this description so much that in the next class, he started the lecture with my remark. On the dumbness of people, I later read somewhere that Kahneman's earlier fellow Israeli co-author Amos Tversky once said when asked what he was working on, 'My colleagues, they study artificial intelligence; me, I study natural stupidity.'

Of course, by dumbness or stupidity, in this context, economists really mean departures from rationality, and knowing that people are often irrational, behavioural economics is really about the systematic departures from rationality which give the subject its analytical coherence—that there is method in the madness as Polonius says in 'Hamlet'. And in the departures from self-centred individual rationality, social norms and fellow-feeling (like empathy and sympathy and social solidarity) often play an important role in individual preference formation. In Berkeley, I had a friendly colleague for many years, Matthew Rabin (now at Harvard), from whose talks and writings I have learnt a great deal on fairness in social preferences in a modified game-theory framework, apart from common human errors in probabilistic reasoning and human frailties like individual self-control problems. These are big changes in traditional ways of thinking in economics.

I might as well take this occasion to make a brief comment on the ongoing changes in economics as a discipline. Over the last fifty years, it has been transformed into a discipline that is highly nuanced, multifaceted, socially conscious, quite aware of the absence of self-regulating markets or of the benevolent state, wary of informational traps and uncertainty beyond measurable risks, and deeply learning from insights from other disciplines. While there is much more to learn and discover in ways of handling the complexity of social processes, one cannot help pointing out that the lay public and journalists, and even academics from some other disciplines, go on criticizing economics in ways and with caricatures that are often decades outdated—it feels like, as Keynes so memorably expressed in 1936, they are 'distilling their frenzy from some academic scribbler of a few years back', maybe 'some defunct economist'. Nevertheless, there is something in what my friend Perry Anderson, the British historian and essayist in the New Left tradition, tells me. He says that he misses in modern economics, the grandeur of the great books in economics in the past (say, from writers like Adam Smith to Joseph Schumpeter). I told him that there are at least two reasons for this. One is, of course, the extremely specialized nature of current economics which makes it very difficult for one writer to fully grasp the whole subject in all its refinements. The other reason probably has something to do with the American predominance in the subject in the last fifty years or more. I have noted that for various reasons even the most brilliant American economists seem to lack the grand sense of history that was there in some of the earlier (European) economists.

There was one important branch of economics, environmental economics, where I wanted to take some courses, but did not get around to doing it, partly because there was no course offered in our department (as it was left to the separate agricultural and resource economics department in the campus). I myself did quite a bit of research on the local environmental resources (irrigation water, forestry, fishery, etc.) which are crucial to the livelihoods of the rural poor all over the world, and on how the management of these local commons depends on the socio-economic characteristics of the community (including inequality). In this connection, I once participated in a detailed study of forty-eight irrigation communities in Tamil Nadu (one of the few times I took part in village surveys outside West Bengal) with the help of my collaborators in the Madras Institute of Development Studies.

But on the *global* commons, I think initially I used to underestimate (or did not pay enough attention to) the severity of the effects of global warming—a problem mainly caused by the rich of the world over many decades and that the world's poor would bear the main brunt. Here is another policy problem where the contours of some of the major solutions are by now reasonably well-known, but the political economy of the needed international coordination and collective sacrifice and climate aid (even reparations) to the poor is extremely difficult to manage.

Looking back, I think it was the senior Japanese economist Hirofumi Uzawa who, in conversation, first made me conscious of the seriousness of the global environmental problem (long before I read the papers of environmental economists like Bill Nordhaus, Nick Stern, Marty Weitzman or Partha Dasgupta). I came to know Uzawa first when we were both working on the theory of economic growth. We used to correspond when I was still a student at Cambridge, England, and we finally met at Cambridge, Massachusetts, at the initiative of my friends George Akerlof, Joe Stiglitz and Mrinal Datta Chaudhuri (all three of them had gone from MIT to attend the summer workshop on economic growth organized by Uzawa in Chicago just a few weeks before that).

Politically, he was on the left, and when he resigned from his position at the University of Chicago at the end of the 1960s, he told me he had mentioned the Vietnam War as one of the reasons why he decided to leave the US and go back to Japan. Earlier, I had also heard a bizarre story about Uzawa's interaction with the econometrician Marc Nerlove when they were both at Stanford. This must be the early 1960s. Apparently, they were neighbours, and when Nerlove reportedly once proposed that they should share costs in building a common nuclear shelter underneath their homes, Uzawa refused to have anything to do with this. This enraged Nerlove and he said, as and when the nuclear war would break out if the Uzawas at that point wanted to take refuge in the shelter Nerlove was going to build underneath his house, they'd definitely be denied access. After some time, Nerlove had second thoughts, and came back and said that he'd allow Uzawa's children to take refuge in his shelter, but not Uzawa and his wife. To which Uzawa apparently said that he'd not allow his children to go there, as when the Nerloves would run out of food in the shelter, they might eat up the Uzawa children!

Uzawa became an environmental activist when he went back to Japan (starting with his participation in the protests against the construction of Narita airport). He once visited our home in Berkeley. By that time, he had grown a long white beard, and I told him that he looked like the 'wise man from the East'. Other Japanese economists had told me he was by then a guru of the active environmental movement in Japan.

In Berkeley, over the years, I have had the good fortune to have many talented Ph students. My style of PhD supervision is a bit of the laissez-faire kind; I do not enjoy breathing down the necks of students urging them to perform, I let them be, and when they have something to show me I read it carefully and give them comments. This leads to some sorting out; I think I attracted more students who prefer this style—of course, in my areas of specialization, like economic development, political economy or international trade.

My academically successful students from Berkeley whose doctoral dissertation committees I chaired include Eric Verhoogen and Suresh Naidu (both now professors at the Columbia University), Ken Kletzer (at the University of California, Santa Cruz), Bruce Wydick (at the University of San Francisco), Eric Fisher (at Cal Polytechnic), Jeff Dayton-Johnson (now dean at the Middlebury Institute of International Studies), Leonard Cheng (now president of Lingnan University in Hong Kong), Lemin Wu (at Peking University), Michael Kevane (at Santa Clara University), and Maurice Kugler (at

George Mason University). Of these, I have published joint papers with Kletzer and Dayton-Johnson. A larger number of my PhD students have been at international organizations like the World Bank (for example, John Giles, Margaret Miller, and Yongmei Zhou, who has now left the bank and is at Peking University). One of my PhD students, Marcelo Tokman, was for a time the energy minister in Chile.

Something unusual happened in the case of Michael Kevane. He was a good student, and after passing the PhD qualifying test, he went off to Burkina Faso to research on structural aspects of the rural economy there. But shortly after he reached there, there was a bad famine as a result of which the whole economy almost collapsed, and there was no way he could collect the kind of data that he needed and carry out the various aspects of his interesting research proposal. He sent an SOS to me and George Akerlof, the other member of his dissertation committee. He had two options: one was to come back and do a dissertation on something completely different, and the other was for him to stay on and still do it on the Burkina Faso economy, but the famine would not allow him to do a standard economics dissertation—it would be more like how a society coped with such an economic disaster. The latter option would produce something like a treatise in economic anthropology, which was not usually accepted as a doctoral dissertation in an economics department. George and I took the tough and risky decision of letting him follow the latter option, and after some time, he got his degree. This also is an example of an important difference between a doctoral dissertation in the US and that in the UK. In the US, the Ph supervisors have a major say on the acceptability of a dissertation, but in the UK the supervisors cannot be the examiners of a thesis—the latter, one internal from the university and the other from outside, take the decision and you do not know who they will be at the point when you submit the thesis.

There is, however, one aspect of my career choice as a teacher I have always somewhat disliked, which is the examination system and my role in it. I understand the need for it in some form, but I have always taken part in it with some reluctance (my students have sometimes complained to me that I have not given them enough exams and tests during the course). For one thing, during the class exam time, students who hardly ever practise any handwriting on any other occasion have to provide handwritten answers to exam questions, which for many are barely legible. So it is a strenuous job to read what they have written. (I have often suggested the need for the campus to arrange silent typewriters made available to students at exam time.) Secondly, students who have diligently followed the class and taken notes, often reproduce them in a way that makes the teacher feel that he or she is looking at oneself through some kind of funhouse mirror—you recognize in their writing what you said in class, but not quite, it comes to you in a slightly distorted version, which is not a pleasant experience.

In Berkeley, my office was on the sixth floor of a building that housed the mathematics, statistics and economics departments. During the exam season, there was a regular hazard. In many rooms when exams were in progress some unprepared student or other would inevitably want to disrupt/delay the process and deliberately trip the fire alarm. And when the fire alarm went off and you were to evacuate the building, you were not supposed to use the elevator. So with unpleasant frequency in the exam season, I had to walk down six floors and wait outside until— after a considerable length of time—the firemen would give us the all-clear to go back to our offices.

After exams, there is the matter of grading, which is another unpleasant task. The (University of California at Santa Cruz, for a time, adopted the system of not letter grading the student, but that of the teacher writing a short essay on the student's overall performance in the whole term. But such narrative evaluation in place of letter grades has its own problems, even for small classes, including comparability with other places where letter grading is used at the time of admission.) For some (usually undergraduate) students, the grade is considered a negotiable matter, and they'd try hard to ambush you in your office on attempts to jack it up. Sometimes in the case of students with Asian parents, the excuse was that the grade I had given them—even if it were okay with them, they said, would be simply unacceptable to their parents ('If I take this grade B home, my mother will stop eating!').

In the final analysis, I dislike being in the power-asymmetrical situation of me being the grade-giver and this harried young person as the grade-receiver. When I was teaching at MIT, I once had an occasion when I could not refrain from admiring a female graduate student who dramatically turned the tables on this power asymmetry between the examiner and the examinee. This was the day of her PhD qualifying viva test, where we were supposed to ask her questions on her dissertation proposal and her general abilities as an economist. We were four examiners waiting for her to appear. She arrived a little late, but as soon as she entered the room, she went on the offensive. She said: 'Shame on you guys! Shame! You've made me so nervous. I feel jumpy, twitchy, my stomach is queasy, and my palms are all sweaty. Feel 'em, feel 'em! Here!' She outstretched her palms to each of us, one after the other, and we sheepishly had to feel them. In the rest of the hour, she made us hesitant to ask her any tough questions.

15

An International Research Network and Travels

In the mid-1990s, my friend from the September Group Sam Bowles and I were invited by the Chicago-based MacArthur Foundation to form an interdisciplinary and international research network to study the effects of economic inequality, with the two of us as co-directors. I have known Sam for nearly four decades now. He is one of the brightest economists I know, with a large vision and wide-ranging interests that are often lacking in many bright economists. His landmark 2013 book *A Cooperative Species* with his frequent co-author Herb Gintis uses experimental data and evolutionary science to show how genetic and cultural evolution has produced a human species where large numbers make sacrifices to uphold cooperative social norms.

He himself has been socially alert and active in public causes all through his life, starting from writing background papers for Martin Luther King's 1968 Poor People's March to most recently providing leadership in the revamping of undergraduate economics curriculum to include upfront non-standard issues like inequality, the environment and reciprocity and altruism in human behaviour, and making it available free online worldwide. He is also one of the most generous and genial people I know.

When his father was US ambassador to India, his parents sent him to a local Indian school, which, at that time, did not even have a building, only a large tent. Prime Minister Jawaharlal Nehru, his father's friend, once invited the family to tea in the garden at his home and encouraged him and his siblings to explore the interior of the house. At that time, he discovered on Nehru's bedside table a framed passage from Robert Frost's poem ('I have promises to keep/And miles to go before I sleep'), which the eleven-year-old immediately recognized, as Frost was a fellow New Englander he knew about. Sam says he was pretty average in his Delhi school, and there were some Indian kids who were smarter than him, and yet, he asked his mother one day, why were most Indians so poor? (In his small Connecticut home town where he had grown up, there were only two people who were really poor—one was an alcoholic, the other had mental problems.) The same question kept on bugging him when, about a decade later, after his undergraduate education at Yale, he started teaching in a school in northern Nigeria.

The question that Sam and I posed in our research proposal to the MacArthur Foundation was why inequality—contrary to the impression created in traditional economics as being necessary for the incentives for people to strive towards economic prosperity—can actually be quite harmful for the economy; in many important situations, equity and efficiency can be complementary. In particular, we spelled out the need for theoretical and empirical work in both rich and poor countries on four questions:

- How do inequalities affect the efficiency and productivity of farms, firms and other entities, and are there more efficient forms of governance that can be promoted?
- How does inequality affect cooperation in local communities, and thus have an impact on the local environment and other public goods, like neighbourhood safety and other residential amenities, irrigation water, fisheries, forestry and grazing lands?
- How do economic disparities among citizens affect bargaining, policymaking and economic performance at a national level?
- What principles can guide the design of efficient and politically viable policies to alleviate poverty and enhance economic opportunity for the less well off?

Our network had economists, sociologists, anthropologists and political scientists from different countries looking at these questions from different angles. Some of the economists in our group have now become quite well known, like Thomas Piketty from Paris or the recent Nobel laureates Esther Duflo, Abhijit Banerjee and Michael Kremer from Cambridge, Massachusetts. Our group funded some of the early work of Piketty in the tax archives in France, just as we funded a lot of the experimental work of those Nobel laureates in India, Kenya and elsewhere. (Esther was the youngest member of our group; she had not yet finished her PhD at MIT when she joined.) We also had well-known sociologists like Erik Olin Wright, anthropologists like Katherine Newman and political scientists like Adam Przeworski.

The group was generously funded by the MacArthur Foundation for more than ten years starting from the mid-1990s and administered by the Institute of International Studies in Berkeley. Twice a year we had meetings in different parts of the world, where we presented our research results for critical scrutiny and also invited other scholars working on related subjects to present their results. In the US, we mostly met in Berkeley, Chicago or Cambridge, Massachusetts, but we also met in some cities in developing countries, including Beijing, Delhi, Rio de Janeiro and San José (Costa Rica).

We had taken a decision to let individual authors publish their research papers as they saw fit; we had no collective output where our results were centralized (except in a summary form for our periodic research reports to the foundation). A few of us did edit some collections of essays, like Sam and I (and the late Michael Wallerstein) edited a volume called *Globalization and Egalitarian Redistribution* and (with Jean-Marie Baland) a volume titled *Inequality, Cooperation* and *Environmental Sustainability*, both published by Princeton University Press; Abhijit Banerjee, Roland Bénabou and Dilip Mookherjee edited a volume titled *Understanding Poverty*, published by Oxford University Press. Looking back, not having a central reference volume or point of publication for the whole group may not have been a wise decision, as—in its absence—many people now do not know that some of the major work on inequality was done under the auspices of this network, long before the current upsurge in work on inequality.

My own research work in this network was mainly of two kinds. One was the study of the impact of inequality on cooperation in management of irrigation water, particularly in the resolution of water conflicts among farmers (both the theoretical and empirical work was published as some chapters in my 2004 book *Scarcity, Conflicts and Cooperation* published by MIT Press), and on some empirical projects on deforestation in the Himalayan foothills (in collaboration with Dilip Mookherjee). The second kind was on the political economy of governance, in particular with respect to decentralization, in a large multi-year project with Dilip Mookherjee. We collected detailed survey and administrative data from eighty-nine villages in West Bengal, and analysed them and published papers in journals both in India and abroad. In 2006, Dilip and I edited a collection of essays on decentralization in different countries in Asia, Africa and Latin America, titled *Decentralization to Local Governments in Developing Countries: A Comparative Perspective*, published by MIT Press.

As a political and institutional economist, I had been interested in decentralization for a long time, as I was sceptical of the easy reliance of my leftist friends on the top-down or centralized state. (Among the major leftist political leaders in India, a persistent advocate of decentralization was E.M.S. Namboodiripad, who was the chief minister of Kerala between 1957 and 1959 and again between 1967 and 1969. When I was in Kerala, K.N. Raj introduced me to him—I did not have much chance to talk with him, but I had read several of his articles on decentralization.) Yet, unlike some Gandhians and other communitarians I knew, I was wary also about the pitfalls of local governments and communities. Some of these conflicting issues needed detailed empirical work to resolve.

I knew Dilip had been interested in theoretical issues of decentralization in the context of corporate governance of a firm. I talked intensively with him to make him interested in issues of decentralization in the context of development governance. I consider it as some achievement on my part to persuade an accomplished theorist like Dilip to take the plunge into the messy matter of village data collection and analysis to glean insights on the pros and cons of decentralized development. West Bengal, at that time, provided an appropriate locale for this research, as the ruling left government had carried out some significant steps towards decentralized governance. With some local collaborators (particularly Sandip Mitra at the ISI) we carried out large-scale village and household surveys in the state, mainly to study the impact of elected village councils (panchayats) on land reforms and various types of anti-poverty programmes, along with general agricultural performance.

Apart from our own research, for more than ten years the eighteen-member MacArthur network gave me the opportunity to interact with some of the finest minds in social science, and to benefit from the extremely high quality and analytical rigour of the discussion. There were quite a few differences of opinion, cogently argued and expressed, examined and dissected, but there was a degree of convergence on some passionate intellectual commitment to do something about the excruciating problems of inequality and social injustice in the world.

For me, my work with Dilip in West Bengal was also, in some sense, a continuation of my earlier work there with Ashok Rudra, when we had tried to understand the various land relations and institutions at the ground level on the basis of surveys of 110 sample villages. Even as the MacArthur projects ended, Dilip and I continued studying some of our sample villages. Altogether, about three decades of detailed micro-level village survey data analysis had given me some understanding of the ground realities in West Bengal economy and polity.

The left government ruled the state for much of this period, continuously for thirty-four years (1977–2011)—an unprecedented case in the world of a democratically elected communist party rule over a size of population much larger than that of France or the UK, at the state, district, municipal and village council levels. To be frank, it was not really a communist party except in rhetoric and some Leninist methods of intra-party discipline and control; on major policies, it was trying at best to be a social democratic party and often fell short. On the basis of my perception of the ground realities and citing our survey data, I wrote from time to time in the popular Bengali newspapers about things that the left government was doing right, and, more often, what it was doing wrong or when it was doing an inadequate job. The young people who were working in our village survey team sometimes reported to me how they saw even in remote villages people at tea stalls discussing my articles, with the newspaper pages open in front of them. I personally knew many of the leaders in the government (including top ministers), and, needless to say, the leading left party often bristled at my pieces. (One minister openly told me: 'Our party does not consider you a friend.' I told him that I was not keen on the party's friendship, but I wanted it to pay attention to what I was saying for its own good.)

Let me narrate now some of my intensive interactions with the party, particularly in the 1990s and the decade after. Once, in Kolkata in the early 1990s, I got a phone call from the personal secretary of Chief Minister Jyoti Basu; he said that both Amartya Sen and I were in Kolkata at the same time, so the chief minister wanted to take this opportunity to have a lengthy discussion with the two of us together. We agreed and went one morning to a hotel room where the CM, some party leaders and ministers were present in a small private gathering. Jyoti Basu said that after the fall of the Soviet Union, they wanted to understand which way things were moving, and if and how their party should change directions in the face of this storm. Amartya-da wanted me to start.

I decided to take this opportunity to be quite blunt, particularly as the media were not there, and discussed the international situation rather cursorily, and concentrated on the kind of mistakes and wrong directions in my judgement they were taking in West Bengal. I spoke for almost an hour; the leaders were mostly silent, except for occasional interruptions by the chief minister, who pleasantly surprised me by seemingly agreeing with me and even giving examples from his experience to supplement some of the points I was making. Then Amartyada spoke, and after that general discussion followed. I was struck by the remarkable measure of agreement in the room or at least silence on the part of those who disagreed. The meeting went on, with a short lunch break, until late in the afternoon, when the chief minister excused himself as he had to go and give a public speech in a large gathering in the city centre. The next morning, I read his speech in the party newspaper; it was full of the usual stale rhetoric and catechisms. I noted the gulf between their public front and the internal unsettled state of thinking. Later, I also faced the same public front from other ministers when I spoke in public panel discussions with them on different occasions.

Another time, an important minister (Nirupam Sen, who rose in the party from the grassroots level and whom I found out to be one of the most thoughtful among the leaders) called me and said that he'd like to come over to my apartment in Kolkata and privately discuss various controversial issues arising at that time out of land acquisition for building new industries. We had a good and candid discussion. A few weeks later, the Bengali newspaper where I used to contribute regularly arranged for a long conversation between me and Nirupam Sen, and with only some small changes requested by Sen, they published the transcript. This was in 2009, and I could see that by then the days of the left party were numbered. Nirupam Sen showed me some unpublished articles he had written on the issues we discussed—he said even if their party were to be defeated in the next election, he wanted to leave for posterity some evidence that he had thought through some things, just could not implement them.

One of the central contradictions I have repeatedly pointed out to the party leaders was that they, and particularly their militant trade unions, were anti-capitalist in their ideology, and yet they had not shown in their programmes and actions any viable positive alternative to capitalism. For example, the left in India have very few successful cases of running cooperatives or other such non-capitalist organizations like worker-owned or -managed firms or farms on any large scale. Their usual slogans for nationalization and state takeovers of firms are not credible any more with a long history of state failures in business where there is competition, and, in the case of some public monopolies, the profits, if any, are often dissipated in different forms of political patronage distribution. Successful management of some state firms under leftist rule would have improved their credibility and created useful examples for people to look up to.

After the party was defeated in 2011, Dilip and I analysed the reasons for the defeat from some data and opinion polls in our subsequent village surveys. I also wrote up a couple of pieces in the popular Bengali press. After the fall of the Soviet Union, I had written an article in *EPW* titled 'The Avoidable Tragedy of the Left in India'; after their defeat in West Bengal, I wrote up a sequel to it. Now, of course, both the left and the liberals in India (along with assorted Gandhians) are facing an even more harrowing tragedy with the triumphal march of the marauding right, pushing the agenda of hateful sectarianism and thuggish tyranny.

In connection with our research and meetings in the MacArthur network, we did a considerable amount of international travel. Let me now turn to a whole series of my travel-related stories—some in connection with this network, but mostly outside it and in different periods of my itinerant life.

When I start thinking of my travels, the first thing that comes to mind, as it does for many others from India, is a whole series of anecdotes relating to authorities in Western countries trying to block or hinder our travel in various ways. Let me unburden here some of them. Many decades back, before I got the much-coveted 'green card' (it actually looks rather pink, not green) for permanent residency in the US, I was standing in the long line for the American visa one early morning in New Delhi. The line started forming even before daylight, hours before the embassy doors opened, and it soon snaked around the building, under the scorching sun. When I finally reached near the counter in the air-conditioned interior, in front of me there was one other person, a woman of probably twenty-seven or twenty-eight years of age. She had told me that she had been admitted in a graduate school in the US with a fellowship, and we discussed her prospective area of research. But when she reached the counter, the surly visa officer looked at the file, examined all her documents, then for a minute or two looked at her, and suddenly closed the file with a thump, and said, 'You don't look like a student to me [he probably meant that she was a few years older than the usual graduate student]. No Visa for you! Next!' Standing there, she started silently weeping and I was next. I reached the counter and asked, 'Is this how you decide on a visa? By the looks of people?' The man growled at me and said, 'Do you want your visa or not?' Things may have improved since then, but, at least in those days, it entirely depended on the arbitrary decision of one visa officer, and there was hardly any scope for appeal. While in the line, I had already overheard some students discussing that the visa officer at the American consulate in Chennai was rumoured to be a bit kinder than officers on duty elsewhere in India at that time, and many students were making a special trip to Chennai to try their luck there.

When, a few years later, I applied for the green card, it took more than a year to be processed by the US Immigration Service (I am told it is much longer now). If, during the processing period, the applicant had to go out of the country (as I had to in connection with my lectures and conferences), you had to get a special permission, which gave you a status of what the service sweetly called 'parole' (which ordinarily means early conditional release of a prison inmate). So during that year, several times I waited at the immigration line on my return to the US, and when the immigration officer saw my file, they'd loudly say, 'Oh, you are on parole! Step aside and wait for the parole officer to come and talk to you.' I stood there trying to avoid the stare of the other people in the line probably speculating about the nature of my crime.

My next story is about the British consulate in Los Angeles, involving the British visa for Titash. He, by then, was working for a software company in the Bay Area and had the green card. The company asked him to attend a meeting in New York, and then move on to a meeting in England. He sent all the documents for a British visa to the Los Angeles consulate for the short trip to England more than two months before he was to go for those meetings and enclosed a paid express mail envelope for the passport to be sent back. But even after two months the visa did not come, and it was of little use to call the consulate as it was almost impossible to get a human on the phone. So when Titash left for his New York meeting, he asked me to express mail the passport to his hotel in New York in case it arrived in the next two or three days; if not, he'd have to cancel his trip to England.

The next day, I desperately tried to get a human at the Los Angeles consulate by phone; after a full hour or so of pressing this or that button and getting only unhelpful machines to talk to, I finally managed to get hold of an extremely bored woman with a British accent, and explained the urgency of the situation. Through numerous suppressed yawns, she told me that the visa would be processed 'in due course', and nothing could be done to expedite it. Then, rather offhandedly, she asked, 'What's the name again—Titus? Where did I come across the name Titus?' I said she might be thinking of *Titus Andronicus*, the Shakespeare play, where Titus was an extremely violent Roman general. Then I added, 'If you want, I can tell you the story of a different, and a much softer, Titus.' She perked up and encouraged me to tell the story.

I said, 'Titus was the name of the son of the Dutch painter Rembrandt. He was Rembrandt's only surviving child, and soon after he was born, Rembrandt's wife, Saskia, died. A woman named Geertje was hired as a wet nurse for Titus; soon, she became Rembrandt's lover. I have at my home the reproduction of a 1660 painting by Rembrandt, which I procured from Rijksmuseum in Amsterdam, where he had dressed up a teenage Titus in a Franciscan monk's habit. In this painting, the downcast eyes of Titus, with his face bathed in light, suggest quiet introspection.' I sensed some thawing at the other end of the phone; she abruptly told me that I was going to get my son's visa immediately. I asked, 'When should I expect it?' She said, 'Tomorrow.' Such is the power of storytelling, as Scheherazade knew well! (I did not bother to tell the British lady that my son's name was not Titus, it was Titash, which is the name of a river in Bangladesh, not very far from my father's ancestral village; there is a famous Bengali novel, *A River Called Titash*, about the life of the fisher community along this river, written by someone from that community. Kalpana had translated this novel, which the University of California Press published, and had given it as a graduation gift to Titash.)

Once, at Heathrow airport, a British immigration officer was lazily leafing through the multiple pages of my well-worn, much-travelled passport, and suddenly chanced upon a page with an old stamp from Bogota airport. He suspiciously asked me, 'What were you doing in Bogota?' I felt like saying, 'Replenishing my supplies', but I knew immigration officers looked down upon such humour (I once saw in Houston airport a big board spelling out the different 'Don'ts' for passengers, and one of them was: 'Do not make jokes'), so I told him that I went there to give a lecture at the university. A Colombian friend once told me that on his passport he used to be always interrogated about drugs in foreign airports, but after 11 September 2001, for a period, he got some respite—the airport authorities were so busy looking for Muslim names that Colombian passports were waved away. A Pakistani economist I know, who has been a professor at Harvard for many years, told me that after 2001, he was regularly taken out in airports to a separate room for interrogation, not just when he was entering the US, but even when he was going out of the US.

Another time, at Heathrow airport, the immigration officer did not quite believe me when I told him that I was invited to give a lecture at a British university. He asked me if I had the paper that I'd be presenting. It so happened I had the printout of the paper in my bag, so I gave it to him. But that was not enough; he started to make a show of reading it and made some inane comments on the paper. The next morning at the lecture, I started with my Heathrow experience and expressed my confidence that my lecture would elicit better comments there.

My next story is about the German consulate in San Francisco. I was invited to give a lecture at Heidelberg University. They were going to put me up in a hotel, but my British friend, Clive Bell, then a professor there, and whom I have known for many years both in England and the US, had graciously asked me to stay with him. At the consulate, they told me that if I was not going to stay in a hotel, my host in Germany had to go to a police station and register there the information about my staying with him. They'd not issue a visa without some proof of that registration.

I did not feel like harassing Clive with this, so I sternly told the officer that I was withdrawing my visa application, and I'd tell Heidelberg University that I was going to cancel my trip for this reason. In a day or two, the university might have done something or made some special request, as the consulate soon called me, and asked me to come and pick up my visa. (Later, my Indian friends told me that this requirement of a hotel stay was there with some other European countries as well. So even when they were actually staying with friends, they'd routinely make a reservation in a reputed five-star hotel, get the visa and then cancel that reservation.)

I also know of many cases of cynical opportunism of some Indians and their attempts to game the system. Let me just mention one somewhat related case. I was once going from San Francisco to Delhi via Hong Kong. After arriving in Hong Kong, I found out that my connecting flight was delayed by five or six hours. It was late at night, I went to the gate area of that flight, found it rather deserted, and decided to lie down on a sofa in a dimly lit area. I fell asleep and woke up when I found a turbaned young Indian sitting down on the same sofa. He seemed eager to talk and asked me where I was going. When I said, India, he said, 'Oh, you've been deported too?' Apparently, he had been in Canada for the last few years, overstaying his temporary visa there, was finally caught and deported. It was not clear to him why any Indian, unless deported, would willingly go back to India.

One time, a kind and alert train conductor saved me from possible deportation. I was invited by Prince Hans-Adam of Liechtenstein to a conference on Indian democracy to be held in his palace (the conference was mainly organized by Atul Kohli, a Princeton political science professor—I know him since the days when I was on his doctoral dissertation committee in Berkeley). Apparently, the prince was interested in political issues like democracy and had written books. I knew that Liechtenstein was a tax haven like Switzerland but was not fully aware of its location. I found out that it was a tiny kingdom, on a short train journey from Zurich, and a Swiss visa would be enough for entry. When I bought my train ticket in Zurich railway station, nobody told me that there was no train station in Liechtenstein. In the train, the conductor had checked my passport and saw that I had a Swiss visa. A short while later, in one small Swiss train station when the train was about to depart, he ran to me and asked me to get off. He told me that I should take a taxi from that train station to Liechtenstein, as the next station was in Austria, and my passport did not have an Austrian visa. If he had not warned me in time, apparently, I was in some danger of being deported from Austria. (Those were the days before the introduction of the Schengen visa, by which a visa for one West European country would serve as visa for a few others as well.)

I have heard an interesting deportation story about illegal Mexican immigrants in California's Central Valley. This is from the days when if the illegal immigrants were caught, they were punished, but not their employers. So from time to time, the immigration authorities were organizing large-scale raids in the valley's agricultural fields to catch illegals. One time, the valley's producers told the authorities that this was much too disruptive for their production or harvesting, and much too inefficient as the immigration agents had to run and chase workers through the mud and dust ultimately catching only a small number of illegals. So they made a deal: instead of raids by the authorities, the employers would agree to hand over to them every month a stipulated number of illegals. (I remembered the story of Bakasura, the man-eating demon in a side-story in the epic Mahabharata, where the villagers periodically ravaged by Bakasura made a deal with him that they'd send to his den in the forest every week a man along with other food.) Every month, there'd be a lottery drawn among workers on a farm and a small number of them would be handed over to the authorities—the workers who lost in the draw would be arrested and deported; while saying good bye to the others on the farm, these unlucky few would place their hats for donations, which would be used to pay the 'coyotes', who were to help them to migrate again.

My last story in this chain is not about immigration, but about the police and foreign visitors in the US, and it is about a German woman. I heard this story from an American friend who was a professor at an east coast university. He had a sister who was mentally ill and, for a time, was assigned to a mental institution. My friend used to go and visit her on some Sundays. One Sunday, in an open area inside the institution, he was waiting for his sister when he found a woman aimlessly loitering in the area and muttering audibly to herself in German. My friend knew German and thought that somehow she did not quite belong there. He started talking to her in German and found out her story. She lived in a remote town in Germany and was coming to the US for the first time to attend the wedding of a relative. She did not speak a word of English, but some relatives were going to pick her up from JFK Airport. Immediately after she cleared immigration and customs, and before she could come outside to look for her relatives, she was mugged and the mugger ran away with her handbag which had the passport, money and all the local contact information she had. After the mugging, she went hysterical. The people around and then the policemen who were called did not understand what she was saying. Nor did she have any local contact information to give them. So, in their wisdom, the police decided to put her up in a nearby mental institution. If my friend had not come to her rescue, she would have rotted in that institution for a much longer time.

The international academic conference circuit—for an amusing account of such circuits, one may read the British writer David Lodge's novel *Small World*, which is second in his trilogy of campus novels, the first of which, *Changing Places*, is largely on Berkeley in the 1960s—also brought me occasionally to some potentially hazardous situations. Once, a reception given for us conference participants by the king of Spain indirectly helped me in what could have been a serious loss from a pickpocket in Madrid. The public reception hall was not far from the hotel where we were staying. I was walking there from the hotel with a fellow conference participant. I was busy explaining a particular point to her in conversation when I had a half-sense that two young women who brushed by seemed a bit too close, and I ignored that for a minute. The next minute, I felt the inside of my jacket pocket and it was gone—a wallet containing not just money and credit cards, but a few important documents (since then I have been careful not to put everything in the same wallet or pocket). So I excused myself from my companion and ran to a nearby uniformed policeman, and told him about it. He brought out a whistle and made a signalling sound. Within five minutes or so, another policeman from the opposite pavement came towards me with my wallet and asked me to check if everything was in place. Those two unlucky young women did not realize that as the king was to be there soon, the whole area was thick with plain-clothes policemen.

My conferences sometimes took place in cities where more violent robberies were quite frequent even in broad daylight. I remember the first day we were in our MacArthur network conference in Rio de Janeiro, at the lunch break, we were told that the lunch would be in a restaurant just one block away. When we came out of the building, we saw that some giant commandos were guarding us all along the road as we were walking to the restaurant. I was told that this was part of the conference arrangement. I thought the organizers were overdoing it. But in the afternoon, during the conference, one woman in our group, who without telling anyone went to the store just next door to the building main gate, came back in tears saying that she was mugged. I saw a roughly similar situation in Nairobi and also in a couple of cities in South Africa; during the lunch break, I thought I'd just go out for a short walk around the big hotels where our conferences were, but the hotel guards would refuse to let us go out for the sake of our safety. It crossed my mind that this situation might not be unrelated to the fact that in all three countries—Brazil, Kenya and South Africa—the level of inequality is extremely high.

Having talked about visa troubles and muggings connected with travels, let me now turn to their more pleasant aspects. Apart from exposure to rich varieties of culture and landscape, one simple feature of international travel was the different kinds of delectable food that it brings to your easy reach. I could never get tired of Italian, Peruvian, Chinese or Thai food. In China, however, I have noted a sharp difference between the food you get at regular restaurants (particularly in some of their vegetarian dishes, the subtle combination of taste and nutrition value achieved is unparalleled for any cuisine) and when on special occasions there were official 'banquets' (*yànhuì*). In the latter, you often get strange and exotic dishes, some of which I did not much care for. I remember during our MacArthur network dinner banquets in Beijing, I'd make sure to have Abhijit Banerjee next to me at the dinner table. Abhijit is a great cook and connoisseur of food, but another side of him is that he is highly adventurous in exploring food, and would try everything on offer (be it a reptile or a 100-year-old quail's egg or bird's nest). So seated next to me, he'd whisper to me what the banquet dish he had just tasted was, and what it could possibly be made of. I'd then decide if I'd touch it or not, as the rotating food table with more than a dozen dishes went past each of us.

In general, food plays a special role among Indians—in India or abroad—and the predominant culture is one of foodies. Even Indian women often express their love through food, making their loved ones overeat. (I have also already referred to a tussle between Mahalanobis and Sukumar Ray in Kolkata in the early part of the previous century about disentangling serious intellectual discussion from enjoyment of food delicacies in the discussion venue.) Talking of food connoisseurs, I cannot resist narrating here a story I read in the *New York Times* about an Indian-origin man from Guyana. The story goes something like this.

This Guyanese-Indian came to New York to seek his fortune, but his luck ran out. He ended up having no job, no income and soon no friends. But his love for good food never left him. So he worked out a strategy. He'd dress himself in his only remaining good suit and choose a posh restaurant in one part of New York. In the restaurant he'd order the choicest of wine and the best delicacies in food. His expensive choices would impress the waiters and they'd go out of their way to make this gourmet with good taste happy. At the end when the large bill came to him, he'd calmly tell the waiter that he did not have any money. After the initial ha-ha among the waiters, soon the truth of his statement would dawn on them. So the police would be called, while the man unflappably would go on using the toothpicks and wait. He'd be arrested and, in the trial, convicted, and when the judge would ask him if he had anything to say before he was to be sentenced, he'd politely request the judge if possible to assign him to a particular jail in the area (because they do 'Swedish meatballs rather well'). Then he'd get released after a few months. And he'd repeat the same thing—arriving at an expensive restaurant in a different part of the city in his suit—and New York City is large enough for one restaurant to not know what happened in a restaurant in another part of the city. The cycle would thus continue for some time this way. The *New York Times* reporter commented: 'In the long and checkered history of serial crimes in New York, this is the first case of a serial diner.'

To pick a story from almost the opposite end of the food scale, in the lunch break of a conference in Cambridge, England, I was once approached by three non-local women participants. They said that they had decided to skip the usual college lunch arranged for the participants and that they had heard there was a good farmers' market somewhere in the city centre. They wanted to know if I'd like to join them in having an informal lunch there with helpings from fresh fruits and vegetables in the stalls in that market, direct farm-to-mouth as it were. This was not quite my idea of a lunch, but I decided to accompany them, particularly since, as a Cambridge ex-student, I knew precisely where that farmers' market was located. The women enjoyed their skimpy lunch there, something that I could not say I did, but I enjoyed their company. When they were gobbling their tomatoes directly from a shop, one of them naughtily pointed me to a sign that the tomato-seller had put up in the tomato heap, which said, 'Don't squeeze me until I'm all yours.'

The first time I went to New Zealand on a lecture tour, Kalpana and Titash accompanied me. It is not just a beautiful country, the nature there gives you a completely different feel as the flora and fauna are so unlike what we are used to in the northern hemisphere. We took a special one-day nature tour from Auckland, and I asked them to take us to the rainforest which I had seen in the recently famous and award-winning film by Jane Campion, *The Piano*. In the film, after a long voyage from Scotland, all the belongings (including a piano) of the mute pianist Ada—sent on an arranged marriage to a farmer in the outback—had been dumped from the ship on a beach, and the strong Maori workers manually carried the piano through a trek in the rainforest, with Ada and her daughter, Flora, following them. The tour took us to that rainforest and we walked through the forest all the way to the beach where the scenes were actually filmed.

When our conference met in Costa Rica, we stayed in a rainforest villa. The frequent, but brief squalls and rain there and the colourful birds fluttering around guava trees were quite a sight—however, there is no comparison with the memory I have of the majestic monsoon rains, accompanied by the drumbeats of thunder, rushing through green paddy fields in Santiniketan (no wonder Tagore composed more than a hundred monsoonal songs; many of his poems, short stories and letters are also suffused with the rainy season). When I was in Ecuador, after my lecture in Quito, I tried—for variation—staying in a cloud forest resort in the north, but there were too many mosquitoes throughout the day there for us to enjoy the outdoors.

I have enjoyed long walks in many cities of the world. In Oslo, my Norwegian friend Karl ('Kalle') Moene, a major economist there, once took me on a long, pleasant walk through the city, which included going through Frogner Park where there is a large collection of open-air sculptures by Gustav Vigeland. He also took me to the Munch Museum where I discovered that Edvard Munch had made many kinds of paintings, which were quite different in style from his iconic painting *The Scream* (for example, many of his late paintings celebrate farm life). Kalle also accompanied me when I took the scenic train journey from Oslo to Bergen. (Incidentally, I have learned a lot from talking to Kalle and reading his papers on the specific features of Scandinavian social democracy.)

Among metropolitan cities, Paris is a city where I have always liked walking aimlessly through the streets (once, my walk was so aimless that it caught the attention of a plain-clothes policeman who approached me and asked for my passport to check that I was not an illegal immigrant). It is a small enough city for you to stroll through the central arrondissements in two or three hours. This is the city of the flâneur, celebrated by the nineteenth-century bohemian poet Charles Baudelaire. For him, the flâneur was the passionate spectator of the multifarious life forms of the city. In the previous century, Jean-Jacques Rousseau's last book, *The Reveries of the Solitary Walker*, about ten walks in the outskirts of Paris, was a meditation on solitude and society. Of course, there is a difference in the flânerie by a native and that by a visitor. Walter Benjamin once said that in observing a city, outsiders concentrate mostly on the exotic and picturesque, while the natives always see the place through layers of memory.

Feminists have pointed out that flânerie by oneself is often a male privilege. Social conventions, inconveniences and dangers limit the freedom of the flâneuse. Still, Virginia Woolf in her 1927 essay, 'Street Haunting: A London Adventure', celebrates rambling through the streets of London, pretending that she needed to purchase a pencil in order to justify what is in effect an aimless stroll through the city. In her novel, Mrs Dalloway strolls through central London, as Leopold Bloom in James Joyce's *Ulysses* does in Dublin, and the city bustle stimulates streams of thoughts and memories. In the 1962, movie *Cleo from 5 to 7* by Agnès Varda the protagonist Cleo has an afternoon of flânerie, when she walks by herself into cafés, crowded streets and gardens of Paris, and the city mainly mirrors Cleo's inward journey. Of course, such solitary flânerie in a city by a woman is almost unthinkable in much of India, or for that matter most parts of the world.

Once, in Paris, my friend the economist François Bourguignon took me to dinner at an old café-restaurant and motioned me to sit in a particular corner. Once seated, he told me that the place where I was sitting was precisely where Honoré de Balzac, one of France's greatest writers, used to come and sit many afternoons in the first half of the nineteenth century. I have heard that Balzac, when he was writing a book, used to subsist on little more than coffee, but after the publication of the book, he used to gorge himself (I read a description: 'in a single sitting, a hundred oysters, four bottles of wine, twelve lamb cutlets, duckling, a brace of partridge, sole, and pears by the dozen'; the bill was charged to the publisher). There is a lovely 2010 book *Balzac's Omelette*, where the author, Anka Muhlstein, shows how in his novels food could evoke character, atmosphere, class and social climbing more suggestively than money, appearances, etc.

Over dinner, when I told François that in public life in Kolkata a poet or writer was more valued than an economist, he said the same was true of Paris. I then told him about an incident in my life. Once, a well-known Bengali writer/poet friend of mine, Sunil Ganguly, and I were walking in a Kolkata street, where every few minutes he'd be surrounded by young women asking for his autograph. While obliging them, he saw me waiting at a distance with a bored look and told these women that I too was a well-known person. At this, a couple of women came towards me and asked me what I did. As soon as I said I was an economist, they turned around and rejoined the crowd around Sunil. This put me and my discipline in our place.

When in Paris, after a day of meetings or museum-hopping, I used to go in the late afternoon all the way up to the Basilica of Sacré Coeur (I did not know then that the Basilica was erected on the spot where the Paris Commune uprising was crushed in 1871). There, seated on the steps, you have a panoramic view of the whole city. With the setting sun in the background and the birds flocking back to the trees nearby or to the nooks of the basilica, you could have some moments of serenity. Talking of serenity, one of the best places in the world in my experience to savour quietude is in the gardens of the shrines in the city of Kyoto in Japan. I have seen some visitors deep in meditation there. Meditation does not quite work for me, but sitting silently in a tranquil, scenic place is good enough.

In the 1960s, I used to see a lot of people practising what was called 'transcendental meditation'. (By the way, the first word of mantra in this meditation, 'Om', is called Pranava mantra, which is the Sanskrit origin of my first name.) Then, in the 1970s, I heard people talking about 'dynamic meditation', introduced by Osho or the Indian godman Rajneesh. Once, in the middle of the 1970s, I had a brief encounter with a couple of disciples of Rajneesh in Pune, India, where I went for an international conference. I was put up at the Blue Diamond Hotel. One evening, I was reading a magazine in the bar lounge of the hotel, when two blonde German girls in identical crimson robes came and sat down near me. When we got talking, they told me that they were disciples of Rajneesh, whose ashram was around the corner outside the hotel. They said they could not have beer in the ashram, so they regularly came to that hotel to have a beer. I then asked them about life in the ashram. They were in general quite reverential about Rajneesh, but their cult seemed to me somewhat hedonistic compared to most other cults.

Noticing my curiosity, they offered to take me and give me a guided tour the next day. At the appointed hour, when they came to pick me up from the hotel, they said they forgot to ask me something the previous day: did I use shampoo to wash my hair? I said, yes—like most other people, I do use shampoo. In that case, they said, I'd be denied entry. This was because Rajneesh was extremely allergic to the smell of shampoo. I then suggested that we could go to other parts of the ashram where Rajneesh was not nearby. They once again said no, and that they were very strict at the main gate. Apparently two six-foot-plus Scandinavian women stood guard at the gate and regularly sniffed every entrant's head. So I missed my chance to have an inside look at the cult I had heard so much about.

Another cultural benefit of my travels, particularly in the early days, used to be my exploration of international cinema. I have already mentioned how, after leaving India, I became exposed to a riot of European art films. In later years, I also saw some superb art films from Argentina, Brazil, Iran, Japan, South Korea and Taiwan. In the US, in many cities, some of these art films were not always easily available, and I sometimes saw them on visits to New York or London, though with some lapse of time, the Pacific Film Archive in the Berkeley campus showed some good international films. Every time I went to Kolkata, my friend Samik Banerjee told me about the new Bengali art films that came out in the months I was away and sometimes took me to their special screenings. Through him, I came to know some of the major film directors and actors in Kolkata. Meanwhile, the quality of American films improved a great deal. But the general commercial film world in the US largely catered to adolescent fantasy worlds or antics of superheroes from comic books or dystopian science fiction—none of which held much attraction for me. Even in more grown-up American films, one often missed the sharp, witty, historically informed, and politically engaged conversation of friends and also a kind of cerebral sexuality that I used to associate with French films, for example—a character in Godard's film *Contempt* famously said in bed: 'I love you totally, tenderly, tragically.'

Then, of course, came the days of DVDs, and I became an avid member of several video stores in Berkeley. Different video stores, particularly the smaller niche ones, gave me the opportunity to savour a wide variety of international movies. I remember once when I heard about a new video store opening in a corner of Berkeley, in the very first week, I went there and tried to see in what way their international DVD collection was distinctive. I got to talk to the young man who was the store's owner-manager, and soon, we were deep into our respective likes and dislikes in movies. I told him that there were some international movies which were in everybody's list of all-time greats, but not in mine (to take examples just from the 1960s, Godard's *Breathless*, or *Last Year at Marienbad* by Alain Resnais—I actually liked the latter's film *The War is Over* much more—or *L'Avventura* by Michelangelo Antonioni). Similarly, there were some movies that critics or film scholars did not quite rave about, but I wanted to see them again and again (say, *The Double Life of Véronique* by Krzysztof Kieślowski from Poland, or *We All Loved Each Other So Much* by Ettore Scola from Italy, or *Landscape in the Mist* by Theo Angelopoulos from Greece)—I think it was more a matter of harmony with my temperament than the technical qualities of the films. The young man gave me his preferred lists and we animatedly discussed them. At one point, he shouted towards an inner room in the store where his wife was busy sorting out their new arrivals of DVDs. He told her, 'You call me a movie maniac; come and see, here's another one!'

Once, I was telling a Romanian student of mine how I had liked some recent Romanian films. She was thrilled to hear that, and a couple of weeks later, her mother in Romania sent me a gift package of DVDs of about a dozen recent Romanian films which were very difficult to get outside the country. Then, after some years, the days of DVD subsided, their stores folded one after another, and the era of streaming services took over. But, in the latter, while I appreciate the convenience of not having to go to stores, and of exploring content and watching what I wanted to online, I miss the multitude and diversity of international movies I was used to—earlier in my travels and later in the DVD days. Maybe there are specialized streaming services catering to tastes like mine, but I have not yet quite found them.

Let me end my travel stories by narrating some experience of hotels where I stayed in various journeys. The interior of big hotel rooms these days often looks similar all over the world with only some token flourishes of local culture—in the flower arrangements or some of the furnishings (in Japanese hotel toilet commodes, for example, there are arrangements for water sprays from inside them, with different angles and temperature, washing your bottom). There is somewhat more variation in the food in the hotels (for example, in East Asian hotels at breakfast time, I much prefer the lighter Asian offerings to Western breakfasts) than in the interior arrangements. In these lookalike hotels, waking up in the morning, I sometimes had to think for a minute to remind myself where in the world I was.

Once, in a hotel in Pattaya, Thailand, very early in the morning, I was woken up by a lot of commotion from the hotel swimming pool a few floors down. I saw from the window a Japanese tour group of elderly people having their swimming adventure orchestrated by a group leader with a whistle and a flag, and people jumping in and out of the water together following the whistle. I have always been struck by the ease of collective action in Japan under different circumstances, particularly in contrast with the easy indiscipline of groups in India (where it is more like 'herding cats').

Another time, I was similarly woken up very early in the morning in an Indian hotel. My mother wanted me to take her to the Himalayan foothills where she had heard that the water in the river Ganges was clean and blue, compared to the muddy and dirty Ganges in the plains she was familiar with. I took her to Rishikesh, where the Ganges was quite blue and swift-flowing. We stayed in a hotel by the river, and the sound of the rushing water was soothing for sleep. But, early in the morning, we were woken up by the loud sound of what seemed like a continuous metallic sound of things hitting one another, like giant cymbals clashing. I could not figure out what it was. I went out of the hotel to the riverbank and saw something strange. Then, talking to people, I realized what it was. Upstream, near the temple, large numbers of pious pilgrims throw coins into the holy river, and a few miles downstream, some resourceful people have put up big magnets where the masses of coins in the swift current hit and get stuck. I saw a few people collecting the coins with big nets. I thought this upstream–downstream system was a neat, mutually beneficial one, with pious people upstream gaining in virtue, and the not-so-pious people downstream gaining in more material terms.

Recently, I reached a big hotel in central London from the airport a bit late in the evening. I was hungry, but the hotel restaurants were about to close, so they advised me to go to the bar where they served food until quite late. I sat down there with my food and drink. After some time, a young brunette with dark attractive eyes entered the bar and was obviously looking for someone. Her make-up and high heels suggested some edginess in her appearance. Within a minute or so, she came over to my table and asked if I was Ashok. I told her that was not my name, but asked if I could be of any help. She said,

'Ashok had asked me to come to this hotel; I knocked at his door for a few minutes, but there was no response. So I thought I'd check in the bar. You look Indian, and Ashok is an Indian name, right?' I said that neither she nor I seemed to know any Ashok in the bar. She said she'd try Ashok's room again after a little while. Then she gave a tired look at my food and drink, and said that as this was a big hotel, beer must be quite expensive. I then asked her to sit down and said that I'd treat her to a glass of beer. She seemed glad to sit down.

Her drink came and we talked. She was from Romania, where she had finished college. But there was hardly any decent job there, so she had come to London to try her fortune in the call-girl business. She had enlisted in several escort agencies, and they sent her to customers, often in big hotels, and charged 40 per cent of her income as their commission, but they took care of advertising online and some other overhead costs. While we were talking a phone call came, and she took it and spoke in her own language for a few minutes and seemed to hurriedly finish the call. She said the call was from her mother in Bucharest, and, with a wry smile, commented that her mother thought she was in London for her studies, and would 'kill' her if she knew what she was doing.

I asked her if she was sufficiently aware that she was taking a big risk of disease. She said she was and got frequent medical check-ups. Then, after some moments of brooding silence, she said she had come to this 'line' neither out of any particular self-generated eagerness nor had anyone really forced her; she sort of drifted into it. While in college, she had fallen in love with a town boy with roguish charm, a motorbike, tattoos, and 'bad' friends; they used to take her to dazzling nightclubs and wild parties, where she got initiated into casual sex and some drugs.

When she finally got over the spell of this company and tried to get a regular job, she realized the kind of jobs she could scrape would not allow her to maintain some expensive habits in clothes and accessories she had meanwhile acquired. Then, with her tired eyes, she gave me a prolonged, upfront gaze, and said, 'I figured out that spreading my legs for a short while would earn me a lot more than those trite jobs I'd otherwise slog in.' So with a couple of other similar-minded Romanian girls, she headed for London. She liked London (except for the infernal patchy rain and cold); in particular, it was much safer for her than Bucharest in the kind of life she had chosen. Then, abruptly, she shook her rolling dark hair, thanked me for the beer, and went away in search of her customer.

I remembered my earlier experience in a Bangkok hotel in the late 1970s. Those were the days when the Vietnam War had just wound up, and Bangkok as a centre of 'R&R' (rest and recreation) for American GIs was in some decline. There were more pimps and painted girls in the streets than customers—a brothel in decline was a sad sight. The organizers of the United Nations conference I came for had put me up in a five-star hotel. Even there, lying in your bed, you could see the ceiling framed in glass mirrors where you could watch yourself whatever you were doing in bed. One night, I was a bit tired, and went to bed a bit early, around 11 p.m., and quickly fell asleep. Shortly after midnight, I was woken by soft but insistent knocks at my door. With sleepy eyes, I opened the door and found a little miniskirted, high-heeled teenage Thai girl who asked me if I needed a body massage to relax me. I loudly said no and slammed the door shut. But going back to bed, I thought I should not have been so rude with this unfortunate girl, and did not sleep much for the rest of the night.

This stab of regret at my rudeness came back to me when, much later, I read a poem by Robert Hass (my ex-colleague in Berkeley English department, and an American poet laureate):

> ... in the thick heat
> Of the Bangkok night. Not more than fourteen, she saunters up to you
> Outside the Shangri-la Hotel
> And says, in plausible English,
> 'How about a party, big guy?'
> Here is more or less how it works:
> The World Bank arranges the credit and the dam
> Floods three hundred villages, and the villagers find their way
> To the city where their daughters melt into the teeming streets,
> And the dam's great turbines, beautifully tooled
> In Lund or Dresden or Detroit,
> Have become hives of shimmering silver
> And, down river, they throw that bluish throb of light
> Across her cheekbones and her lovely skin.

Incidentally, a few years back, I was surprised to receive an invitation from a women's collective in Kolkata named Durbar (the Bengali word for 'unstoppable'), the by now widely recognized organization of more than 65,000 sex workers in West Bengal, for an event at the Kolkata Book Fair where I'd have to ceremoniously release some of their published books. This is an organization, established in 1992, that is active in promoting the rights and dignity of sex workers and issues of their health, education for their children and access to financial services (earlier, due to social ostracization, these workers had problems even in opening bank accounts or getting their children admitted to schools). I readily accepted their invitation. At the book fair event, I met Dr Smarajit Jana, a physician and public health specialist, who was the founder and the pioneering leader of this movement, totally dedicated to the cause. He presented me with several of his own books and pamphlets. At his urging, apart from releasing the books, I also had to address quite an enthusiastic and colourfully dressed gathering of sex workers there. This was a new experience for me. (Unfortunately, Dr Jana succumbed to Covid-19 in 2021, which was a big blow to the movement.)

16

At Journey's End

Following the mantra of *charaiveti*, I have travelled extensively in this wide world—the northernmost point I have been to was Trondheim in Norway (I gave a lecture at the university there), not very far from the Arctic Circle, and the southernmost point for me was Dunedin in New Zealand (where I gave a lecture at the University of Otago), not very far from the Antarctic Circle. Starting from the obscure crevice of a poor neighbourhood in north Kolkata, I have traversed a stretched-out, rather cosmopolitan life—the many memories and anecdotes of which I shared in these pages. Memories are, of course, by nature too multi dimensional, elusive and unstable to be easily captured this way. In his highly perceptive Booker Prize–winning short novel, *The Sense of an Ending*, the English writer Julian Barnes meditates on the malleability of memory and its construction by an unreliable narrator. This should actually apply to all narrations of memories including this one.

As I look towards the Pacific Ocean from my hilltop house in Berkeley, with its panoramic view, I sometimes feel like the Polish poet Czeslaw Milosz, who, when he was teaching at Berkeley, lived in a house down the road, about half a mile away from mine—he described his chosen self-isolation in the Berkeley hills as comparable to the isolation that Thomas Mann's hero Hans Castorp in the novel *The Magic Mountain* chose by pretending an illness so that he could stay in the Swiss sanatorium at Davos in the Magic Mountain, far removed from the world.

Yet, even here, as I get to the end of my journey, amid the darkening shadows, it seems three things in particular preoccupy my weary mind. One is the memory of the number of people, friends, relatives and valued acquaintances I have lost along the road. The curse of old age is the paralysing sense of pervasive loss, more than one's own physical infirmities and indignities. I pine at the thought of so many things I still wanted to talk to the lost ones about, so many feelings and emotions I wanted to share with them, but they were snatched away from me. I remember one brief section of the 1976 Italian animation movie *Allegro Non Troppo* by Bruno Bozzetto, where against the background music of Maurice Ravel's *Boléro* you see the inexorable journey of evolution of different creatures whereas many drop off by the roadside, others, the survivors, carry on in the onward trudging to their destiny. One also remembers that at the end of the epic *Mahabharata*, as Yudhishthira walks up the Himalayas his brothers and Draupadi fall by the wayside and he continues his desolate journey. The chorus in *Agamemnon*, the famous play by the Greek playwright Aeschylus, tells us: 'He who learns must suffer, and, even in our sleep, pain that cannot forget falls drop by drop upon the heart …'

The second thing is special to first-generation immigrants like me, their particular restlessness, that they are at home nowhere. In his novel *Snow*, Orhan Pamuk writes about his character Ka, a Turk living in Germany, thinking of the nineteenth-century Russian writer Ivan Turgenev:

> Ka loved Turgenev, and his elegant novels, and like the Russian writer Ka too had tired of his own country's never-ending troubles and come to despise its backwardness, only to find himself gazing back with love and longing after a move to Europe.

This longing on the part of the deracinated in melancholy exile and yet disappointed with one's origin country is not unfamiliar to me. I also think about Saadat Manto's satirical Urdu short story where, after the Partition, India and Pakistan exchange the inmates of each other's lunatic asylums; and one Sikh inmate from the Lahore asylum, the man from Toba Tek Singh a town now in Pakistan, decides to lie down in the no man's land between the barbed wire fences of the two countries, refusing either country. Sometimes, I feel like that man from Toba Tek Singh; other times, I feel like belonging to all countries.

Finally, a kind of deep political despair makes the footsteps in my remaining journey increasingly weary. When I was young I could never imagine that I'd live through a day when a hateful intolerant majoritarian and authoritarian poison would vitiate the air of many countries in the world, would be a serious challenge to the pre-existing (flawed) liberal order, and also retard the progress towards meeting our new challenges of environmental degradation, public health crises and corrosive inequality and insecurity. Faced with these challenges and the dysfunctionalities of our current social and political institutions in meeting them, some social commentators are turning to apocalyptic terms to describe the future, which I cannot bring myself to share, but I have deep worries. I have now written a book for a general readership, titled *A World of Insecurity: Democratic Disenchantment in Rich and Poor Countries* (Harvard University Press, 2022), where I try to discuss a diagnosis of the problems as well as tentatively indicate some possible though narrow and slippery pathways out. I have adopted there an attitude of what might be called an upbeat scepticism: pushing for things to get better while being aware that they may not—this is somewhat akin to what Antonio Gramsci, writing in Mussolini's prison, called 'pessimism of the intellect, optimism of the will'.

I hope against hope that my grandchild will grow up in a better world.

Index

Abbott, Megan, 261
Acharya, Nirmalya, 30
Adams, Ansel, 87
Addy, Premen, 30, 58–60, 259
Adelman, Irma, 136
Adiga, Aravind: *The White Tiger, Between the Assassinations*, 199
Adorno, Theodor: *The Authoritarian Personality*, 129
Aeschylus, 341
agrarian-relations in India, 113–116
Ahluwalia, Montek Singh, 136, 275
Ahmed, Bashiruddin, 124
Akerlof, George, 72–73, 79, 96, 150, 155, 233, 281, 295, 300, 303, 305

Akhmatova, Anna, 213
Alejandro, Carlos Díaz, 226–231, 280
Alibaba and the forty thieves, 171
Allen, Woody, 173
All Souls College, Oxford, 13, 203, 245-51
Almodóvar, Pedro: *Talk to Her* film, 18
Ambedkar, B.R.: democracy in India, 217; on Indian village community, 125
American Economic Association (AEA), 144
American Statue of Liberty, 183
Amis, Kingsley, 26
Anand, Sudhir, 253

Anderson, Perry, 113, 302
Anscombe, Elizabeth, 253
Antonioni, Michelangelo, 173
Aoki, Masahiko, 176-77, 179, 193; perspective on Japanese corporate governance system, 176; *Transboundary Game of Life*, 177
Arachchi, Uswatte, 57
Aragon, Louis, 172
Aristotle: *Politics*, 33
A River Called Titash novel, 319
Arjun, Tan, 181
Arrow, Kenneth, 53–55, 150–151
associative democracy, 221
Atkinson, Tony, 251
Attlee, Clement, 11
Ayyub, Abu Sayeed, 83

Baez, Joan, 57
Baker, Laurie, 131
Bakunin, Mikhail, 85
Balzac, Honoré de, 330
Bandyopadhyay, Kanika, 5
Banerjee, Abhijit, 41–42, 109, 273, 277, 310, 325; *Understanding Poverty* (co-edited with Roland Bénabou and Dilip Mookherjee), 311
Banerjee, Dipak, 41–42
Banerjee, Nirmala, 41–42
Banerjee, Samik, 26, 332
Bangiya Sahitya Parishad (Bengali Literary Society), 40
Bannister, Roger, 248
Banville, John, 262
Barcelona, 168–171, 173; Picasso Museum, 172

Bardhan, Pranab, 206–213, 223–224, 265–267; academic life in Berkeley, 293–307; gave Ashok Rudra Memorial Lecture, 119; *Awakening Giants, Feet of Clay: Assessing the Economic Rise of China and India*, 180, 192–193; *The Contested Commons*, 121; *Conversations between Economists and Anthropologists*, 121; data manufactured for some countries, 234; *Decentralization to Local Governments in Developing Countries: A Comparative Perspective* (co-edited with Dilip Mookherjee), 312; decentralized development supporter, 128; *Development Microeconomics* (co-author Christopher Udry), 161; Dipak Banerjee Memorial Lecture, 42; on economic reform, 218; *The Economic Theory of Agrarian Institutions*, 174–175; Ford Research Professorship, 150; on globalization, 218; *Globalization and Egalitarian Redistribution* (co-edited with Samuel Bowles and Michael Wallerstein), 311; *Handbook of Income Distribution*, 251–252; historical time, concept of, 228; *Inequality, Cooperation* and *Environmental Sustainability* (co-edited with Jean-Marie Baland and Samuel Bowles), 311; interest in political economy

Index ❧ 347

of comparative-systemic issues, 202–203; international research network and travels, 308–339; invited to give V.K.R.V. Rao Memorial Lecture at ISEC, Bangalore, 140; *Journal of Asian Studies*, 180; La Casa Mila, 173; *Land, Labor and Rural Poverty*, 174; liberal democracy, 221–222; *The Political Economy of Development in India*, 225; *Poverty and Income Distribution in India*, 109; on privatization, 218–219, 221–222; Ramaswami Memorial Lecture at DSE, 276; *Redistribution with Growth*, 136; Samar Sen Memorial Lecture, 118; *Scarcity, Conflicts and Cooperation*, 311;Sukhamoy Chakravarti Memorial Lecture at DSE, 148; T.N. Srinivasan Memorial Lecture, 108; visited China in 1989, 181–194; lectures at Tsinghua University, Peking University and at Renmin University in Beijing, 192-3,195; visited Maison des Sciences de l'Homme, Paris, 169–170; visited Vietnam, 201–202; visiting fellow assignments, 245–258; *A World of Insecurity: Democratic Disenchantment in Rich and Poor Countries*, 343
Barnes, Julian: *The Sense of an Ending*, 340–341
Basu, Jyoti, 314
Basu, Kaushik, 277
Baudelaire, Charles, 329
Bayley, John, 253–254
BBC, 185, 259–260
Bell, Clive, 320–321
Bengali encyclopaedia, 40
Bengali literature, 25, 93, 127; *Abyakta*, 287
Bengalis among Indian economists, 41
Bentham, Jeremy, 286
Berkeley, University of California, 20, 39, 42, 68–69, 73, 83, 119, 150–153, 155–156, 161–162, 165–167, 169, 177, 192, 215, 225, 227, 229, 231, 237–238, 243, 254, 269–270, 291; Blackwell Hall, 178; Budget Committee, 236–239; *Changing Places*, 324; Consumers' Cooperative of Berkeley, 154; Institute of International Studies, 311; Pacific Film Archive, 332; undergraduate classes in, 158–159
Berlin, Isiah, 203
Berlin Wall fall, 174
Besley, Tim, 236, 258
Beteille, André, 100, 123–124, 127, 138, 256
Bhagwati, Jagdish, 44–45
Bhatia, Bela, 272
Bhattacharya, Ananyo, 298
Bhattacharya, Bhabani, 33–34
Bhattacharya, Sudipto, 166-67
Bierce, Ambrose, 27
Binswanger, Hans, 230
BJP government, 124
Black Panther, 294
Blackwell, David, 178

Bliss, Christopher, 53, 251, 265
blue-collar workers, 77
Bose, Amar, 71
Bose, Amitava, 89
Bose, Buddhadeb, 30
Bose, Jagadish Chandra, 286–287
Bose, Jyoti, 71
Bose, Kalpana, 42–43
Bose, Nirmal, 100–101
Bose, Sanjit, 66, 100, 123
Bose, Satyen, 43, 71, 233, 286
Bose, Subhas Chandra, 71
Bose, Swadesh, 57
Bose, Uttara, 66
Boston Experimental Film Society, 85
bourgeois democracy, 125
Bourguignon, François, 277
Bowles, Sam: *A Cooperative Species* (co-author Herb Gintis), 308
Bowles, Samuel, 206, 308-9
Bozzetto, Bruno: *Allegro Non Troppo* film, 341
Brahmo sect, 7, 91, 119
Braudel, Fernand, 169
Brecht, Bertolt, 284
Brenner, Robert, 206, 208
Brexit, 261
Brighouse, Harry, 206
British Communist Party, 32
British Council, 27, 30, 45
Browning, Robert, 40
Bruno, Michael, 277
Buendía, Colonel Aureliano, 228
Burma (Rangoon), 227–228

Calcutta University, 44

Cambridge Arts Theatre, 62
Cambridge University, 45–54, 62, 64, 66, 76, 91
Campion, Jane: *The Piano* film, 328
Camus, Albert, 30
capitalist democracy, 196
Cárdenas, Mauricio, 161
Cardoso, Fernando, 216
caste in Indian society, 126–127
Castro, Fidel, 226
Catholicism, 16
Cecco, Marcello de, 56
Center for Development Studies (CDS), 131–132
Chakrabarti, Arindam, 244
Chakravarty, Suhas, 58
Chakravarty, Sukhamoy, 41, 123, 138, 148–149
Chakravorty (Spivak), Gayatri, 26
Chameli, Tan, 181
Chanda, Nayan, 202
Chandrasekhar, S., 92–93
Chandra, Vikram: *Sacred Games*, 20
charaiveti (keep moving), 1, 340
Chatterjee, Elizabeth and McCartney, Matthew: *Class and Conflict: Revisiting Pranab Bardhan's Political Economy of India*, 249
Chatterjee, Soumitra, 30
Chaudhuri, Binod, 35–36
Chaudhuri, Hiten, 38
Chaudhuri, Mrinal Datta, 72–73, 79, 138, 146–147, 215, 303
Chaudhuri, Sachin, 36–39, 45, 71, 149
Cheese Board Collective, 154–155

Cheng, Leonard, 304
Chetty, V.K., 100–101
China/Chinese, 231, 235;
  advancement in technology,
  190–191; artificial intelligence
  use by, 191; capitalist
  development in, 199; China
  Center for Economic Research,
  190; *China Economic Review,*
  180; Cultural Revolution, 185,
  189, 193–195; Deng Xiaoping's
  economic reforms, 179–180;
  New Left in, 199; People's
  Liberation Army (PLA), 183–
  184; performance indicators,
  180; public-private ownership,
  220; social engineering project
  in, 191; Tiananmen Square
  protest and killings, 182, 186,
  188; ultra-nationalism, 195
Chomsky, Noam, 84-5
Chubais, Anatoly, 211
Chung, Tan, 181
Churchill, Winston, 11
Cipolla, Carlo, 167-8classical
  liberalism in India, 125–126
Cohen, Jerry, 150, 164, 203,
  206–207, 281
Cohen, Joshua, 206, 221
Cohn, Bernard, 223
college: debates, advantages of,
  26–27; life in, 24–25
College Street agitations, 35
colonizer-colonized cultural
  interaction in Western
  academia, 291
Communist Party, 14

conclave economy, 81
Congress party, 198
Congress Socialist Party, 137, 145
Conrad, Joseph, 288
Cooter, Robert, 165
Corden, Max, 252
Cornwell, Ronnie, 262
COVID-19 pandemic, 192, 339
CPI government in Kerala, 132
Cultural Revolution, 59

Dandekar, V.M., 137, 158
Dantwala, M.L., 137
Dasgupta, Amiya, 149–150
Dasgupta, Buddhadeb, 117
Dasgupta, Dipankar, 100–101
Dasgupta, Partha, 58, 149–150, 303
Dasgupta, Sonali, 256
Dasgupta, Sudhangshu, 27–28
Das, Veena, 123–124, 139
Datta, Amlan, 31, 37, 83; *For
  Democracy,* 31
Datta, Bhabatosh, 40–41
Datta Chaudhuri, Mrinal, 72-3,
  122-23, 146-49
Dayton-Johnson, Jeff, 304–305
Dead Peoples' Society, 158
de Beauvoir, Simone: *The
  Mandarins,* 25
De, Bishnu, 30
decentralization, 125
de Janvry, Alain, 161
de Cecco, Marcello, 56
Delhi (New Delhi), 6, 42, 44–45,
  80, 91, 96–99, 102, 109–110,
  123–124, 134–135, 140–144,
  148, 151

Delhi School of Economics (DSE), 45, 53, 89, 106, 122, 137–142, 147, 151, 156, 256, 272, 276; Agro-Economic Research Centre, 265–266
Desai, Meghnad, 258–260
Desai, Padma, 45
de Silva, Nalini, 57
Desiraju, Sucharita, 58
Deutscher, Isaac, 30
Deutscher, Tamara, 30
development economists, 27, 72, 82, 122, 136, 175–176, 226, 230, 236, 252, 258, 279–280
Devi, Mahasweta, 116–117
Devi, Siddheshwari, 209–210
Dhaka, 8
Dhaka University, 35
Dhar, P.N., 123–124, 209
Dhar, Sheila, 209
Diamond, Peter, 72
Dickens, Charles, 25
disillusioned communists, 37
Dixit, Avinash, 73, 151
Djilas, Milovan: *The New Class: An Analysis of the Communist System*, 37
Dobb, Maurice, 32, 56; *Studies in the Development of Capitalism*, 28
Doniger, Wendy, 223-4; *The Hindus: An Alternative History*, 224
Doordarshan, 284
Dowry Prohibition Act of 1961, 126
Drèze, Jacques, 267

Drèze, Jean, 265–274
Duflo, Esther, 139, 169, 172, 277, 310
Dutta, Bhaskar, 138
Dworkin, Ronald, 281

Eagleton, Terry, 128
Eaton, Richard, 223–224
Eckaus, Richard, 72
Economic Weekly (EW), 35–36, 107
Economic and Political Weekly (EPW), 35–36, 38, 135, 149, 188, 284, 316
Egypt, 72
Einstein, Albert, 43, 164, 233, 299
elections in democracy, 217
electoral sanctions, 217
Elster, Jon, 203, 209–210, 247; *Making Sense of Marx*, 204–205
Engels, Friedrich, 25
Enlai, Zhou, 92, 235
Evans, Peter, 165

Faguet, Jean-Paul, 258
February Revolution, 177
Federal Reserve, 74
Feminist crime novels, 261
Ferrante, Elena, 15; *My Brilliant Friend*, ix
Feynman, Richard, 299–300
films/movies/TV series: *Amarcord*, 153; Bombay (Bollywood), 72, 99–100; *Bonnie and Clyde*, 66; *Breathless*, 333; *Calcutta 71*, 117; *Charlie's Angels*, 212; *Cleo from 5 to 7*, 329; *Contempt*, 333;

Dooratva (Distance), 117; *The Double Life of Véronique*, 333; *The Graduate*, 66; *Grihajuddha (The War at Home)*, 117; *Heat and Dust*, 250; *Hour of the Furnaces*, 143–144; *Iris*, 253; *Landscape in the Mist*, 333; *Last Year in Marienbad*, 333; *L'Avventura*, 333; *Padatik (The Guerrilla Fighter)*, 117; *A Passage to India*, 257; *The Passenger*, 173; *Quills*, 249; *Tinker, Tailor, Soldier, Spy*, 263; *Vicky Christina Barcelona*, 173; *Viridiana*, 269; *The War is Over*, 333; *We All Loved Each Other So Much*, 333
Findlay, Ron, 227-8; *Power and Plenty: Trade, War, and the World Economy in the Second Millennium*, 227
Fischer, Stan, 74–76, 277
Fisher, Eric, 304
Fishlow, Albert, 136, 150, 160, 229
Foley, Duncan, 66
Foley, Helene, 66
Foot, Philippa, 253
Forster, E.M.: *Passage to India* or *Howard's End*, 62–63, 229, 257
Fox, Kate: *Watching the English: The Hidden Rules of English Behaviour*, 257
Foxley, Alejandro, 136
Frédérique Marglin, 80, 128
free-market capitalism, 196
Friedman, Milton, 71, 92
Frost, Robert, 309

Fudan University, 188
Fudenberg, Drew, 298

Galbraith, John Kenneth, 15, 71, 82; *The Affluent Society*, 81
Gambetta, Diego, 241
Gandhi, Indira, 109, 124, 145–146, 149, 295
Gandhi, Mahatma, 23, 125–126, 203, 268; decentralization, 137
Gandhi, Rajiv, 59
Gandhi, Sanjay, 59, 146–147
Gandhi, Sonia, 59, 197–198
Ganguly, Sunil, 330
Gaudi, Antoni, 173
Ghatak, Maitreesh, 258
Gide, André, 5
Giles, John, 305
Ginsberg, Allen, 30
global commons, 302
globalization, 67
Godard, Jean-Luc: *La Chinoise*, 59, *Contempt*, 333
Goldman, Robert, 165
Goldman, Steve, 150
Goldsmith, Oliver, 297
Gorky, Maxim, 25
Gramsci, Antonio, 66, 343; *Prison Notebooks*, 56
Gramsci, Piazza, 154
Guha, Ranajit, 115–116
Guinness, Alec, 263
gully cricket in Kolkata, 19
Gupta, Sisir, 146

Haberler, Gottfried, 81
Hahn, Frank, 49, 51–52, 54, 258

Haldane, J.B.S., 95
Hamid, Mohsin, 200
Hamied, 60–61
Hammett, Dashiell, 152
Hansen, Bent, 90
Harcourt, Geoff, 56
Harriss, John, 258
Harsanyi, John, 298
Hart, George, 165
Harvard Square, 65–66, 76, 79, 81–82, 85
Hass, Robert, 338
Havel, Václav, 27
Hayek, Friedrich, 211; *Road to Serfdom*, 74
Hegel, Georg Wilhelm Friedrich, 288
Herring, Ronald, 223–224
Hinduism, 16
'Hindu rate of growth', 138
Hirschman, Albert, 122
honour killings, 267
Hoselitz, Bert, 36
Hua, Yu: *Brothers*, 199
Hui, Wang, 196–199
Hurwicz, Leonid, 177-78
Huxley, Aldous: *Point Counter Point*, 25

IBM computer, 104, 106
India-Italy comparison, 14-5
Indian Council of Social Science Research (ICSSR), 137, 151
Indian Institute of Management Calcutta, 89
Indian Statistical Institute (ISI), 90–96, 99, 101–105, 107, 110, 122, 144, 178

India Policy Forum, Delhi, 108
Industrial Revolution, 79
innovation: pattern of, 221; rate of, 221
Institute of Advanced Study, Princeton, 298
Institute of Development Studies, Sussex, 135
Institute of Social and Economic Change (ISEC), Bangalore, 139
institutional economics, 175–176, 179, 193, 214
International Crop Research Institute for Semi-Arid Tropics (ICRISAT), Hyderabad, 230
International Labour Organization, Geneva, 56
International Monetary Fund (IMF), 74, 214, 277
international politics, 77–78
Iraq War, 294
Islam, Nazrul, 288

Jain, Devaki, 124
Jain, Lakshmi Chand, 124, 145
Jana, Smarajit, 339
Jayawardena, Lal, 137
Jefferson, Thomas, 203
Jenner, W.J.F.: *The Tyranny of History*, 197
Jhabvala, Ruth Prawer, 250
Jinglian, Wu: *Chinese Economic Reform*, 195
Johnson, Boris: *I Got Views for You*, 255
Johnson, Harry, 92
Johnson, Samuel, ix

Index ❧ 353

Journal of Development Economics
 (JDE), 225-6, 231-4, 236
Judt, Tony: *New York Review of Books*, 78–79

Kahneman, Daniel, 300
Kairon, Partap Singh, 79
Kaldor, Nicholas, 56
Kalidasa: *Meghaduta*, 288
Kalpana, 43-44, 52–53, 56–57, 60, 76, 87, 98, 131, 137, 160, 167, 169–170, 181, 183, 230, 243, 271, 319
Kapczynski, Amy, 206
'Kashmiri mafia', 147
Kaviraj, Sudipta, 259, 288
Kelkar, Vijay, 275
Kelly, Erin: *He Said/She Said*, 261
Kemp, Murray, 148
Kerala, 132–135
Kerr, Clark, 162–163
Kevane, Michael, 304–305
Keynesian economics, 50
Khan, Aziz, 57
Khullar, Rahul, 138
Kindleberger, Charles, 70
King Henry VIII, 243
King, Martin Luther: Poor People's March in 1968, 309
Kletzer, Ken, 304–305
Kohli, Atul, 321
Kolkata/West Bengal (then known as Calcutta), 1–2, 7, 11, 83, 143, 151, 154, 156–157, 183, 186, 213; agriculture in, 114; collective action/mobilization for religious festivals, 13–14; corpulent man in neighbourhood, 15–16; Durbar (women collective), 338; Kolkata Book Fair, 338; left government rule from (1977-2011), 313–314; mafia (mastan) fiefdoms, 19–22; Naxalbari movements, 114–116; politics, 19, 114; pre-Partition Hindu-Muslim riots in, 21–22; show of East European films, 47; upper-caste hegemony in, 127
Kolmogorov, Andrey, 104
Kothari, Rajni, 124
Kremer, Michael, 277, 310
Krishna, K.L., 138–139
Krishnan, T.N., 135
Krishna, Raj, 138
Krugman, Paul, 233, 281
Kugler, Maurice, 304
Kumaramangalam, Mohan, 133
Kumar, Dharma, 123–124
Kumar, Lovraj, 124
Kuper, Simon: *Chums: How a Tiny Caste of Oxford Tories Took Over the UK*, 254–255
Kushari (Dyson), Ketaki, 26

Laffont, Jean-Jacques, 237
Lahiri, Jhumpa, 279
Laitin, David, 216
Lange, Oskar, 211
Laxman, R.K., 147–148
Lean, David, 229
le Carré, John, 26-4; *Silverview*, 262; *Tinker, Tailor, Soldier, Spy*, 263
leftists, 30, 37, 56, 110, 124, 127, 141, 145, 179, 209, 220, 293, 295, 297

left politics, 35
Lenin, Vladimir, 25
Leontief, Wassily, 79
Lerner, Abba, 211
Leruth, Luc: *Rumble in a Village*, 266
Lewis, Arthur, 280
Lin, Justin Yifu, 181–182, 190, 192, 195, 277
Lippman, Laura, 261
Lodge, David: *Changing Places*, 324, *Small World*, 324
Lohia, Ram Manohar, 34
London School of Economics (LSE), 167, 245, 257–258, 260, 265, 268, 271
Lord Macaulay: *Minute on Indian Education*, 288

MacArthur Foundation, 309–311
MacArthur network, 313, 316, 324–325
Madras Institute of Development Studies, 302
magazines/newspapers/journals: *American Economic Review*, 112, 226; *Asian Development Review*, 226; *Biometrika*, 95; *California*, 281; *Cambridge News*, 46; *China Economic Review*, 195; *Daily Telegraph*, 247; *Desh*, 188; *Economic and Political Weekly (EPW)* (earlier *Economic Weekly (EW)*), 4, 35–38, 40, 107, 110, 135, 149, 188, 284, 316; *Economic Development and Cultural Change*, 36; *The Economist*, 191, 259; *Ekshan*, 30; *Encounter*, 83–84; *Far Eastern Economic Review*, 202; *The Financial Times*, 259; *Frontier*, 118; *Ganashakti*, 188; *The Guardian*, 247, 261; *International Economic Review*, 226; *ISM* (Indian Students' Magazine), 31; *Journal of Development Economics (JDE)*, 225–226, 229, 231–232, 234; *Journal of Economic Perspectives*, 211, 226; *Mankind*, 34; *New Statesman*, 30; *Newsweek*, 70; *New Yorker*, 128–129; *New York Times*, 76, 82–83, 166, 196, 229, 287, 295, 326–327; *Politics, Philosophy and Economics Journal*, 241; *Quarterly Journal of Economics*, 40; *Quest*, 83–84; *Review of Social Economy*, 226; *Sandesh*, 287; *Wall Street Journal*, 259; *World Bank Economic Review*, 226
Mahalanobis, P.C., 90–94, 101, 103, 108, 110, 235, 286, 326
Malfa, Giorgio La, 56
Mann, Thomas: *The Magic Mountain*, 341
Manto, Saadat, 342
Marglin, Steve, 79–80, 128
Márquez, Gabriel García: *One Hundred Years of Solitude*, 228
Marx, Groucho, 155
Marxism, 209; Catholic, 14; 'non-bullshit', 203; rational-choice, 205

Marxists, 14, 25, 28–30
Marx, Karl, 25, 70, 203, 207; class struggle, 70; *Das Kapital,* 258
Mas-Colell, Andreu, 167–172, 174, 177
Masood, Syed Ross, 229
Massachusetts Institute of Technology (MIT), 36, 38–39, 45, 49, 55, 64–89, 96, 122, 150, 176, 196, 226–227, 273, 298, 307
Matilal, Bimal, 249-251, 254; *Epistemology, Logic and Grammar in Indian Philosophical Analysis,* 249
Matthews, Robin, 52
Mazzucato, Mariana: *The Entrepreneurial State,* 220–221
McEwan, Ian, 262
Meade, James, 48–49, 51, 149–150, 196, 251–252; social dividend idea of, 196
Melville, Herman, viii
Meng, Xiao, 193–194
Menon, Achutha, 132–133
Merton, Robert, 74–75
Midgley, Mary, 253
Miller, Margaret, 305
Milosz, Czeslaw, 341
Minhas, B.S., 100
Mirrlees, Jim, 52-3, 243, 251–252, 265
Mitra, Kamal, 42–43
Mitra, Sandip, 313
Modi, Narendra, 128, 259, 273
Moene, Karl ('Kalle'), 328
Mookherjee, Dilip, 128, 236, 311–313, 316

Morgenstern, Oskar, 297
Morton, A.L.: *A People's History of England,* 28
Muhlstein, Anka: *Balzac's Omelette,* 330
Mukherjea, Kalyan, 58, 65
Mukherjee, Bharati, 166
Mukherji (Badal and Swapna), 123
Munch, Edvard, 328
Mundle, Sudipto, 138
Murdoch, Iris: ix; *Iris: A Memoir of Iris Murdoch,* 253
Murthy, Narayana, 140

Nagar, A.L., 138
Naidu, Suresh, 206, 304
Naik, J.P., 137
Naipaul, V.S., 288, 291
Namboodiripad, E.M.S., 312
Nandy, Ashis, 43, 123–124, 126–129, 147
Nandy, Manish, 42–43
Narayan, J.P. (JP), 109, 145
Naser, Sylvia: *A Beautiful Mind,* 299
Nash, John, 298–299
National Advisory Council for Sonia Gandhi, 273
National Health Service, UK, 65
National Sample Survey (NSS), 91, 101–102, 108–111, 156, 158
National Statistical Office, 236
National Theater Live programme, 261
National Theatre on the South Bank, 260

nation-state, 127
NDTV, 138
Needham, Joseph, 59; *Science and Civilization in China*, 60
Nehru, Jawaharlal, 7–8, 23, 36, 59, 71–72, 91, 125, 181, 309; *Discovery of India*, 286; *Glimpses of World History*, 295
Nehru Museum, Delhi, 59, 197
Nerlove, Marc, 303–304
New Hampshire, 66
Newman, Katherine, 310
Newnham College, 45, 57
New York Review of Books, 253
Nicholas, Ralph, 223
Nietzsche, Friedrich, 204
Nilekani, Nandan, 140
Nilekani, Rohini, 140
No.1 Clapham Road: The Diary of a Squat, 270
Nordhaus, Bill, 303
North, Douglass, 175

O'Donnell, Guillermo, 216
Olson, Mancur, 13, 214–215
Osborne, John, 26
Osho, 331
Ostrom, Elinor, 13
Oxford Union, 27

Pal, Prasanta, 25–26
Pamuk, Orhan: *Snow*, 342
Panchatantra, 236
Parashar, B.N., 94
Parfit, Derek, 281
Parikh, Kirit, 100–101
Paris Commune uprising in 1871, 331

Partition of India, 7, 23
Pasinetti, Luigi, 56
Pasolini, Pier Paolo: *Gospel According to St. Matthew*, 14
Pasternak, Boris: *Dr Zhivago*, 84
Patel, I.G., 275
Pattanaik, Prasanta, 138
Pearce, Ivor, 104
Pembroke College, 45
Perkins, Dwight., 192
Picasso, 172-3
Piketty, Thomas, 190, 310
Piore, Michael, 66
Pirandello, Luigi: *Six Characters in Search of an Author* play, 86
Planning Commission (Yojana Bhavan), India, 82, 90, 95–97, 103, 122, 148
popular culture, 12
positive feedback, 10
Posner, Michael, 45
poverty, 11; culture of, 12
Presidency College, 24, 33, 39–41, 58–59, 81, 91, 148, 166, 297; Dipak Banerjee Memorial Lecture in, 42; Marxist history tradition, 29
Primakov, Yevgeny, 263
Princess Diana car accident in 1997, 257
Proudhon, Pierre-Joseph, 85
Przeworski, Adam, 196, 206, 208, 215-217, 310; *Sustainable Democracy*, 216
psychic income of California residents, 240
public and private in Indic culture, 12

Index ❦ 357

public debate, 28
public firms' performance, 219-220
public universities in India, 237
Punjabi mafia, 147
Putin, Vladimir, 212
Puzo, Mario: *The Godfather,* 20

Qian, Yingyi, 192–193, 195

Rabin, Matthew, 301
Radhakrishnan, S., 58, 245–247, 249
Radner, Roy, 156
Rajaraman, R. and Indira, 123
Raj, K.N., 45, 89, 129–132,134, 167, 312
Rajneesh (Indian godman), 331–332
Ramanujan, Srinivasa, 91
Ramaswami, V.K., 123, 275
Ranis, Gus, 136, 280
Rao-Blackwell theorem, 178
Rao, C. R., 102, 109, 178
Rao, V.K.R.V., 139
Ravel, Maurice: *Boléro,* 341

Ray, Isha. 121
Ray, Satyajit, 93, 253, 285–287; *Charulata,* 118; *The Hero,* 285; *The Home and the World* film, 34; *Shatranj Ke Khilari (The Chess Players),* 119
Ray, Sukumar, 93, 326

Reagan, Ronald, 163
Real Utopias project, 221

religious hypocrisies, 16
resident alien, 77

Resnais, Alain: *Last Year in Marienbad,* 333
Robertson, Dennis, 32
Robeson, Paul, 57, 269
Robinson, Andrew, 253
Robinson, Joan, 50–51, 55, 59, 70, 228
Robinson, Neville, 253
Roemer, John, 203, 211, 267; *Analytical Marxism,* 206
Rogers, Joel, 221
Roland, Gérard, 167, 173–174, 176, 179, 193
Rosenstein-Rodan, Paul, 39, 71-2
Rosenzweig, Mark, 236
Rossellini, Roberto, 256
Rothenberg, Tom, 300
Roth, Philip: *A Perfect Spy,* 262
Rousseau, Jean-Jacques: *The Reveries of the Solitary Walker,* 329
Rowse, A.L., 246
Roy, Aruna, 273
Roy, P.K., 7
Roy, Prabir, 58
Roy, Prannoy, 138
Roy, Ram Mohan, 286
Roy, Sarala, 7
Rudra, Ashok, 110-114, 118–120, 156, 270, 287
Rumpole of the Bailey (British TV series), 36
Rushdie, Salman, 253
Russell, Bertrand, 84, 95
Russian privatization, 211

Sadoulet, Elisabeth, 161
Salvador Dalí museum, 172

Salvati, Michele and Bianca, 56
Samuelson, Paul, 45, 69–71, 73, 239
San Francisco International Film Festival, 290
Sanskrit, 5, 8, 165, 223, 244, 249, 286, 288, 331
Sarkar, Sumit, 29
Sarkar, Susobhan, 29
Sarkar, Tanika, 123
Sartre, Jean-Paul, 30
Satz, Debra, 206
Schmitt, Carl: Totalstaat, 191
Schneider, Maria, 173
Schultz, Ted, 280
Schumpeter, Joseph, 217, 302; methodological individualism, 204
Scott, James: *Two Cheers for Anarchism*, 85
Scott, Jim: *The Good Soldier Švejk*, 105
Second World War, 172, 227
Seeger, Pete, 57
self-hating Jews, 78
Selten, Reinhard, 298
Sen, Amartya, 5, 9, 41, 45, 50–51, 53, 73, 87, 89, 123, 137, 243, 246–248, 254, 270–273, 279–280, 282–285, 314–315; *Development as Freedom*, 281; Western admirers of, 286
Sen, Arun, 25
Sengupta (Arjun and Jayashree), 123
Sen, Kshitimohan, 5
Sen, Mrinal, 117, 123–124, 129
Sen, Nilima, 5
Sen, Nirupam, 315
Sen, Samar, 118
September Group, 203, 205–208, 210, 215, 221, 223, 308. Seth, Vikram: *The Golden Gate*, 152
sex-repressed society, 143
Shakespeare, 25, 246, 319
sharecroppers' movement (tebhaga), 117
Shaw, Bernard, 279
Shell, Karl, 72
Sheth, D.L., 124
Shiffrin, Seana, 206
Shleifer, Andrei, 211–214, 220, 295
Shudraka: *Mricchakatika* play, 288
Sidrauski, Miguel, 66
Simic, Charles, 22
Singh, Ajit, 56
Singh, Manmohan, 275
Sino-Indian war, 181
Smale, Steve: founded Vietnam Day Committee, 165; *The Smale Collection: Beauty in Natural Crystals*, 165
Smith, Adam, 302
social dividend, 49
Social Science Research Council, New York, 121
Solow, Robert, 53–55, 64–65, 71, 77
South Asia Committee of the Social Science Research Council (SSRC), New York, 223–225
Soviet Union, 145; fall of, 210
Spender, Stephen, 83
Sraffa, Piero, 55-56

Srinivas, M.N., 139-40
Srinivasan, T.N. (TN), 90–91, 95, 101–103, 105–106, 108-9, 112, 137, 161, 182, 233
Stalin, Joseph, 25
Stanford University, 54, 100, 150, 176, 237, 240, 303
Steiner, Hillel, 206
Stepan, Alfred, 216
Stern, Nick, 258, 265, 277, 303
Stiglitz, Joe, 66, 73, 78–79, 113, 175, 194, 211, 277, 281, 303
structural adjustment, 214
St Stephen College, 115
Summers, Larry, 75–76
Sutch, Richard, 159
Swatantra Party, 125
Swiss stamps, 6
Szanton, David, 225

Tagore, Rabindranath, 3, 5, 7, 23, 25–26, 35, 63, 91, 110, 117, 125, 135, 164, 181, 253, 286, 288; *Char Adhyay,* 34, 117; *Charulata,* 118; *Ghare Baire,* 34; *Gora,* 34; *Nationalism,* 34; Santiniketan, 3–9, 25, 91, 119, 122, 149, 244, 270, 283, 285; *Vishwa Parichay,* 43
Taylor, Lance, 80, 136
teachers' insurance, 159
Temin, Peter, 72
Tendulkar, Suresh, 100–101
Thapar, Romila, 169, 228–229
Thatcher, Margaret, 259
The Indian Econometric Society, 101

Thomas, Dylan, 17
Thorbecke, Erik, 136
Thorner, Daniel, 107, 109
Tiananmen Square, 181-84, 186
Titash, 98, 150-1, 155, 253, 255, 287, 294-5, 318-9, 327
Tokman, Marcelo, 305
Tolstoy, Leo, 25, 160
Tomaselli, Sylvana, 288
Townes, Charles, 163, 165
trade unions in formal sector, 132–133
transcendental meditation, 331
Trinity College, 95, 243-44
Trinity High Table, 244
Trotsky, Leon, 30, 59; *The Revolution Betrayed,* 37
Turgenev, Ivan, 25, 342; *Fathers and Sons,* 117
Tversky, Amos, 300

ul Haq, Mahbub, 137
Unger, Lisa, 261
United Nations: Development Programme, 135; General Assembly, 234
universal basic income (UBI), 49, 196–198, 251, 274
University of California, 57, 163, 239–240
University of Glasgow, 45
University of Minnesota, 177–178
Upadhyay, Brahmabandhab, 117
US: American academia, 242; Central Intelligence Agency (CIA), 82–83; civil rights movement, 126; Congress

for Cultural Freedom (CCF), 83–84; culture of constant competition, 241; National Institute of Health, 82; National Science Foundation, 82; USAID, 214
Uzawa, Hirofumi, 73, 139, 150, 303–304

van der Veen, Robert, 206
van Parijs, Philippe, 198, 206
Varaiya, Pravin, 165, 274–275
Varda, Agnès, 329
Varma, Ravi, 134
Veblen, Thorstein, 81
Veneziani, Roberto, 206
Verhoogen, Eric, 304
Vietnamese economic reform ('doi moi'), 201
Vietnam War, 64–65, 77, 82, 151, 201-202, 294–295, 337
Vigeland, Gustav, 328
von Neumann, John: 297-99; *Theory of Games and Economic Behaviour,* 297
von Weizsäcker, Christian, 53, 55

Wade, Robert, 258
Wain, John, 26
Wajda, Andrzej, 47, 215
Wantchekon, Leonard, 278
Waters, Alice, 293
Watts, Michael, 165
Weber, Max, 21, 204
Weibull, Jörgen, 299
Weiner, Myron, 223–224

Weitzman, Martin, 73-74, 113, 303; *The Share Economy,* 113
Weiwei, Ai, 199
Wenders, Wim, 67
Westerners, Indians' thoughts on, 209
Whitehead, Alfred, 207
Whitman, Marina, 298
Wilson, Francis, 56–57
Wilson, Lindy: *The Guguletu Seven* film, 57
Winslet, Kate, 249
Wittgenstein, Ludwig, 56
Woolf, Virginia, 257, 329
World Bank, 74–75, 135, 214, 276–277, 305
World Peace Congress (1949), Paris, 172
Wright, Erik Olin, 206, 221, 310
Wu, Lemin, 304
Wydick, Bruce, 304

Xiaobo, Liu, 199
Xu, Chenggang, 195

Yadav, Yogendra, 198
Yale Club, 227
Yao, Yang, 195
Yellen, Janet, 165
Yun-Shan, Tan, 180

Zedong, Mao, 37–38, 189
Zhang, Xiaobo, 195
Zhiyuan, Cui, 196
Zhou, Yongmei, 305
Ziyang, Zhao, 182

About the Author

Pranab Bardhan is Distinguished Professor Emeritus of Economics at University of California, Berkeley. Educated at Presidency College, Kolkata, and Cambridge University, England, he had been a part of the faculty of MIT, Indian Statistical Institute and Delhi School of Economics before joining University of California, Berkeley. He is the author of seventeen books, including *Awakening Giants, Feet of Clay: Assessing the Economic Rise of China and India* (Princeton University Press, 2011) and *A World of Insecurity: Democratic Disenchantment in Rich and Poor Countries* (Harvard University Press, 2022). A collection of his Bengali essays has been published by Ananda Publishers in Kolkata in 2020.

HarperCollins *Publishers* India

At HarperCollins India, we believe in telling the best stories and finding the widest readership for our books in every format possible. We started publishing in 1992; a great deal has changed since then, but what has remained constant is the passion with which our authors write their books, the love with which readers receive them, and the sheer joy and excitement that we as publishers feel in being a part of the publishing process.

Over the years, we've had the pleasure of publishing some of the finest writing from the subcontinent and around the world, including several award-winning titles and some of the biggest bestsellers in India's publishing history. But nothing has meant more to us than the fact that millions of people have read the books we published, and that somewhere, a book of ours might have made a difference.

As we look to the future, we go back to that one word— a word which has been a driving force for us all these years.

Read.

Harper Collins

HARPER PERENNIAL

HARPER BUSINESS

HARPER BLACK

हार्पर हिन्दी

HarperCollins *Children'sBooks*

HARPER DESIGN

HARPER VANTAGE

Harper Sport